NUMBER FOUR

THE CORRIE HERRING HOOKS SERIES

BIRD STUDENT

BIRD STUDENT

An Autobiography

George Miksch Sutton

UNIVERSITY OF TEXAS PRESS

Austin and London

Requests for permission to reproduce material from this work
should be sent to Permissions, University of Texas Press,
Box 7819, Austin, Texas 78712.

Library of Congress Cataloging in Publication Data

Sutton, George Miksch, 1898–
    Bird student.
    (The Corrie Herring Hooks series; no. 4)
    1. Sutton, George Miksch, 1898–
    2. Ornithologists—United States—Biography.
    I. Title.
    QL31.S96A33   598.2′092′4 [B]   79-20196
    ISBN 0-292-70727-4

Frontispiece:
Ookpikjuak   *Direct-from-life portrait of a snowy owl caught in a trap set by the Eskimos for foxes on Southampton Island in the winter of 1929–30. Translated freely, ookpikjuak* means "something soft and big."

CONTENTS

Pied-billed Grebe   Drawing made directly from life at Bethany, West Virginia, of a bird that had been unable to take off from a wet road on which it had crash-landed. While being drawn, it floated peacefully on water several inches deep in a bathtub.

George Miksch Sutton

PREFACE

THE CHAPTER "Sheldrake Springs, New York" in this book appeared some years ago, though not quite word for word, in *Audubon* under the title "Fuertes Remembered"; it also appeared in *To a Young Bird Artist*, recently published by the University of Oklahoma Press, a little book containing all the letters that Louis Agassiz Fuertes wrote me between 1915 and the year of his death, 1927. No other chapter has heretofore been published verbatim, though in my book *Eskimo Year* (1934) I did tell of my memorable sojourn with the Inuit of Southampton Island at the north end of Hudson Bay, and in another book, *Birds in the Wilderness* (1936), I wrote of my crawl through a hollow log after a turkey vulture's nest, of the rearing of young roadrunners, of the expedition down the Labrador coast in 1920, of the Blue Goose Expedition to James Bay in 1923, of my visit to the Florida Everglades in 1924, and of the expedition to Churchill, Manitoba, in 1931.

I am indebted to several persons for their help with the manuscript, especially my sister Dorothy (Dr. Dorothy S. Fuller, of Topeka, Kansas), whose memory for detail is beyond belief; my sister Evie (Mrs. Harry Swartz, of Cuernavaca, Morelos, Mexico), who does not remember my boyhood very well for, being ten years younger than I, she belonged to a vastly different age group; Dr. Olin Sewall Pettingill, Jr., of Wayne, Maine, who shared my days at Cornell University while I was a graduate student there, who became a more and more important part of my life at Churchill on the west coast of Hudson Bay in 1931, in a tropical part of Mexico in 1941, and in Iceland in 1958, and whose friendship has been a continuing source of inspiration year after year; John ("Jack") David Ford, of Port Hope, Ontario, with whom I wintered on Southampton Island in 1929–30, who therefore came to know me extremely well and who liked me despite my assorted shortcomings; Dr. Kenneth C. Parkes, of the Carnegie Museum of Natural History in Pittsburgh, Pennsylvania, a

brilliant ornithologist who could, had he so chosen, have been successful in any field whatsoever; Michael Harwood, of Washington,
Connecticut, who gave me important information about Pennsylvania's
wonderful Hawk Mountain; and Dr. Sally Hoyt Spofford, of Portal, Ari-
zona, who helped me remember just who my fellow graduate students at
Cornell were in 1930, 1931, and 1932 and what these lively, talented
persons have been up to.

BIRD STUDENT

Kigavik   *Head and foot of an immature gyrfalcon drawn from a specimen shot at the Hudson's Bay Company's trading post on Southampton Island in the winter of 1929– 30. According to Amaulik Audlanat, one of the island's ablest hunters,* kigavik *means "it picks at a bone."*

THE BEGINNINGS

IS IT NOT REMARKABLE that the human mind, for all its much touted acumen, has so much trouble distinguishing between what it truly remembers of early childhood and what it has only been told? So often, as a growing boy, was I told of a ruffed grouse that drummed on the windowsill of our cabin in the woods near Aitkin, Minnesota, of a porcupine that upset a jar of dill pickles in the cellar there, of wild blueberries gathered in tin cups, and of a deer that we saw swimming across our little lake that today I cannot for the life of me be sure that what I remember is the grouse, porcupine, blueberries, and deer themselves. I am not even sure how we happened to be in Minnesota. Were we there only in summer? Was the rent there lower than anywhere else? Did we have any other place that we could call home? *I'll just ask and find out*, I say to myself—eagerly and confidently—whereupon I recoil as I remember that those who know are gone. My beloved parents have long been dead, Mother since the summer of 1937, Father, whose prediction that he'd live to be a hundred often amused us, since 1962, when he was almost ninety-six. There is no one, not a soul, who can tell me why we were living in Minnesota. A chapter I wrote for a book published recently by the National Geographic Society reads as if that Minnesota cabin had been among the minor luxuries of a well-heeled family. Well-heeled? I am not sure that we had heels of any sort.

I believe I remember, truly remember, the drumming grouse. It came to the window every day, marched back and forth, with tail grandly spread and wings drooping. Then, presumably after making sure that it approved of what it saw through the glass, it stood still, straightened up, and thumped its chest with its wings. The thumps were separate at first, then became a whirr. Hidden behind a chair, I watched and listened, fascinated. If I let myself be seen, off went the grouse. I remember, too, being awakened in the middle of the night by the odor of a skunk.

3

Whether the skunk was arguing with the porcupine over the pickles, or whether the poor creature had been cornered by a great horned owl and was resisting as best it could, I shall never know. Or . . . may I someday find out? Almost every Sunday during boyhood I heard that, for those who were "good," for those who were "saved," there was heaven and eternal life after death. The idea, be it ever so unscientific, be it ever so fantastic, clings. If by inexplicable chance or Divine Plan I do continue to exist "for ever and ever," I shall certainly ask my Creator and Omniscient Friend what happened to that skunk.

I wasn't born in that cabin by the little lake, but my sister Dorothy was. I was three years old then. I have only two clear memories of the town of Aitkin. I consider these genuine memories, for I can't recall ever being reminded of them by my parents. One is of a collection of bird skins owned by a man named Albert Lano—row upon row, drawer after drawer, of red-winged blackbirds, jays, orioles, tanagers, hawks, owls, sandpipers, and ducks, even a flamingo! The other is of an experience on the iron bridge across the Mississippi. Father and I were standing on the bridge, close to one end. The river was up, the water brown and sinister-looking. A blackbird of some sort, probably a grackle, alighted on the railing not far from us. Father lifted me up onto the railing. I stood there, feeling shaky, wondering if he really loved me. "Look at that blackbird," Father said. "He doesn't seem to be afraid, now does he?" Father was not trying to scare me to death. The thought must have crossed his mind that if I crumpled he'd have to catch me ever so quickly. But he let me stand there, completely on my own, because he wanted me to be self-reliant. I must have been a timid sort. Very timid, perhaps.

No, I wasn't born in Minnesota—I was born in southeastern Nebraska, in Bethany, at the time a suburb of Lincoln, on May 16, 1898. How long we lived in Bethany before going to Minnesota I do not know—a year or so perhaps—then back we moved to Bethany. We lived in a small frame house at the edge of town, not far from the campus of Cotner College, in whose one and only building Father taught English, church history, exegesis, and elocution. I'm not sure that he taught all of these concurrently, but from the roaring we heard from him I'd say he gave elocution the lion's share of his attention. He memorized great stretches of Shakespeare—notably from *Macbeth*. Asked by Mother to take a message to Father, I would find him on the second floor of the big building, declaiming behind closed doors. "Hail, Macbeth, Thane of

Cawdor!'' would greet me like a clap of thunder as I peeped in. Father, annoyed no doubt, embarrassed perhaps, would be forced to leave his beloved Birnham Wood, Dunsinane, and "yon battlements" with their croaking ravens to pay attention to me. "What is it, son?" An element of resignation was in his voice.

"Hail, Macbeth, Thane of Cawdor" gave my life a theme song. Using a willow switch, I drove my sister Dorothy about, shouting "Hail, Macbeth!" at her until she whimpered and the Parental Powers commanded me to stop. Dorothy was a flaxen-haired, gentle girl given to an almost idolatrous adoration of such creatures as honeybees. A bee, in response to my "Hail, Macbeth!" might leave its clover blossom, head straight across the yard, and sting me properly on the nose. The same bee, approached and talked to by Dorothy, would submit to being caught, held in her cupped hand, and *stroked* with a finger as she carried it about, showing it to everyone—not with pride, not with the slightest pomposity, but with deep affection for her brown, shiny-winged, tiny friend. There you have an essential difference between Dorothy and me. Dorothy was goodness and gentleness incarnate, always was, always will be. I was something else.

I cannot remember just when another sister, fragile little Pauline, was born—but she was there in Bethany when I was about five and Dorothy two. Pauline was beautiful. Dorothy and I loved her dearly, but this younger creature was so delicate, so like a shadow, that we never romped with her. Dorothy and I, playing fox, got down on all fours with chicken bones in our teeth and scuttled under the big black piano to our "den," there to crunch away, growling savagely at each other. Pauline never played fox with us. I wouldn't have dreamed of shouting anything from *Macbeth* at her or chasing her with a switch. She would sit in the swing in the box elder tree near the house, smiling happily, a little wistfully, as if she had things she wanted to say but never quite had strength or courage enough to say them . . .

Dorothy and I hauled Pauline around in a little wagon. On certain days I owned the wagon, on other days Dorothy owned it. When the weather was just right—no wind, no rain—and the wagon was mine, I hauled my pintail duck around for all to see. This prized possession, a nicely mounted specimen, my parents had bought for me at the taxidermist's shop in Lincoln. I was inordinately, even disagreeably, proud of it. I recall how infuriated I was by a remark from an out-of-town boy to the effect that "that pintail" wasn't much, that his father owned "millions of pintails," all better than mine. No doubt I had been bragging a little too loudly about my specimen.

The walk leading from the back porch of our house to the woodshed was lined with gooseberry bushes. The berries became quite large before turning dark, but many had no chance to darken since Dorothy and I, as well as sundry other kids of the town, consumed them. We vied with each other, seeing who could swallow the largest one without chewing it up.

The birds of the neighborhood that impressed me most were not the blue jays, whose colors were so fine, or the meadowlarks, with their exuberant songs, but the thousands upon thousands of blackbirds that passed over in late summer and fall. These awed me, for the supply seemed inexhaustible. They always flew in the same direction, day after day, in a band several yards wide, and the flock seemed to have neither beginning nor end. I looked hard, even from the top of the woodshed, trying to see where they were coming from, where they were going, but could never tell. To this day I wonder just what those blackbirds were— redwings, grackles, and cowbirds probably, perhaps some yellowheads, but no starlings. Starlings had not yet spread that far west.

I climbed to a blue jay's nest and took one of the stub-tailed babies. The old birds attacked me fiercely, alighting on my head and pecking hard; when I reached the ground, blood was running down my face. I kept the jay in the screened-in part of the back porch. It became a winsome pet.

A boy named Grant Aspinwall, who lived on a farm across the creek from our house, joined me in what promised to become genuine bird study. Together we watched the nighthawks on summer evenings as they traced their chirography across the sky. These graceful birds were called bullbats by most people. Once, we admired a dead bee-martin that someone had found in a puddle. We washed the mud off its feathers at the pump on our back porch, blew on the plumage and shook it until it dried, and marveled at the brilliance of the partly concealed patch of orange on the top of its head. "That's the bird's crown," said Mother. "Maybe that's why the books call the bee-martin a kingbird. It has its own little crown of gold."

Grant and I had our "laboratory" under the bridge between the Aspinwall house and ours. Here, where the ground was soft and the air cool even on the hottest days, we buried the kingbird after pulling its wing and tail feathers out and examining them carefully. Here—be it set down for all to read—we killed a half-grown chicken, cut it open, and removed its esophagus, crop, gizzard, liver, gallbladder, and intestines, not knowing a thing about the function of these several organs but vastly interested to see how they were all attached to one another. And their colors were intriguing. We had decided against killing my pet Bantam hen and had stolen one of the Aspinwall chickens instead.

My Banty, a dear little creature, speckled black-and-white all over, had been in for trouble the moment it became mine. People named Wilkinson, who had been missionaries in the West Indies, gave it to me. Interested in whether or not it could swim, I threw it into the creek and watched it paddle out. It did right well, too, using only its feet, never its wings, but when I took it, soaking wet, back to the house, it was badly done in. Mother wrapped it in a cloth, warmed it in the oven, and brought it back to life. No, my Banty could not be sacrificed, no matter how important the investigations under the bridge might be.

Beyond the Aspinwall farm, not far from a little-used road, was a shallow impoundment called Brewer's Pond. Here Dorothy and I surprised a coot which, disinclined, or perhaps unable, to fly off, dived repeatedly. We went in after it. The water was muddy, so we couldn't follow the bird's movements when it went under. Neither could it see us, so when it popped to the surface it was sometimes very close. Try as we did to catch it, we failed. We were good and wet when we started for home; not so the coot, whose plumage was wonderfully waterproof. Rumor has it that a bull chased us out of the pasture that day—a circumstance I do not seem to remember. Let us dismiss the matter by saying that but for the bull we would surely have caught the coot.

A holy of holies for me was the tower of the big building on the Cotner campus. Here, after the climb on all fours up a rickety ramp, I could count on seeing two barn owls. The pigeons stopped cooing and flapped noisily off when they saw me approaching. But the barn owls stayed, watching me from their lofty, shadowed perch, so white throughout their underparts that I could see them distinctly, bowing, looking at each other as if in consultation, then boring holes through me with their sad dark eyes. They probably nested somewhere in the tower, though I never found any eggs or owlets.

A dog ran across the campus one day, carrying something that looked very red. *A red-headed woodpecker*, thought I, as I gave chase. The dog must have wondered why this hot pursuit, but it did not drop the woodpecker. I threw a stick, threw it hard, almost hitting my target. Still no relinquishment. The dog started around the big building. *Ah*, I thought, *now I can surprise him*! I raced through the building, looked out a window on the opposite side, and saw the dog hastily burying its prize—a bone. Thus did I learn that even the best of amateur ornithologists can misidentify a bird.

Recognizing birds and giving them their correct names were becoming important to me. I used our big dictionary a great deal. Here I found tiny, uncolored pictures of many strange species that I knew I'd never see near our house, or in Nebraska, or even in North America, but all these wrynecks, crocodile birds, cockatoos, bustards, and other exotic forms interested me deeply nonetheless. My parents indulged in pardonable hyperbole when they told the neighbors that I could correctly name every bird pictured in that huge book, and they revealed profound understanding of my needs when they gave me a bird book of my very own—Frank M. Chapman's *Bird-Life*. This little volume, with its many color plates, I looked at every day, many times every day, and quite literally wore out.

One bird that this new book told me about lived in tall weeds along the creek in back of our house. It had a black mask across its face, and it sang *witchery*, *witchery* so very clearly that I knew it could be nothing but a Maryland yellowthroat. It struck me as strange that a Maryland bird of any sort should be living in *Nebraska*.

At school I was to bring shame upon the family by having to stay in one whole recess period, writing on the board a word that was new to me. I had never attended a funeral—had never even heard the word. At home we had better things to talk about. In reciting "The Psalm of Life," with its line about "funeral marches to the grave," I had pronounced the word "funeral" as if it were a prolongation of the word "fun." The teacher must have thought that I was ridiculing funerals, life and death in general, perhaps especially her—so in I stayed and wrote, wrote, wrote that word "funeral."

I had a long white stocking cap that I wore in winter. It was warm, tight-fitting (it made my forehead itch), and useful. Useful especially when Bertie Austin, an older boy who lived across the street from us, gave me a dead marsh hawk, a specimen so wonderful that I could not bear to be parted from it. I slid it tenderly, head first, into the stocking cap and took it to school with me. At my seat I pulled it out, smoothed its plumage, and put it in my desk, where I derived comfort from its beautiful patterns and its softness when arithmetic problems became boresome or overly difficult. I don't remember burying that lovely bird or taking it to the laboratory under the bridge. I do recall standing on our front walk, admiring the spread wings, when Dr. David Hilton, our family physician, having finished a routine call inside the house, asked where I'd got it. "Whoever shot that hawk made a bad mistake," he said. "Hawks are good birds, especially marsh hawks, for they eat rats and mice." Thus did I receive my first lesson concerning the economic value of birds of prey; thus began a friendship that lasted to the end of Dr. Hilton's life, many years later.

Ours was a busy household. Mother practiced hours on end. Her piano was not a grand but a bulky, rectangular instrument that looked like a high, very thick table. One of her pieces was that pyrotechnical Liszt opus called Hungarian Rhapsody no. 2 in C-sharp minor. We kids especially enjoyed the parts in which Mother's right hand made leap after leap from a high note to a low. Though not much of a musician, I sensed how bad it would be if that finger failed and one of those important notes turned out to be the wrong one. Mother taught piano, too. She was not, I believe, on the Cotner faculty, but she spent a great deal of time training a campus chorus to sing Handel's *Messiah*. Father, whose principal work was teaching, was busy writing a play called "The Temptation," a tragedy dealing with the stricken conscience of Judas Iscariot.

Mother, who read stories wonderfully well, held us spellbound with chapters from Ernest Thompson Seton's *Wild Animals I Have Known*. The stories about Raggylug the cottontail, Silverspot the crow, and Redruff the ruffed grouse or "partridge" of the Don Valley were so touching that Dorothy and I could not hear them through without shedding tears. A story titled "The One Who Was Hated," by another nature writer of the day, convinced me that no living thing was safe while a weasel was abroad. One day I learned that the Austins across the street had killed a weasel in their chicken house. When I looked at the limp, slender carcass and was assured that the animal was full-grown, I felt much more comfortable about weasels.

Father's marvelous voice, his ability as a speaker, and his firm convictions concerning such evils of the day as the saloon led him to enter politics. We youngsters had only a vague idea as to what he was doing, but we knew that he was forever on his way to some town called Superior or Scottsbluff or Beatrice (pronounced not as the girl's name was pronounced but as Be-át-rice, with the accent on the second syllable), and we must have felt a certain pride as we looked at the big photograph of him under which someone had written "The Governor." He ran for the office on the prohibition ticket. He did not win, but he did what he thought was right, namely, denounce in no uncertain terms what he considered bad. He was a saintly man whose occasional lapses into less than saintly behavior included sound thrashings administered to his children.

Handel's *Messiah* and Father's "The Temptation" were presented in the auditorium on the second floor at Cotner. Church services were held there, too. These I found hard to endure unless a hat on some woman in the pew in front of ours happened to have a bird (or part of a bird) on it. With pencil in hand and hymnbook in lap, I could draw to my heart's content. For a wonder, no one chided me for this vandalism. I recall especially a veritable whorl of terns, each footless and with spread wings, encircling the crown of a straw hat. Perspective and foreshortening did not bother me in the least those days. I wonder if one of those "illuminated" hymnals is still in use anywhere today. Probably not.

Another clear-cut memory of church is of a well-to-do man named Kimball who habitually reached into his pocket when the collection plate was passed, brought forth a whole handful of change, and poured it all into the plate. The sound of the many coins was so audible throughout the room that the Lord Himself must surely have heard it.

On rare occasions, Dorothy and I went with our parents on the "Interurban" to Lincoln, where we had to be careful every time we crossed the street, where there was a bakery whose display of pies, cakes, cookies, éclairs, ladyfingers, and cream puffs was downright demoralizing, and where there was a streetcar pulled by a team of big horses. No one pointed out this last, calling it passé; it was not a tourist attraction; but I noticed that when we returned to Bethany the neighbors asked, "And did you see the horsecar? Are they still using it?"

On the other side of town was what everybody called the campground, and beyond that—big, noticeable, jutting above the horizon like a grain elevator of sorts—was the home of William Jennings Bryan, a man famed for his silver-tongued oratory and his never-say-die political aspirations. Our family had a tent at the campground, and there we lived for part of a summer, though how the five of us disposed ourselves at night I cannot remember. Mother was busy composing a piano piece called "Bryan's March." It was tuneful, optimistic, and catchy. She played it with vigor. On a memorable evening when Bryan himself spoke in a big tent, Mother played her march and the broad-faced would-be president bowed his thanks to her. I remember the bowing but not the speech.

In early summer, we visited one of Father's prohibitionist friends who lived on a farm near Fairbury, Nebraska. Not far from the house was a big orchard inhabited by many birds. The trees were easy to climb, so I found and examined nests. The eggs were so beautiful and it was so exciting finding that what my beloved book had said about their color and shape was all correct that I decided to gather them. When I returned to the house I had a whole boxful of robin, catbird, kingbird, flicker, and dove eggs, only a few of which were broken. For this, my first egg collecting, I was severely reprimanded. I felt that the scolding was not quite fair. No one seemed to realize that obtaining those eggs was of importance to me.

At home I asked Father how it happened that I was so much interested in birds. He made no attempt to answer. Instead, he told me of his own boyhood in Illinois; of the hordes of plovers he had seen while plowing, of wild ducks and geese by the thousand, of prairie hens and snipes. "Draw me a snipe," I begged. Father found a pencil and a piece of newspaper and drew a long-billed, long-legged bird. "There you are, son. That's a snipe," he said.

Father's snipe and the dictionary's were much alike in several important ways. If Father's drawing could be as good as the dictionary's, why couldn't mine be? I decided that the time had come for me to make *good* drawings, not in hymnbooks but on separate sheets of paper. So I found paper and crayons and proceeded to draw redbirds, blackbirds, and bluebirds, contenting myself with images that were in truth red, black, and blue and not much else. These I considered a distinct improvement over anything I had ever done. Putting them in the jointly owned wagon, I peddled them from door to door, selling them at a penny apiece. I am not sure that I gave Dorothy her share of the money, but she did eat some of the "likkerish" candy that I bought with it.

A big haul came for me at a state fair to which our whole family went. There we rode the "roly coaster," ate such exotic treats as cotton candy, saw a huge Mississippi catfish in a glass tank barely big enough to hold it, and came upon a magnificent barred Plymouth Rock rooster that had won a blue ribbon. That rooster was too much for me—I could not get away from him. He looked me straight in the eye, precisely as if sizing me up. "You can tell that I'm the real thing," he seemed to say. "You know you like me. Why don't you stay here and make a picture of me? You can see for yourself that I'll not be going away.''

So stay I did—after finding a pencil and some paper. No crayons this time, just pencil. My subject wasn't gaudy; he was merely beautiful, very beautiful. Where the family went while I worked I do not know, but they must have kept an eye on me. A well-dressed, middle-aged man hovered over me, watching intently. No crowd gathered, for the man waved people off. I had to use the eraser a lot, but the picture took shape. I could tell that the man liked it.

When I had finished, the man—who could have been the rooster's owner—asked me what I intended to do with the drawing. "I want it,'' he said, "and I'll pay you for it.'' I hated to part with the heart-to-heart portrait, but the offer was too much for me. I capitulated. The man gave me a dime. Even in those days, a dime wasn't much. But it meant a great deal to me.

OREGON

WHEVER FATHER'S REASONS were for moving his family of five to Oregon, I remember no regret at the thought of leaving Nebraska but, rather, excitement at the prospect of seeing a new part of the world. There would be mountains, real mountains, in Oregon, I had been told, and rivers with salmon in them, and the shore of the great Pacific. There would be a snow-capped Mount Hood and a river with the intriguing name of Rogue, in whose valley grew apples famous for their beauty and flavor.

We traveled by train, carrying a good deal by hand, my load being a satchel and a guitar, the latter in a dark green cloth bag. So big was the guitar—or was I so small?—that until very recently I have insisted that what I carried was a contrabass viol. My sister Dorothy, whose memory for detail is sometimes embarrassing, has set me straight on this. Of course it was a guitar, the instrument Mother played while singing "Come ol' Aunt Jinny, git de hoe-cake done" and plaintive ballads, one of which was about "bonnie sweet Bessie, the maid of Dundee."

I can hear Mother singing even as I write. I feel not sorrow so much as tender gratitude as I listen. Her voice was not angelic. Indeed, very little about Mother was angelic. She was too much of a fighter for that. Her singing voice was neither rich nor resonant. This I know for, because of that fine woman's love of music and her determination to pass some of it on to her children, I have heard many of the world's very best singers. Mother played the piano well. A graduate of the great Oberlin Conservatory in Ohio, she could have had a career as a concert performer, but she decided to be a mother instead. That guitar and her singing were a part not of career but of motherhood.

The trip was long and a bit stuffy, but the tedium was relieved by visits to the dining car, where it was thrilling to be waited on while looking out the window. The fresh figs I ordered proved to be less palat-

13

able than I'd expected them to be, but as I ate them I beheld the wonders of the Snake River's canyon—by far the most spectacular scenery I had ever seen. And capping all the excitement of that particular day was a big hawk that plunged into the river not far from the train, caught a fish, and flew alongside us for quite a while. The train was moving rather slowly upgrade, so we all had a marvelous look. "That bird's a fish hawk," said Father. "Another name for it is osprey." I could remember the dictionary's tiny picture of an osprey clearly enough. What a far, far cry from the drab drawing was the magnificent bird itself—in action!

Following us as freight came not the ponderous black "square" piano, nor the marble-topped table, washstand, and dresser, nor the fragile little melodeon (now in the collection of the Nebraska Historical Society), nor that much loved possession of mine, the mounted pintail duck, which had, by dint of much handling and carting about, fallen to pieces, but Mother's new "mission-style upright" Gabler piano, the whole of the library of George Frederick Miksch, my maternal grandfather, and, of course, my precious copy of *Bird-Life* by Chapman. In Grandfather's library were the complete works of Dickens, Thackeray, Macaulay, Gibbon, Shakespeare, Scott, Coleridge, Hawthorne, and James Fenimore Cooper, not to mention scores of authors less fully represented.

I was named for Grandfather Miksch. His real surname was as I have just given it, but in Ohio and Minnesota he had had so much trouble with the outlandish spelling that he had shortened it to Mix, an abbreviation that my mother, proud of her Moravian ancestry, could not bear. Balancing the account, she bestowed Miksch as a middle name on each of us children, and I have spent a fair part of my life spelling, pronouncing, and explaining the strange name, of which I too am proud. The Moravians were, and are, a wonderful people. The name Miksch is honored in the annals of Gnadenhutten, Ohio, where Mother was born, in Winston-Salem, North Carolina, and in Bethlehem, Pennsylvania. Of the Miksches, more later; now a word about the George Mix library. As his collection of books grew, Grandfather decided that he wanted a bookplate all his own. The quaint, unpretentious label that he had printed was 3¼ inches wide and 1⅔ inches high. It had a small illustration at the left—a pen-and-ink drawing of a hook-beaked dragon climbing an urn. I have wondered about this little picture from time to time, finally deciding that the urn must have been filled with the nectar, wine, or stronger drink of knowledge and that the dragon was thirsty. At the bottom of the bookplate, to the right of the urn and dragon, was a quotation from Sir

Walter Scott—two sentences that must have been part of Scott's own bookplate: "And please return it. You may think this a strange request, but I find that although many of my friends are poor arithmeticians, they are nearly all of them good bookkeepers." My own bookplate, in use throughout my ornithological library today, was designed many years ago by my sister Evie. Knowing how much I had enjoyed the George Mix bookplate, Evie incorporated the whole of it into mine.

In Oregon we lived a year or so in Ashland, in the southwestern part of the state about twenty miles from the California line, and a year or so in Eugene, the seat of the University of Oregon. My memories of Ashland center not in any school that I attended nor in any college building in which Father taught but in the sparkling creek that ran through the town. At a bridge we had to cross in reaching the business district, I could look down at the wonderfully clear water and the thousands of lovely pebbles on the stream's bottom. These seemed to be of remarkable brilliance and smoothness, as if selected and polished and put in place solely for my delight. I stood there and looked, simply looked, wondering what made me feel as I did. Was I puzzled because the wet pebbles were more colorful than the dry ones on the bank? Was I spellbound by the patches of reflected light that came and went so endlessly and that shut the pebbles from sight when flashing? Was I psychologist enough to sense that the water's gentle babbling would always be part of what seemed at the moment a purely visual experience? My mind may have been ever so callow, but it captured an important something there on the little bridge in such a way as to make that something a continuing part of me—a part that would refresh me when I needed refreshing and calm me when I needed calming. No other stream in my whole life would do this for me.

One thing, one thing only, do I remember clearly about the furnished house that we rented in Ashland: a slab of dark gray rock in the front hall, a doorstop. In it, visible when I looked closely, were scattered garnet crystals whose deep red beauty affected me almost as powerfully as the pebbles on the creek's bottom did. What gave me those strange feelings? Was it the light that flashed from their little facets, or the richness of their color, or the fact of their being where they were—perfect little bits that would have been hidden away in a matrix forever but for the chain of accidents that had exposed them, led someone to preserve them, and somehow brought them and me to this house, thus making them mine to behold and admire? They awed me.

My interest in ornithology continued, though I do not remember a single bird seen or heard in our neighborhood. I do recall, and vividly, capturing two adult male western tanagers on a slope well away from town. One of these had been chasing the other fiercely, but the pursued about-faced, the two locked horns in midair directly above me, and to the ground they tumbled, almost at my feet. All I had to do was throw my cap over them. Holding one in each hand, I watched them glare at each other. Neither intended to give in, oh no, not that. Then the expression on their faces changed; they seemed to acknowledge that there were problems in this world other than those having to do with vanquishing rivals; and they started biting the fingers that held them. They bit hard.

I let the tanagers go—but not without qualms of a sort I had never felt. I didn't know what the birds were, and this ignorance hurt. Their lustrous black, white, yellow, and scarlet plumage was the most gorgeous I had ever held in my hands. All that beauty, that exquisite beauty, I wanted to keep, to have for reference, to show to people by way of making clear how wonderful birds could be. Here was an opportunity of a lifetime. But what was I to do with them? How could I preserve them? As they flew off, I felt that I had not quite played fair with an important part of myself.

Sister Dorothy was with me when I caught the birds. We had taken a long walk. Toward evening we found ourselves in country we had never seen before. At a house along a dirt road, we asked where we were and were invited to supper. The warmth of this hospitality, not to mention the pangs of hunger, must have prompted us to say that it would be all right for us to stay a while. Our hosts were good enough to hitch up their horse and buggy and drive us back to town in the dusk. Here Dorothy, whose accounts never fail to entertain, must take over. According to her, our parents had been agonizing, a posse searching, and sirens screeching by the time we got home. I venture to guess that our kindhearted friends never again invited stray children in for supper.

The day Father and I climbed Ashland Butte, we returned through a cemetery in which we found great numbers, literally dozens, of dead birds, victims of an ice storm. The only ones that I could identify were robins, though I now know that white-crowned and golden-crowned sparrows, juncos, warblers, hermit thrushes, and kinglets were among them. There were no jays, chickadees, or woodpeckers. Every blessed tree had dead birds under it. Some were lying on tombstones. I picked up as many as pockets and hands would hold and took them home. All were somewhat decomposed, so I did not try to skin them, though I pasted some of the feathers on cards and wrote names that I thought were right on the cards. Some names I had to make up, for my *Bird-Life* dealt with eastern, not western, birds.

In Ashland I joined the Christian church. While the congregation sang "Just as I am, without one plea," I went to the front pew and professed my belief in God and His Son, Jesus Christ. I couldn't quite understand why I should consider myself sinful, but the idea of having sins "washed away by the precious blood of the Lamb" was somehow appealing, genuinely appealing, and everyone seemed so happy over my decision to be "saved" that I felt an inner glow. I was immersed in the baptistry by Reverend Mellinger. A pair of hawk wings given me by a member of the church seemed, in its way, a reward for good behavior. "We've had these a long while," said the woman who gave them to me. "We all know how interested you are in birds."

In Eugene we lived not far from the University of Oregon campus and next door to the long-since-defunct Eugene Bible University, where Father taught. I was old enough to have certain chores, among them chopping wood for the kitchen stove.

Bird study demanded more, ever more, of my attention. Not content with saving feathers picked up here and there, with taking an occasional egg from a nest, and with doodling birds while going through the motions of solving mathematical problems and memorizing the capital cities of Europe at school, I tried stuffing birds—the first a handsome Steller's jay someone had shot in the woods along the Willamette River. What a glorious creature it was, with its flowing crest, the neat little brush of feathers over each nostril, and the rich blue of its wings and tail! I had no trouble removing the skin, but I failed to open the skull and remove the brain. Ladies' hats in those days were held in place with long pins, each of which had a black, shining glass ball at one end. This ball would, I foresaw, serve perfectly as an eye for my jay. Since I had no way of cutting the ball from the pin, I decided to let the ball serve as an eye on one side while the pin supported the specimen on the other. So my jay, complete with one fine, glittering eye and dangling legs, wings, and tail, all supported by the pin stuck firmly into a board, was presentable enough until flies laid eggs in its brain, maggots hatched, and the head fell apart.

Mother helped with my taxidermic work by furnishing thread that would match the colors of the birds I planned to obtain. She gave me a spool of yellow silk for goldfinches and orioles and some black for crows.

I did not realize that thread used properly in sewing up a specimen never showed, no matter what its color.

From now on, I decided, there'd be no more of this amateurish stealing of a bird egg now and then, so down from a tall spruce came a Brewer's blackbird nest and its four eggs, each of which I blew free of its contents after pricking a neat hole in each end with a needle. This blackbird was new to me, though I may have seen it in Nebraska without knowing what it was. I found a brief description of it in Florence Merriam Bailey's *Handbook of Birds of the Western United States*, and it was nicely represented in the collection of bird skins at the university. Mrs. Bailey's book I did not own, but whenever I went to the biology building on the campus I pored over it. Especially did I enjoy the full-page halftone plates by an artist named Louis Agassiz Fuertes.

Professor Sweetser, of the university staff, was kind to me. Sensing that I was more than casually interested in those bird skins, he let me arrange them for him and complimented me on my ability to put all the swallows together, all the sparrows, all the warblers. I had trouble with the thrushes, for bluebirds and robins were said to belong to the thrush family, though they didn't look like thrushes. I greatly enjoyed the biology laboratory. I came to feel that I was welcome there, even needed, for I kept the bird skins in order. Alas, the highly polished wooden stair railing, down which my young friends and I swooped from third floor to first, was my undoing. A campus policeman informed us that we were not to hang around the building anymore.

Being denied access to the bird skins at the university forced me to build up a collection of my own. A goldfinch that I found attached to a thistle had been dead so long that I did not try to skin it but kept it as a mummy, thistle and all. Some nests that I brought home I could not identify, but I kept them nevertheless, arranging them not in a case, for I had no case, but on the floor in one corner of an upstairs room. The floor was covered with linoleum. Sister Dorothy, convinced by what I told her that my bird work was of great importance, felt it her duty to scrub the linoleum for me.

One day while she and I were playing in the yard, I teased her by sticking a fluffy feather in her hair. A puff of wind lifted the feather and a violet-green swallow swooped past, almost within touching distance, seized the feather with a snap of its bill, and made off. Dorothy and I looked at each other with profound understanding. Off we rushed, in complete harmony, after feathers. We found many in the woodshed, where chickens had been plucked, but a great many more, and fluffier ones, in pillows in the house. Swallows responded by the dozen. Never for the following week or so did we emerge from the house without being followed by the graceful birds. If we opened an upstairs window, a flock gathered almost immediately. Rarely did a feather blown from there reach the ground. Seated at meals in the dining room, we perceived that the swallows were watching us as they flew back and forth just outside the window. Occasionally one tapped at the glass as if to remind us of our duty.

So excited was I by the swallows that I wrote William L. Finley, whose column on nature appeared in a little magazine called *School and Home*. Mr. Finley replied. Indeed, I believe he published something about our swallows. He may even have quoted from my letter.

A pair of swallows had a nest in a cranny below one of the gables of our house. Moving cautiously, rafter by rafter, in the hot, dusty, dimly lighted space between roof and rafters, I reached a crack through which I could look directly out on the brooding female, who became so tame that she accepted flies from the tips of my fingers. I could not get my whole hand through the crack.

A colony of cliff swallows nested under the eaves of a barn about a quarter of a mile from our house. The birds gathered mud for their nests at the edge of the millrace nearby. I was enough of an ethologist to wonder why the violet-green swallows should come to us daily, while the cliff swallows never did.

In September of 1908, Dorothy, Pauline, and I made room in our world for a new baby sister, Evie. I was ten years old, Dorothy seven. Dorothy and I both stayed home from school the day Evie was born. How wonderfully happy we were when we learned that Mother and the baby were safe!

In Eugene I started drawing birds in earnest. My intense admiration for the Fuertes halftones in Mrs. Bailey's book had a good deal to do with this. The best of my drawings I pasted together, end to end, and kept in two rolls. All were in pencil, for I had neither crayons nor paints. The subjects in one roll were, from left to right, the Screaming (Steller's) Jay, the Cliff Swallow, the Flycatcher, and the Least Pheode (*sic*), in the other the Screaming Jay (a little better this time, except for the right leg), the Red Wing, the Gairdener (*sic*) Woodpecker, the Brewer's Blackbird, the Dwarf Chewink, and the Vaired (*sic*) Thrush. Lord knows where I got some of these names, but I'd never even have tried to spell Gairdner had I not remembered to some extent what I'd seen in Mrs. Bailey's fine book. All the drawings were crude, crude beyond belief, but they were the result of sincere interest, and I am glad now that I was conceited enough to save them. The prize of the lot was the Red Wing, whose legs each had a tibiotarsal bone, a tarsometatarsal bone, and a fine short *extra* bone in between the two—providing the bird with a grand total of four ankles (and heels) rather than two. What a bird!

I look at the drawings today and remember the upstairs room in which I had my museum—-on the wall what was left of the Steller's jay; several rows of nests on the floor in one corner, a few of them with eggs; the big dry thistle with its mummified goldfinch; the two hawk wings; and cards galore, each with feathers pasted neatly on it.

ILLINOIS

FATHER COULD NOT have received much salary in Eugene—or in Ashland either, for that matter. I wonder now how he managed to keep the bills paid. Eugene Bible University was very small. Its one and only building continued to be unfinished; indeed, I am not sure that it was ever finished. There was no real campus, none at all, not even a lawn or tree in front. I am not sure that Father actually met classes there, nor do I know what he taught. In any event, we, his family, learned that we were to move again, this time to Illinois. I was bewildered, but excited too, at the thought of another long ride on the train. We would be living in a town called Eureka, and Father would teach at Eureka College. I thought, ever so jauntily: *Well, here we go again!*

Once more our hometown was small—about the size of Bethany, Nebraska. Our house was tall and ugly, with leering front windows. It had been painted a dark greenish shade of gray. Whoever chose that miserable color must have felt that the world was in dire need of sobering down. My room was on the second floor. I kept my copy of *Bird-Life*, a set of bird cards with which a game could be played, and my collection of birds' nests and eggs in a glass-fronted bookcase.

In a big vacant lot next to us a neighbor's cow grazed. I found that I could rouse this animal to genuine hostility if I swooped about her with an empty mattress cover held up on outstretched arms. The cover filled with air and flapped grandly. Dorothy assisted by pumping away on an accordion. The cow's eyes rolled, showing their whites; her lowered head swung balefully from side to side; her front feet pawed the ground. Little sister Pauline and the other kids of the neighborhood heartily approved of the show, so we staged a bullfight whenever life showed signs of coming to a standstill.

During one fight I stepped into a bumblebee nest. This was a tactical error, but it did not spoil the show, for the bees that were not stinging

21

hung menacingly near my face, and my efforts to elude them amused the gallery greatly. One bee got under my shirt and stung away for all it was worth. Pure joys of this sort had, of course, to end. There were complaints, lectures on cruelty to dumb animals, and a rueful return to a calm as dark greenish gray as that of our house.

Summer was almost over, but the orioles that had nested along our street had not yet left for the south. The gorgeous black-and-orange males scolded harshly and sang short, clear songs on cool mornings in early September. I found but did not collect two empty oriole nests, each near the end of a drooping elm branch, well out of reach. The young birds had all fledged long since. A third nest that I did collect I found after the leaves had fallen. It was in the very top of a tree in front of our house. It was double—two nests side by side, inextricably woven together and hung between vertical twigs. To this day I do not know whether two pairs of orioles had shared the double nest or whether one female had built both nests and used only one. Conceivably there had been one male bird with two mates.

One morning I found a dead thrush on our front porch. It lay there on its back, as perfect a specimen as I'd ever seen. It had killed itself flying into a window. With such instruments as I could find, I tried to skin it. Alas, it was exceedingly fat, the delicate skin tore badly, and handfuls of feathers came out.

Someone told me of a man who knew all about stuffing birds, so I took a blue jay that I had found dead to him and received a lesson. He skinned the jay out quickly, using only a pocketknife. With cotton and a piece of wire, I finished the specimen and put it in my bookcase to dry. When Professor James S. Compton at the college told me of a sora rail whose skin he wanted to preserve, I persuaded him that I could do the work. This time the bird was not fat, its skin was fairly tough, the feathers stayed in, and the specimen turned out surprisingly well.

Our house was not far from the college campus, but the focal point of my life was neither the college nor the public school I attended but a big sycamore in which barn owls nested in the heart of town. Here, after dark, the clamor of the hungry owls was beyond belief. I could hear them blocks away. People told me that the owls had nested there for years, that this was the second, perhaps even the third, brood for that year. Only occasionally did I see one of the old birds, but I found quantities of pellets under the tree, and I wondered as I gathered these whether they had been regurgitated by the parent birds only or by the young ones, too. I picked the pellets to pieces. With the tightly matted fur I found perfectly clean, beautifully shaped bones of small mammals. The lower jaws were especially neat and pretty. Only occasionally did I come upon a feather or any other part of a bird.

I did not enjoy school. I felt that my teachers did not like me: the thought that any of them might learn to love me, or be truly interested in me, never entered my mind. A teacher who had charge of us during a study period was something of a celebrity, for she had spent the preceding summer in France. Her last name, an unusual one, rhymed with rice (and therefore with mice, lice, etc.), thus begging to be used in snide doggerel, some of which I composed. She often tossed off French words and phrases that, whether correctly pronounced or not, had our young heads spinning. On one occasion, just after she had seen me passing a note across the aisle, she bewildered us all by calling me something we had never heard of—"a perfect noo-ee-sawnce!" She had become very French indeed. She was calling me a nuisance, which doubtless I was. She wound up her remarks, as her face reddened, with this: "George Sutton, if I had a nice fat ruler, I'd whack that hand of yours good and hard!" There was nothing mysterious, nothing exotic, nothing in the least Parisian about this statement. Everyone understood it perfectly.

At school I fell madly, hopelessly, in love with a girl named Lillian Callahan. I wrote sentimental poems about her and broke rules sending these to her desk, which was quite a way from mine. My infatuation centered in a wild desire to buy her a ring more beautiful than any I could find pictured in catalogs. Black-and-white illustrations of rings I colored variously, cut out neatly, pasted on cardboard, and gave to Lillian. She blushed tenderly as she accepted these, whispering about which of them she "really and truly" liked best. I hung around waiting for her after school, so as to see her home. One of my teachers, a towering female with beetling black brows, found me waiting for Lillian with what must have been a forlorn look on my face. Did I receive so much as a pat or a syllable of understanding? "Bah, you two! Calf love!" she snorted.

Christmas had always been gala at our house—a gilding of English walnuts, stringing of popcorn and cranberries, fashioning of ornaments from bright foil and paper, and decorating of the tree. A boxful of tinsel, glittering baubles, and ornate little metal candle holders designed to clamp on to branches came forth from a closet. In Eureka Mother and

Father announced that we'd not be using the candle holders anymore, for lighted candles were dangerous. Dorothy and I were let down by this decision, but Pauline and Evie were too young to care. I recall with shame, real shame, my own behavior on that particular Christmas. On a trip to the city of Peoria—a veritable Sodom or Gomorrah according to the neighbors—I saw a mounted hooded merganser in a hardware store window. The classic black-and-white beauty of the specimen obsessed me. I issued an ultimatum: unless I received that bird for Christmas, I'd *destroy* anything else I might receive. What a brat, what an insufferable brat I must have been! Are eleven-year-old boys in general that contemptible? Surely not. Santa did not bring me the merganser, nor did I destroy my presents. I shouldn't have received a single one. I should have received a good sound thrashing instead.

That Christmas it became painfully apparent that little Pauline was not recovering properly from heart trouble. A severe case of whooping cough had been followed first by nephritis, then by a weakness of pulse. Her continuing illness so baffled the local doctors that Father and Mother decided that their only hope of saving her lay in taking her to Battle Creek, Michigan, where some of the ablest physicians in the country could diagnose the trouble and prescribe treatment. Traveling to Battle Creek and living at the Kellogg Sanitarium there must have been dreadfully expensive, yet for some reason Father and Mother took me along. Strange health foods were served in the hospital dining room—"steaks" made of ground nuts, boiled carrots sprinkled with toast crumbs, and saltless butter. The good doctors did their best, but Pauline did not recover. Father and Mother were with the sweet, pale little thing when she died, and I was in a small room close by. Mother's sobbing cut deeply into me; so did the gentle voice of the doctor, who offered a simple prayer.

The funeral in the tall gray house in Eureka and the burial in the cemetery at the edge of town were perfunctory. During the evening of that sad day, Dorothy and I stood on the back porch, looking at the sky. Somewhere we had read that when a loved one died another star was added to the firmament. We must have known, as we gazed upward, that there'd be no way of recognizing little Pauline's star even if it had been there, but we looked nevertheless . . . and were somehow comforted.

After Pauline's death, we lived for a while in the Dye home. Royal Dye and his wife had been missionaries in a village called Bolenge, on the Congo River in Africa, and he had just been sent back to his station for another term's service. His wife, whom we called Aunt Eva, and two daughters, Polly and Dorcas, remained in Eureka. The Dye house was full of wonderful curios—spears, shields, grass mats, bracelets, anklets, especially a strange pillow carved from dark wood. A gray parrot with a red tail was a noisy part of the ménage. It called chickens with clucking sounds and, having drawn them all close, scattered them pell-mell with a shriek. The wonder of this hilarious farce was that it took place every day, sometimes several times a day, but the chickens never learned.

Well before sunup one morning, I was wakened by the parrot's cries, which included a sound remarkably like the word "George." Thinking that the bird had called me could have been only a dream, of course, or my imagination running wild, but to the cage I went, there to find a mouse, lying on its back under the perch, kicking its last. The parrot must have reached down and nipped the little gray thief of sunflower seeds to death.

In the spring of 1910, we Suttons moved to a small, one-storied house across the street from the big greenish gray one. Here I had no room of my own, but I did have a desk in the living room, and Mother agreed to let me use part of the refrigerator for my specimens. I had a set of colored crayons. I was never praised at school for my art work, but my drawing of an oriole at its nest was reproduced as a halftone in a school publication with statewide circulation. The drawing was not signed, nor was my name mentioned. The picture was used, I daresay, to prove that art education in Illinois was producing results.

Someone told me of a "big, brown, long-legged bird" that a man had shot. I went to the man's house, which was a short way out of town, talked with his wife, and was told by her to take the bird if I wanted it. I surmised from the look on her face that she was glad to be rid of it. It was an American bittern. I was entranced by its yellow eyes, its beautifully marked plumage, and its pale olive green legs. At home, I was about to skin it when a neighbor boy told me that "a man down the street" wanted to see me right away. The man, who must have been afraid to come to the house, said: "If you're the one who stole that shike-poke, you'd better take it right back to where it came from, or I'll have the law on you." I told the man that his wife had said that I could have it. "That there shike-poke's mine, not hers," he shot back. "You get it back to where you took it from!" So sadly, resentfully, I took it back, not wanting to argue further with anyone whose property I had "stolen." I put it on the porch where I had found it, gave it a last, long, loving look, and withdrew.

That spring there was great excitement over Halley's comet. We youngsters wondered whether there'd be a sudden crash when the comet's tail brushed the earth, or a lingering noise like that of huge cymbals striking one another, or an awful roar, worse than that of a heavy freight train. One evening, as neighbors stood with us in our yard looking at the sky, a much respected older person asked what may have been intended as a purely jocular question, but it scared the daylights out of me: "Don't you smell something strange—something like sulphur or some kind of gas?" I went to the far side of the house, feeling very lonely and frightened, convinced that the constriction in my throat was real—that presently we might all be strangled.

Deeply sorrowed by Pauline's death, Mother sought solace in her music. Talented, energetic, ambitious creature that she was, she practiced fiercely every day. She did her best to teach Dorothy and me, too, but we were not faithful in practicing. One day she stunned us by announcing that she intended to go to Chicago to study piano under a famous teacher—Fannie Bloomfield-Zeisler. She and Father had talked it over, of course. Mother would live in Chicago; Father would go on teaching in Eureka; and we children would spend the winter in Minnesota—Dorothy with Uncle Milton Fuller and his wife, Montie, in Albert Lea, Evie with Uncle Will and Aunt Elsie Lobb on a farm near Huntley, I with Grandfather and Grandmother Sutton in Winnebago.

For me, Minnesota was wonderful. Winter was cold and snowy, but I throve on winter weather. I walked about a mile to school, carrying my lunch in a tin box. When spring returned, I went to the woods beyond the town limits whenever possible. The Blue Earth River was beautiful and exciting at that time of year. For a while it was frozen over, but I knew that the ice was unsafe, for it looked wet. Then came the breakup and flocks of migrating waterfowl. At a bend where the water was deep, the current slow, and the gouged-out bank high, I watched mallards and pintails courting among the floating ice chunks. The green on the drake mallards' heads, when struck by the sun, was one of the finest colors I had ever seen. When the ducks sensed danger, they sprang from the water and whirred off. The hen mallards seemed to be the only ones that quacked.

Beyond the river, in the middle of an old road through the trees, I found a woodcock's nest. There were four eggs. So protectively colored were the eggs and the brooding bird that I marked the nest site with a dead branch lest I step on it. Near the road were hundreds of flowers, all coming into bloom at once—spring beauties, bloodroots, dutchman's-breeches, jack-in-the-pulpits, trilliums. The freshness, the flawlessness of their petals impressed me deeply. What could one *do* about so much beauty, so much perfection? What indeed—beyond leaving it all as it was, untouched, untrampled.

Uncle Frank, Father's older brother, who lived on a farm near Huntley, gave me my first real instruction in taxidermy. He shot a crow and I watched him as he skinned it, put a "body" of excelsior and tow inside the skin, stuck wires through the legs and wings, and stood it up on a board as if it were preening its plumage. That crow became an important part of my young life.

I remember Grandfather Critten Sutton, who died while I was living in his house, as a dignified, heavily bearded man who never laughed. I am not sure that I ever saw him smile. People said of him: "He was a good farmer. He kept things in good repair and he was good to his animals." His wife, Polly Ann, was gentle, even-tempered, industrious, and mannerly. Two objects in my grandparents' house fascinated me—a drake green-winged teal that Uncle Frank had mounted and a large blue book titled *The Horrors of Polygamy* on the top shelf of a bookcase in the parlor. By stepping from a chair onto the top of the piano (always in stockinged feet), I could reach this book, whose illustrations of certain ceremonial customs were a bit frightening. Especially so was one of a young woman, with a soulful look on her face, having the skin of her knee snipped with scissors. I derived a strange thrill from this picture, a secret feeling beyond explanation. Certain boys that I knew heard about the picture. Whenever I felt that one of them deserved a special award, I showed it to him.

When our family reunited in Eureka in 1911, we lived in a two-storied white frame house just beyond the edge of town. Here we were close to a big strawberry patch in which a pair of upland sandpipers nested. Father called these birds prairie whistlers. He told me that he had seen thousands of them as a boy. Their call notes and behavior held me spellbound. As they circled above me, their wings seemed to quiver rather than beat or flap. Their most memorable call began with a bubbling sound but trailed off into a windy whistle so beautiful that it made my spine tingle. The birds were especially graceful when they alighted on fenceposts. They held their long, pointed wings over their backs a full second before folding them.

Inevitably someone found their nest, for picking the berries de-manded covering every foot of ground. There were four eggs. The size of these bewildered me, for they seemed about twice as large as they ought to be. Their hugeness became no more understandable when Pro-fessor Compton showed me an upland sandpiper specimen at the college. The upland sandpiper was known as the upland *plover* in those days.

In heavy woods across the road from the strawberries, barred owls nested. We often heard their weird hooting at night. The noise sounded oddly like laughter at times, especially when two birds called at the same time. Occasionally we heard the hooting in broad daylight. The parent owls must have left the woods at times when hunting, but I never saw one flying across the road. Once I found a young owl on the ground in the very heart of the woodland. It was not injured; it could hobble about nimbly, though unable to fly. It made a popping sound with its bill and hissed savagely when I picked it up.

Beyond the strawberry patch was a brook along which I captured a truly rare bird. I was walking through heavy grass at the water's edge when up flew what I thought was a young red-winged blackbird. It flew weakly, with legs dangling. Across the brook it went, I in hot pursuit. Finding no lush vegetation in which to hide, it flew into the woods. I kept after it, for I believed that it had never learned to fly properly. I might never have started after it in the first place had I realized that it was full-grown. Finally, it crash-landed among some roots and tried to hide in a shadowy spot, where I pinned it down. Imagine my surprise when I found in my hands a fully adult *black rail*, the first I had ever seen. Its eyes were bright red. It kicked vigorously, but I held on to it, took it to the house, made a cage for it, and kept it several days. When it died, I decided the time had come for me to become a professional, so I wrote the Northwestern School of Taxidermy, in Omaha, asking them to for-ward their lessons. I paid for these with money earned picking strawberries. The tools they sent with their first booklet were excellent. The sturdy forceps, which I still use almost every day, are like a third hand.

Now I was convinced that I should establish my own school—not of taxidermy but of ornithology. My room, on the second floor, was large enough for at least nine desks. I drafted a plan which made clear just where the pupils' desks would be, just where the teacher's. My collection of feathers, bones, nests, eggs, and the mounted crow were neatly as-sembled on the floor in one corner. Below a window I heaped soft earth into which I could drop in case of fire. I found I could hang on to the crow and land in the earth without the slightest damage to crow or self. I had a sort of fire drill every week or so. What kept my indulgent parents from investing in desks and chairs, all of which were to be fastened down securely, I do not know, but my School of Ornithology never got beyond the blueprint stage.

TEXAS

AN OFFER from Texas Christian University convinced Father that another move was in order, so we went to Fort Worth when I was thirteen. For several months, we lived in a residential part of the sprawling city, close to Magnolia Avenue, an important thoroughfare. What impressed me most in this new habitat was the boundless enthusiasm of everyone for all things Texan—Texas history, Texas politics, Texas cotton, Texas oil, Texas cattle, Texas scorpions, centipedes, tarantulas, rattlers, "horny frogs," prickly-pear cactus, mesquite trees, roadrunners, scissortails, blue northers, and whatnot. Never had anyone in Ashland or Eugene tried to sell me Oregon, nor had anyone in Eureka tried to sell me Illinois. These new acquaintances, proud as they were of their homeland, hastened to caution me of the dangers I would be facing. "If a centipede crawls over you, the flesh will rot from your bones." Such statements kept me alert.

An unbelievably colorful bird of the neighborhood, right there in the city, was the painted bunting—a species some books called the nonpareil. The male was a mixture of bright red, golden green, and purplish blue, the female very dull by comparison. A pair nested in a hackberry tree in the yard next to ours. After the brood had fledged I took the nest, branch and all.

I soon learned about Forest Park—a wild area well out of the city but easily reached by trolley. In the park were many caged animals, notably a collared peccary or *jabalina* who so enjoyed having its back scratched that it pressed close to the woven-wire fence whenever I approached, grunted its satisfaction as the scratching started, and presently flopped to the ground in utter bliss. Its lashes were so thick and long that I could hardly see its eyes. "You want to watch those fellas," someone warned. "They can be *bad!*"

In the vicinity of the park, roadrunners were fairly common. The first one I ever saw sprang from a thicket only a few feet ahead of me, darted across an open space, paused in the high grass long enough to startle me by rattling its mandibles sharply, then leaped into the air, sailed on short, rounded wings across a gully, and disappeared into a tangle of greenbriar. Unexpected and brief though this encounter had been, I had seen the orange and pale blue bare space in back of the eye, the glossy black crest, and the boldly white-tipped outer tail feathers.

Soon I was to find that these strange ground cuckoos, which many people called chaparrals or chaparral cocks, really liked roads. By following their footprints (two toes pointing forward, two backward), I came upon shallow basins in which they had dust-bathed. Occasionally I found a feather. Observed at a distance and undisturbed, a roadrunner might move slowly through sparse vegetation, catching flightless nymph grasshoppers, an almost effortless procedure; but, surprised at the edge of a road, it suddenly became long, low, and horizontal, ran swiftly a rod or so, and bounded into the brush without spreading its wings. A roadrunner could be especially interesting on a chilly morning in early spring when, eager to warm up, it hopped from branch to branch to the very top of a leafless tree, there to perch with tail straight down, wings spread wide, and back plumage so lifted as to let the sun reach the featherless areas. Comfortable at last, it might sing from this high perch, choking out a series of rough coos. This odd vocalization I heard many times before realizing that a roadrunner, not an owl or a dove or a dog, was producing it.

Scissor-tailed flycatchers were whiter on the head than I had expected them to be. The whiteness seemed almost out of place. But how lovely were the pink on their sides and the bright salmon red under their wings, and how graceful their flight as they chased each other high in the air! Perched on a wire, they did not have the upright posture flycatchers were said to have; this bothered me until I saw for myself what an important element of their habitat wind was. Wind *forced* such long-tailed birds as these to be horizontal while perching.

Scissortails had a delightful predawn song that I heard whenever I was afield early. How I loved to listen as I looked toward the sound, hardly able to see the tree in the darkness and wondering just where the singer was! In the fall, great numbers of scissortails gathered at roosts in certain large trees along the edge of the city. The awakening at these roosts was wonderful to witness as the birds, all of them in fresh plumage, scattered noisily at sunrise.

The loggerhead shrike was common in open country. One morning,

I observed a shrike flying laboriously from the ground to its "butcher shop," the top strand of a barbed-wire fence, with a heavy object in its bill. Having no field glasses, I could not make out what the bird was impaling until I was almost within touching distance. To my amazement, the shrike refused to leave its prey—a giant water beetle, the insect we boys called an electric-light bug, since we so often saw one zooming about a streetlight at night. When I reached toward the struggling captive, the shrike reared back, opened its hooked beak wide, and scolded harshly. Not without a scene would that doughty bird give up its hard-earned meal!

In our backyard I built a cage for two owls—a barred and a barn, who lived together amicably enough until one night when, probably because I had not fed them enough, the barred owl killed and ate the barn. I had a young prairie dog, too, a winsome animal whose mischievous grin and shrieked-out cry kept us all laughing. A loud-voiced guinea and a duck, two fowl that belonged to my sisters as well as to me, had the run of the yard.

Near the front window in the attic I kept my collection, which now included a grackle and a white-breasted nuthatch, two cabinet skins beautifully prepared by a man named Willis W. Worthington. I was dishonest with my parents about these specimens. I had arranged with my friend Ramon Graham, a young taxidermist, to pay for them eventually, when I had earned enough money. My parents happened to find a hand-written bill, a statement Ramon and I understood perfectly but they didn't. I lied about this bill when, after burning it, I said that I didn't even know of its existence. What I did know, of course, was that it didn't exist anymore. I felt wretched about telling this lie and never confessed that I had told it, for I feared that Father and Mother would never believe me again if I did tell them.

I attended high school about half a mile from our house. Dorothy and I had a pair of roller skates between us, so I often went to school on one skate. A history teacher whose accent was unequivocally southern pronounced "gods" and "guards" in exactly the same way, leading me to wonder whether the Praetorian defenders of the Roman emperors were graven images that people worshipped or living policemen of some sort. An English teacher made clear that I was not to go beyond assignments. A theme enlarging upon the idea expressed in Robert Burns's line "But pleasures are like poppies spread" seemed to me to need an illustration, so I added some nicely drawn poppies. Proclaimed the red penciling:

"This is a course in Rhetoric, not Art." A kindly man who tried to teach us mathematics had no control over his roomful of teenagers. Facing the board, writing away, he would be struck on the head with a paper glider thrown from afar. "This will have to stop," he'd mutter, as if to the chalk. "You just wait and see. I'll catch you next time." But "next time" it was not a glider; it was a pecan crunched underfoot. "Who did that?" he'd bark. Stalking back through the room investigating, he'd find crunched pecans under every desk.

One day, after several flocks of migrating sandhill cranes had passed low over the building, all classes were dismissed so everyone could watch the great birds. Many of us youngsters went to the roof, which was flat. Hundreds, perhaps thousands, of cranes and white pelicans were moving southward in advance of a blue norther. The cranes trumpeted magnificently. Boys who had been misbehaving badly indoors stood rapt in amazement. I have never ceased to wonder who among all those high-and-mighty, stuffy, unsympathetic teachers was broad-minded enough to suggest that we be dismissed in order to look at those birds.

Father said that he liked Texas. He bought a lot near the university—the three buildings were in the country well beyond Forest Park—and started establishing a real home. First came a small, two-floored barn, in which we camped out. A young Texan, a student at the university, helped Father. So did I, in various ways, especially when shingles were going on. The house seemed ever so much larger than necessary to me, but the screen porches, one above the other at the north end, were delightful on hot days, and the living room was extremely spacious.

Father wanted to panel the whole interior with cypress. He worked hard, at times almost feverishly. When the bathroom was finished, we moved from the barn into the house. Now that we were ensconced, a garden was in order. Next came a cow, a temperamental Jersey named Daisy, whose oddly shaped horns served her well. She could, and did, push at her stake and pull on her rope till the stake came up, then, using those horns, open the barn door without help from anyone, rip open a sack of cottonseed meal, gorge herself, and turn on the water faucet in the yard.

I had charge of this prima donna. She had her own special way of putting her foot into a bucket while being milked, of flinging saliva over me with a toss of her head, of blinding me with flicks of her tail, even of hooking me now and then. She was at times quite unmanageable. I am sure she hated me. She was calm on one memorable evening while a small tornado went over. As the ink black clouds boiled overhead, spitting fire, Daisy stood quite still, gazing respectfully upward.

The family had an infuriating way of laughing whenever I complained about Daisy. My tribulations seemed to be great fun for them. However, Father sided with me when a monthly bill was exceptionally high. Daisy had turned the water on but had not—profligate creature!—bothered to turn it off. When we returned from the city that day, a little stream was flowing between the ties under the trolley rails at our stop a hundred yards downslope from the house. I had given Daisy all she could drink before we left, but she had pulled her stake up, gone to the faucet, turned it on, and delighted her soul with the sound of water running full blast while moistening lips and tongue.

I found comfort of sorts in writing a story about Daisy. The plot was simple. The hero was a hardworking, unappreciated boy and Daisy was the culprit, the evil element, the *bête noire*, who disliked the hero for no good reason at all, a feeling she expressed as often and in as many ways as possible. The years passed. As the hero grew older, so did Daisy. Eventually, when the hero had reached a glorious prime, Daisy had become fit only for butchering, so off she went to the stockyard. But Daisy was not to be outdone. One day while the hero was purchasing groceries, a jar of chipped beef fell from a shelf and hit him hard on the head. It was Daisy.

Our house fronted on an unpaved street that nothing but lizards, grasshoppers, tiger beetles, robber flies, bull nettles, wild verbenas, and sandspurs ever used. Beyond that lay a vast stretch of open prairie—magnificent, untamed grassland with its scattering of yucca, prickly pear, and mesquite, not to forget the ridiculous jackrabbits that popped up as if out of some Great Magician's hat that no mortal could see. Beyond the prairie, not quite far enough off to be purplish blue or hazy, were trees lining a small, usually bone-dry tributary to the Trinity River. This arroyo was known as Bushong's Run.

The prairie was my hunting ground, my laboratory, my library, my sanctuary. I roamed over it, studied it, listened to its sounds, turned over its rocks, dug in it, took parts of it home for careful observation. Never did I cease to marvel at the ways in which it responded to the moods of sun and sky. I watched dark, sunless patches moving across it in early spring and searched among the clouds until I ascertained exactly which ones were responsible for the shadows. Wonder at the special beauty of frost on its brown grass in fall became a side study in physics when I perceived that an opalescent brilliance shone close around my own long shadow early on bright mornings. This I might never have noticed had I not so often walked with the sun at my back. A rising sun blinded me momentarily if I was forced to look in its direction.

The brilliance of the prairie flowers amazed me. Spring triggered rebellion against monotony—a rebellion led by wild flax and blue sky, by yucca blossoms and white clouds, by acre upon acre of red-and-yellow gaillardia daisies. There were times when I sat on a rock and looked at the varicolored panoply for the sheer joy of looking. At times my mind busied itself with trying to comprehend why this mere viewing, this mere drinking in, should be enough. Ought I to be *doing* something about it all? My alter ego, the pragmatist, would remind me that time was escaping, that I was growing old all too rapidly, that I had a very great deal to learn about the cotton rats that lived in the clumps of cactus; the mice, shrews, scorpions, and snakes under the hundreds of flat rocks; the tarantulas in their burrows; the spotted skunk, or spilogale, whose den I had happened upon in the middle of that colorful carpet; and all these new birds, some of which had me so bewildered that I went to bed night after night wretched because I knew so little about them.

One wonderful day, April 13, 1913, in thick brush along the edge of Bushong's Run, I found my first roadrunner nest. I brought home two of the young birds, gave one to my pal Noland Williams, and found an old bucket in which to keep mine. Noland's died from being fed a quantity of dry wheat; mine throve on grasshoppers, crickets, centipedes, scorpions, stinkbugs, beetles, angleworms, tarantulas—in short, anything in the small-animal line that I could find. Grasshopper nymphs, whose wings were mere stubs, were easy to catch, but I had trouble finding enough of them. The ideal meal was an eighteen-inch snake that could not be swallowed all at once.

The young roadrunner grew rapidly. Presently it was looking *at* things rather than merely staring, lifting its glossy blue black crest, and rattling its bill when excited. On April 22, just before it was strong enough to toddle, I put it on a table and made a direct-from-life drawing of it (plate 1). This drawing I saved. It is, I believe, the earliest direct-from-life drawing of mine still in existence.

When my pet began obtaining its own food, it was pure joy to watch. Though slightly unsteady on its feet, it had no trouble catching nymph grasshoppers, many of which made no attempt to escape. It soon learned that, when I turned over a board or a rock, cave crickets were to be captured, and not many days passed before it was whacking to death and gulping centipedes, millipedes, and scorpions. Flying grasshoppers, whose brightly colored wings and clacketty courtship noises had attracted it from the first, it had to learn to capture. After many a futile try, it found that by sneaking up slowly, then dashing in with wings and tail spread, it could snatch the fleeing insects from the air. Very young horned lizards it had no trouble seizing, battering, and swallowing; but mature individuals flattened out, stood high on their legs, and swayed back and forth menacingly, and the roadrunner had to learn the hard way that a half-dead horned lizard was not ready for ingestion. Race runners were at first far too swift and agile for the bird. But at length it caught one by the tail; whereupon the lizard, following a time-honored custom, released its tail and ran on, leaving the roadrunner first with the wiggling tail in its bill, then with the wiggling tail on the ground, finally with a woebegone, utterly bewildered look on its face. It wasn't sure that it wanted to eat this questionable item. When I came up, it turned to face me, crouched, fluttered its wings, and begged hoarsely for food. It was still only a baby. I picked up the quiescent tail, gave it to my pet, and watched the morsel go down. What in this wide, wide world was to be trusted if not a parent?

On a gorgeous May 16, my fifteenth birthday, came a present from my parents that replaced conflict with peace, sorrow with gladness, loneliness with companionship—a copy of the third edition of Mrs. Bailey's *Handbook of Birds of the Western United States*. I unwrapped the package with fingers that would not behave. If words did not express my gratitude, the look on my face must surely have done so.

The bird I most wanted to find out about was a dull-colored little thing. I had seen enough of it to be sure that it was a sparrow of some kind. It was practically invisible on the ground, but it had a way of jumping from the grass, flying upward fifteen or twenty feet, spreading its wings wide, and floating downward, singing one of the most touchingly beautiful songs I had ever heard. I could not for the life of me imitate the song, but I transliterated it into a sort of *Thee, diddle it, diddle it* that had meaning, at least for me. At times several birds sang in a kind of chorus—not in unison but here and there all over the prairie. I turned to the part in my new book that dealt with sparrows. Finally, on page 353, I found the following: "Scattered through the bushes around you the little choristers one by one spring up several feet above the brush and with heads high and wings outspread in a rapture of song give themselves to the air, floating slowly down as they sing." *That* was my bird—Cassin's sparrow!

Its principal field characteristic was the "sandy brown streaking" of its gray upperparts. Its nest was "on ground, in low bushes, or tufts of grass," its eggs "3 to 5, white or bluish white." These I would find as soon as possible and see for myself. Slowly, very slowly perhaps, but also very surely, was the prairie becoming part of me.

During our first winter on TCU hill, I had become acquainted with three other members of the sparrow tribe, but I wasn't dead sure that I knew their names. These were the handsome Harris's sparrow, whose habitat was the woods, and two longspurs, the chestnut-collared and the McCown's, both of which went about in big flocks in open country. The longspurs were, like the Cassin's sparrow, hard to see while they were on the ground. They flew up not far ahead of me, one by one, two by two,

Nestling Roadrunner   Direct-from-life wash drawing, Fort Worth, Texas, April 22, 1913. After learning to capture its own food, this bird became an extremely interesting pet.

or in a flock all at once, and they had a way of swinging about with strongly undulating flight, of climbing higher and higher, of sometimes almost disappearing in the distance, then of returning, circling closer and closer, and finally, after reaching agreement in a fluttering mass—a sort of feathered cloud a few feet aboveground—of settling not far from the spot they had left.

As I proceeded with my study of the prairie, I came to feel that I needed a menagerie. I built cages from planks, chicken wire, and screen—a large one against the side of the barn; a smaller one, on legs, that could be kept on the lower floor's screen porch; and still smaller ones that could be moved about in such a way as to provide the animals with fresh grass every day or so. I didn't keep many of my captives long. Something was forever happening to them. A big striped skunk that the family never quite approved of got away by digging out. A coyote pup became quite a pet but ranged widely and was shot for stealing chickens. An American kestrel that I caught at its roosting spot high on a water tower became surprisingly tame but threatened to batter itself to pieces when frightened in its cage. Mice of various kinds fared well in captivity until I made the fatal mistake of putting a shrew in with them; the shrew simply annihilated the mice. Favorite pets were two gray screech owls, which Mother permitted me to place at either end of the keyboard while I practiced on the piano, as well as a one-winged junco whose little cage I occasionally put into the garden. When I opened the door, the junco hopped out, made a tour of the growing vegetables, filled up on insects and bits of sand, and of its own volition returned to the cage, where it knew it was safe.

To prove to the family that I wanted my zoo to improve the looks of our place, rather than clutter it up, I lugged fossil gastropods to the yard, dozens of them, lining paths to the cages with them. I was annoyed when I noticed that everyone stepped over these paths rather than walking on them, and Daisy's utter disregard of them was hard to bear. My friend Noland Williams, who also had to care for a cow he didn't like, gave me a fine suggestion: "George, why don't you chop her with a hoe?"

My room was on the second floor, near the head of the stairs. At one of its windows were a built-in table and bench. Since the stairs needed light from that window, there was neither wall nor partition directly in back of the bench. I wondered what would happen were I to fall through the opening, but misgivings of this sort were compensated for by the pleasant prospect of listening to what went on in the living room below. I soon learned that conversation there continued no matter how loudly I coughed or shuffled my feet, so I felt that I had a perfect right to hear all. At a meeting of the ladies' missionary auxiliary, a devout soul held forth on the joys of tithing. Her voice was a shade unctuous. "We of my consecrated family have tithed for many years, but we manage somehow. It takes a good deal of self-denial here and some going-without there, but we never fail to give back to the Lord one-tenth of what He has given us. And sometimes, my dears, we even give Him back a twentieth!" The mathematician within me, small though he was, felt like shouting "Bravo!" on hearing that.

I attended classes in the preparatory school at the university rather than at the high school in the city. My mind was not on lectures or on recitations; it was wandering. How could a turkey vulture soar and soar, hour after hour, without ever flapping its wings? Where did the big, solemn-looking birds nest? What did their eggs and young look like? I could read about all this, of course, but reading wasn't the real thing. Did marsh hawks nest anywhere near Fort Worth? I never seemed to see them in summer. When would I have a 12-gauge shotgun of my own? Charlie MacLendon had stirred my imagination with glowing accounts of the ducks he had shot at Katy Lake. Which blackbird was it that nested among cattails—was it always the ordinary redwing, or might it sometimes be the much bigger great-tailed grackle? A crow's eggs were really green, a special sort of pale bluish green, and they were speckled . . . "No, Professor Hamner, I can't remember who Alexander Pope was, and I can't remember what he wrote," I heard myself saying. I had been thinking of a certain crow's nest not very high up in a live oak, a nest easy to climb to. There had been two eggs in it the day I'd found it; there'd probably be a full clutch by now. "George," continued the stern voice, "I shall have to speak with your father about this."

Professor Hamner spoke with Father, and Father spoke with me, and my mind went right on wandering. To keep my mind company, I went along whenever possible. One day, one never-to-be-forgotten day, I learned firsthand about the turkey vulture's nest. I had walked farther than usual, to the very banks of the Trinity, to heavy woods in which flying squirrels, opossums, raccoons, even bobcats lived. I came upon a hollow log about twenty feet long. In that log I could see—bulky, motionless, silhouetted against the light at the other end—a turkey vulture. The big bird did not leave. I decided that it must be at or on its nest. Moving swiftly, I propped two flat rocks at one end of the log and rushed to the other end. No vulture came out. The log was thick and not so *very* long and the vulture was inside it. I would crawl through and get the vulture. The plan was simplicity itself.

About the time my body was inside the log, I decided that reconsideration of the whole business was in order, but I was unable to back out. I could not pull with my toes or push with my hands. My arms were in front of me; there they would have to stay. The only direction in which I could move was forward. I clawed with my fingers, shoved with my toes, inching along. Clothes gave way; buttons snapped; I could feel my belt digging into my skin. Panic seized me. I had sense enough to realize, however, that panic might do more harm than good, for it was forcing me to gasp and there wasn't air enough even for ordinary breathing. I calmed down, relaxed, felt somewhat better. *If I ever get out of here,* I thought fiercely, *I'll show them. They may think I'm a no-account, but they'll learn! They'll find out! I'll show them!*

My hand touched something soft—a conclave of granddaddy long-legs, thin-legged creatures that milled about when I disturbed them. Prancing on my skin, they nearly drove me frantic. Wiping them off by moving my face from side to side against the damp wood was about all I could do. I must have killed or disabled scores of them. Crushed, they had a disagreeable smell. Again a hand touched softness. The mice that scampered out I could not see, but I felt two of them when they raced over my neck and tried to squeeze past me. The vulture must have frightened them more than I did.

When, at length, I came face to face with the vulture, I found to my intense relief that I could move more freely. The log had widened, and my eyes had adjusted to the darkness. The vulture was hissing. Presently it opened its mouth wide, leaned forward a bit, and disgorged decayed flesh. It tried to produce more, but none came, a shortage for which I was grateful. Near my face were a snow-white downy baby and a big egg. Ordinarily I would have considered these lovely. As things stood, however, all I felt was gratitude, profound gratitude, for not being stuck.

Pushing the baby, egg, and wad of decayed flesh ahead of me—the parent vulture needed no urging—I reached the rocks. When I grasped the old bird by its feet, I was surprised by its refusal to bite. It hardly even flapped its wings. Out of the log at last, I bound my captive's feet together with a strip of undershirt and tied it to a sapling with another strip. At a shallow pool nearby, I washed smears of wood and remains of granddaddy longlegs from my face. God in heaven, it was good to be out of that log!

In what was left of my shirt, I found a dead mouse. My pants were fairly intact—there were only one or two bad tears. I felt pretty shaky. I decided not to take the vulture, baby, and egg home so put them back in the log. Again, to my surprise, the old bird made no attempt to fly past me or to dash through the log to freedom. It stood there with mouth slightly open and eyes staring—almost as if it did not see me.

At home I found the house empty. There would be some explaining to do, but I could throw the remains of my shirt away, and torn pants were nothing new for Mother. She would understand. My sisters would laugh, no matter what I said; they considered all my vicissitudes ridiculous. Father might lecture me, but he would take what I told him in stride.

Mother did, indeed, understand: "Why, of course, pants need mending now and then." I had said not a word about the log. She had been attending a meeting of an active musical organization to which she belonged, the Harmony Club. She was elated. She had important news—news far more important than anything having to do with logs, vultures, or torn pants. "Madame Alda will be coming, and Tetrazzini, and even Schumann-Heink!" she announced, proud because her program committee had functioned so well. She was wearing her black-and-white, her daytime best. Her face glowed. The story of my expedition through the hollow log would have to come later.

I was in the audience the evening Frances Alda sang. Madame Tetrazzini's aigrette fascinated me. When Schumann-Heink, responding to thunderous applause, gave us Brahms's tender "Guten Abend, gut Nacht, mit Rosen bedacht" as an encore, the silence of the great hall fairly throbbed. I was on the stage, only a few feet from the diva. A huge emerald in her ring was beautiful, but it flashed less brilliantly than her smile. The train of her dress caught in a splinter. She had to jerk at it a bit with her right hand. Many a time since that memorable moment, I have chided myself for being so slow. I could have made *history* had I jumped from my chair and yanked that dress free for her!

In April 1914, I found another roadrunner's nest. It held five young birds and an egg. The two largest of the brood I took home. I put my new pets in a pail and went after grasshoppers. The gray-skinned, somewhat reptilian babies were slow to respond at first; but when I placed a board over the pail, then suddenly removed it, both birds opened their oddly spotted mouths and begged hoarsely. Once they had accepted a meal from me, all was well.

I knew, from considerable experience, that obtaining food for a young roadrunner was quite a task. Rearing *two* roadrunners would be laborious. I proposed a contest among the smaller fry of the community—youngsters now loftily referred to as the kids—promising a prize for the one who provided "the most grasshoppers and other things" for the roadrunners to eat. The arrangement worked wonders, except that it was I who had to put the grasshoppers "and other things" into the gaping mouths and remove the great gelatinous fecal blobs that the birdlings exchanged for each meal. The prize was a jackrabbit that I had stuffed, a monstrosity with shriveled ears, staring eyes, and a loose tail. We had a little ceremony when the winner was announced. The day was windy. I suspect that the prize lost its tail, or perhaps an ear, on its way to its new home.

When the roadrunners were old enough to toddle about, I took them from the pail. I now decided to name them Titania and Oberon. These names reflected an admirable familiarity with Shakespeare, I thought, but I never used them. I was never entirely sure which bird was which, and I never called either of them anything but Birdie. So completely apt was that name, so often did I use it, so much a part of me did it become, that not so long ago, in the Black Mesa country of Oklahoma, I caught myself holding out my hand and calling "Here, Birdie! Come, Birdie!" to a *perfectly wild roadrunner*!

The process of learning to capture food without help from me was fascinating to witness. I had observed this before. Now, however, there was teamwork—notably in dealing with big, furry tarantulas, many of which I found for the birds by twirling a straw down the great spiders' burrows. When a tarantula popped out, one bird grabbed it by a leg and flipped it, minus one leg, into the air. The other bird snatched it the instant it hit the ground, and off came another leg. Eight small, hollow gulps, one for each leg, then a big gulp for the tarantula itself, and all was over.

A young cotton rat the birds dispatched by whacking it so rapidly and hard that it had no chance to fight back. One bird by itself might have been bitten savagely, for cotton rats are quick-tempered and strong. I had to cut the rat in two after the birds had killed it, for neither would permit the other to swallow it.

Everyone enjoyed watching the roadrunners—everyone except little sister Evie, now almost six years old. The trouble started when Evie, wearing a pair of brown sandals, kicked at one of the birds who had rushed toward her, begging for food. The bird never forgot. When those sandals appeared, the roadrunner attacked their wearer. Evie opened the screen door one day while the roadrunners and I were standing not far away. *She had on those sandals.* The bird's facial expression and behavior changed instantly; its head went up, its crest down. When Evie started walking toward us, the roadrunner flew at her savagely, grabbed her by the earlobe, and hung there shaking and yanking as if trying to pull her ear off. I could scarcely believe what I saw. No wonder Evie squealed and struck at her assailant. I grabbed the bird and flung it to one side. It showed no animosity toward me; neither did it run up begging for food, as it usually did when all was well. Its hostility did not subside until *those sandals* went into the house.

That spring the tide of fortune turned once more. Father had an offer from a small college in West Virginia, Bethany College, an offer he could not turn down. We would be leaving the big, white, still unfinished house. We would be bidding the fine prairie good-bye. But the roadrunners and my two screech owls had become part of the family. They would go with us.

During the flurry of packing, Dorothy was stung by a wasp. Somewhere she had heard that such a sting might prove fatal. Saying not a word, believing there was nothing anyone could do to save her, she had wept, found a piece of paper and a pencil, and written a brief will. I read the document myself. She had left some of her choicest possessions to me.

WEST VIRGINIA

THE MOVE TO WEST VIRGINIA, again by train, was hot and stuffy. My hand luggage was two hardware-cloth cages, one barely big enough for two roadrunners with broken-off tail feathers, the other with ample room for two screech owls. The food supply for these four charges, a sackful of live grasshoppers, soon ran out, so fresh meat had to be obtained in the diner. Replacing soiled paper with clean was a continuing chore. The cages smelled bad. A woman seated not far from us announced that she was about to faint, hurried to the ladies' room, and returned holding smelling salts to her nose. I feared that the conductor would send me and my birds to the baggage car; nor did these fears subside as more and more people came for a look. Not one person on that train, it seemed, had ever before seen a real live chaparral close-up.

The town of Bethany, our destination, was in the state's northern panhandle, only three miles from the Pennsylvania line. It was about as little as a town could be, though it would be lively enough when several hundred college students returned in the fall. Past it, almost around it, flowed the Buffalo, a pretty, unspoiled creek that joined the broad Ohio at Wellsburg, seven miles away as a crow might fly, but more like twenty-one as a kingfisher might, keeping close to its food supply.

When we first saw Bethany, a trolley that everybody called the Toonerville connected the village with Wellsburg. This car's tracks ran over several trestles, some of them quite high, as well as through two tunnels said to be the longest in the world serving both ordinary road traffic and trolley traffic. The trolley had obviously been old a long while. There was only the one car, and everyone seemed a bit awed by the fact that it continued to function. No one ever washed its windows but cracks that had opened along their edges afforded clear looks at the outer world as the car rattled and creaked along—glimpses, I was eventually to learn, of blooming redbuds in spring, of maples and oaks and beeches

44

ablaze with bold colors in fall, of huge icicles hanging from gray shale cliffs in winter, and, off down through the treetops, of the creek itself, whatever the season.

In Bethany at last, pets and all, I considered myself a confirmed ornithologist, for a short article of mine on the roadrunner I had reared in the spring of 1913 had recently appeared in the bimonthly magazine *Bird-Lore*, and the comments of an editor had been so encouraging that I had reared the two birds I now had, I had recorded all manner of notes on the development of the two, and I had made a watercolor of one of them "in an attitude of fright." This drawing had not, of course, been done direct from life. There had been no way for me to force the bird to hold the position that I wanted to show. I had simply done the best I could at putting down what I had seen. Word that this drawing was to be reproduced in *Bird-Lore* gave purpose and importance to all that I thought and did.

The roadrunners were forlorn-looking enough when I let them out of their cage. They limped about on Main Street, the picture of tattered neglect. But their vigor returned; they began showing a lively interest in grasshoppers and crickets; and soon they were capturing and swallowing insects of various sorts with gusto. The screech owls, both old enough to catch their own prey, I liberated that very first evening, for there were many big trees, mostly elms, in town.

Our family lived for two days in a house on Main Street; then for a week or so in a dormitory on the hill; at length in a one-story frame house on "Intellectual Avenue," an unpaved street a block upslope from, and parallel to, Main Street. Our house was between two really old houses, the Tener house and Mrs. Lindsay's house, both brick. In Mrs. Lindsay's yard was a grape arbor. We had no front yard to speak of. Our backyard, along with other backyards on our side of the street, sloped upward first to an expanse of open pasture, then to the college apple orchard. Not far beyond our back fence was a big black walnut tree.

I had a vast new countryside to learn about—new birds, new mammals, new plants, new place-names, new people, new colloquialisms. This "East" I had heard so much about was vaguely hostile. The steep-sided, wooded hills were self-sufficient, secretive, even haughty. They did not accept me, yet there was no getting away from them. The horizon was unbearably close. Even when I climbed the highest hill, the world's rim did not move back as it should have.

Adjusting was difficult, truly difficult. The land about our house in

Texas had been flat and dry. At Bethany, a really flat area was exceptional, and dank, foggy mornings were the rule in summer. The stands of giant ragweed in the Buffalo's bottoms were a veritable jungle. Ironweed and joe-pye weed grew higher than my head. A bit frightening were the partly hidden caves, cliffs, and sudden drop-offs that I came upon whenever I followed little streams back to their headwaters. One wide, shallow cave close to town I decided to name the Amphitheater.

Certain birds, especially of the warbler family, demanded my attention. To my surprise, I found cerulean and Kentucky warblers in almost every mature woodland, the former in the very tops of the trees, the latter close to the ground. Wherever there were berry thickets there were yellow-breasted chats. The singing of these on moonlit nights was fervent. I never heard it without wondering whether the birds were clowning as they often did by day. From any one point in Bethany, I could hear four or five chats calling on slopes above town.

A biology teacher at the college, Milton Hover, took an interest in me and my artwork. Among this thoughtful man's responsibilities was the college farm with its head of about thirty blooded Guernsey cattle, among them a world champion butterfat producer, a cow named Marshall's Lady Dudley. The calves that were born from time to time, handsome little things every one, were valuable stock. The registration papers needed diagrams of the facial markings. These diagrams I made— carefully, meticulously, almost religiously, for I knew that they were important. So it came about that my first really professional drawings were not of birds but of baby Guernseys.

It did not take me long to learn that Buffalo Creek teemed with water snakes. These I caught for the roadrunners. A fairly big snake, cut in two, made a meal that lasted several hours, a meal that, once started, continued to the exclusion of virtually all other activity, for the act of swallowing all but incapacitated the swallower. The birds made no attempt to catch such reptiles themselves, for they were not used to hunting prey near water. In this, their new habitat, there were few if any lizards, no tarantulas, and no scorpions, but there were house sparrows galore, and it was not long before my pets were catching these at a spot where garbage was thrown out in sufficient quantity to attract a flock of the greedy little birds. Fascinating it was to watch the roadrunners, who learned to move closer and closer to the sparrows, behaving all the while as if not in the least predatory, as if wholly disinterested, then suddenly dashing forward, leaping into the midst of the fleeing company, and grabbing a victim in midair. The technique was basically the same as that used in capturing flying grasshoppers, except that the roadrunners sidled, rather than sneaked, closer and closer to the sparrows.

The Bethany of those days took secret pride in the old trolley and the two tunnels; in the trestles, at least one of which was considered dangerous; in the long college building known as Old Main, with its majestic clock tower and outdoor corridor; in Pendleton Heights, the stately house in which the president lived; in the Parkinson Oaks, a magnificent stand of trees on the hilltop above campus and town; in the new circular barn on the college farm, half a mile northeast of town; and in the long, low, white frame Campbell Mansion, a short way beyond the barn. In this house the Campbells themselves had lived—Thomas Campbell, a Scotsman who had broken away from Presbyterianism and established a new sect called the Disciples of Christ, and his son Alexander, who had helped organize the new church and had founded Bethany College in 1840—all this before the Civil War, while West Virginia was still part of the sovereign state of Virginia.

Occupying the Campbell Mansion in the summer of 1914 was a nice old lady, Mrs. Decima Barclay, the tenth of Alexander Campbell's children. How fascinated we youngsters were by "Miss Decima," she of the delicate hands, dazzling rings, and fuzzy poodle who, properly urged, hopped onto the piano bench, struck the keys with his front feet, and sang. The fervor of his performance never waned. Once started, it gained force. The harder the little feet struck the keys, the more the dog suffered, so the more loudly he yelped. Miss Decima stood proudly by, a bright smile on her face, until she felt that everyone had had enough. When she called the dog off, the singing stopped without the slightest hint of diminuendo, and off the shaggy performer dashed as if pursued by Presbyterian ghosts.

Not far beyond the opposite end of town, crowning an eminence about as high as that on which the college stood, was a beautifully groomed estate called Point Breeze. The handsome brick mansion and its parklike surroundings had about them an air of affluence and grandeur that contrasted sharply with the simplicity of the village. We youngsters could not help feeling that Point Breeze stood for that which was secular, wealthy, perhaps even wicked, but fascinating nonetheless, while the Campbell Mansion represented all that Point Breeze did not. At Point Breeze there were gala doings that we read about in the newspapers, stables with fine horses, formal gardens, and two dogs, one a huge, lumpy bulldog of terrifying mien. Too, there was a young lady named Jessica Nave, who had a special way of tossing her golden hair as she cantered gracefully about the countryside, even occasionally along our Main Street, on her thoroughbred. Jessica's beauty was special. She was not much older than we; she might have been our friend; but she did not even know us. We did not in the least dislike her for this. Indeed, we respected her for her aloofness, for this seemed honest and in character. We knew that she had something which we sadly lacked. That something was a combination of poise, elegance, and savoir-vivre.

In July of 1914, a short article by me titled "The Interesting Road-runner" appeared in *The Oölogist*, a folksy, not very scientific little monthly for which I had subscribed since about 1910. The magazine was so friendly in tone that its readers all came to feel that they knew one another. Contributors named Sam S. Dickey and James B. Carter both lived in Waynesburg, Pennsylvania, a town so close to Bethany that I decided I would pay these fellow ornithologists a visit when opportunity offered.

That fall I was not ready to enter Bethany College, for I had not finished high school, but the authorities arranged for me to attend classes and to receive credit for work done, so to college I went. Professor Hover gave me permission to draw birds in the clean, well-lighted biology laboratory in Oglebay Hall, a recent addition to Old Main. I worked with a living model when possible, but as a rule I had to be content with freshly killed specimens or prepared skins. One day, after I had been sweating over the problem of depicting a grackle's iridescent plumage, I found a long-handled mop in my hand and a bucket of hot water at my feet. I had been appointed janitor of Oglebay Hall—work that required only a few hours each day and that meant money in my pocket.

In early November, I went by train to visit Sam Dickey and James Carter. It was a wonderful trip. My report was published in *The Oölogist*. Here the author's name appeared as George M. Suttard, a foible of fate that greatly amused my sister Dorothy.

On Thanksgiving Day Lewis Perry, Mike Taylor, and I, proud of our stamina and eager to proclaim it, went for a swim in the Buffalo. Only the quieter stretches were deep enough for swimming, and here ice had formed. We broke the ice as we lunged about gasping. We might have stayed in for two or three minutes. We came out with feet so numb that we had to look to be sure they were still there.

When the halftone reproduction of my drawing of a roadrunner "in an attitude of fright" appeared in the January–February issue of the 1915 volume of *Bird-Lore*, I was so excited, so exalted, so puffed-up with pride, that I must have been hard to live with. The drawing was crude indeed, yet its proportions were about right, and I am not badly embarrassed when I show it to people today. It has exactly the right number of tail feathers (ten), so these I must have counted. The distal part of the outer hindtoe turns upward precisely as it does in a living roadrunner. And the "attitude of fright" I have witnessed many times when a roadrunner is puzzled, perhaps actually frightened, by the size or behavior of prey with which it does not quite know how to deal.

When I contemplated that halftone, right in the middle of page 59, with my whole name correctly spelled right under it, I felt that I was arriving at last. I was almost seventeen, hence getting along in years. I decided to take the bull by the horns, write the great bird artist Louis Agassiz Fuertes, who lived in Ithaca, New York, and ask for his help. Fuertes's drawings in *Bird-Lore* and in my beloved *Handbook of Birds of the Western United States* I had admired for years. I had worshiped him from afar. His very name had fascinated me. He answered my first letter promptly, suggesting that I send him drawings for criticism. Thus began an important relationship, one that was to continue until his tragic death in 1927.

Fuertes's outgoing, warmhearted reply contained—in response to my derogatory remarks about Audubon's bird drawings—such a wonderful little essay on that towering figure's place in human history that I must quote the whole of the letter here:

Ithaca, N.Y., Feb. 15, 1915.

My dear Mr. Sutton:

Your very kind letter came to me out of a clear sky, and I cannot well tell you how much I was touched and gratified by your warm appreciation of my efforts to come at the truth in bird-painting. Much praise from the uninitiated means little or nothing: a rare tribute like yours, from those who have met some of the difficulties and know them by their first names, is an uplift and encouragement that means more than all the every-day, inexpert praise in the world.

So far as I now know, I shall be in or near Ithaca this summer, and if you should decide to come up, will be glad to help you in any way I can. My methods are not academic, and have been developed to suit the rather peculiar needs of the situation, and I might do you more harm than good.

In the meantime, if you have any study material, or pictures that you have done and would like criticism on, I would be glad if you would send them on, and I will write you more fully than I can now, as to their promise, the field, etc. etc.,—all vital points if you are thinking of going seriously into it. Of course the field is limited, and must in a large measure be created by the one who is to fill it. When I started, about twenty years ago, there wasn't *any* field, but one developed, and now there is considerably more of a one than one man can fill, though there are not many who seem to combine the sympathy with nature, the specific knowledge of their subject, and the technical ability to paint, which are all necessary if their work is to stand up under the test of time and the inevitable competition that is ahead. Say what you will of Audubon (much of what you *did* say is just, too) he was the first and only man whose bird drawings showed the faintest hint of anatomical study, or that the fresh bird was in hand when the work was done, and is so immeasureably ahead of anything, up to his time or since, until the modern idea of drawing endlessly from life began to bear fruit, that its strength deserves all praise and honor, and its many weaknesses condonement, as they were the fruit of his training: stilted, tight, and unimaginative old David sticks out in the stiff landscape, the hard outline, and the dull, lifeless shading, while the overpowering virility of A. himself is shown in the snappy, instantaneous attitudes, and dashing motion of his subjects. While there's much to criticize there is also much to learn, and much to admire, in studying the monumental classic that he left behind him. He made many errors, but he also left a living record that has been of inestimable value and stimulus to students, and made an everlasting mark in American Ornithology. It is indeed hard to imagine what the science would be like in this country—and what the state of our bird world—had he not lived and wrought, and become a demigod to the ardent youth of the land.

I had not meant to write an essay on Audubon—and shall not continue! I *do* want to thank you for the truly great encouragement of your letter, and to assure you that if there is any way I can help you to develop your bird-painting, I am anxious to do so.

Faithfully and gratefully yours,
Louis Agassiz Fuertes

Fuertes urged me to observe closely, to study, to *see*. By way of illustrating his comments on highlights and shadows, he sent me his watercolor of a Flathead Indian's skull. This was not a bird. It revealed a shockingly new and different Fuertes. The impact of that beautiful drawing, done by a famed *bird* artist, yet obviously not of a bird at all, was terrific. Determined to show the master what I could do, I made a drawing of a turkey vulture's skull—a specimen I had brought with me from Texas. This won Fuertes's praise. He perceived that I was taking to heart what he had tried so hard to say.

Many hours each week I devoted to one aspect or another of bird study. I could prepare a fairly acceptable bird skin, but I had not yet started a collection, nor was I cataloging my specimens. Such notebooks as I kept were full of daily lists. In Texas I had mounted a few birds, one of which—a Swainson's hawk with partly spread wings—I still had. One day Lewis Perry brought me a handsome drake hooded merganser he had shot along Buffalo Creek. This I skinned and mounted. It was the beginning of a new collection of mounted birds, one or two of which are on exhibition in the Carnegie Museum of Natural History in Pittsburgh to this day.

With the return of spring, I wandered farther and farther afield—eventually westward into the drainage of Jordan Run, one of Buffalo Creek's major tributaries. One day I came home in great excitement, reporting that I had found a red-tailed hawk's nest high in a big oak. "I must collect the eggs," I announced. "They're important."

Father did not, as a rule, evince much interest in my bird study. He may indeed have been bewildered, even chagrined, by it, for it could not have been clear to him how ornithology might one day become my career. But this time, either because he wanted to see the birds and their nest or because he feared that I'd break my neck, he offered to help. We cut a bundle of cleats, got a hatchet, some big nails, a roll of binder twine, and a little tin bucket with a sturdy handle, and off we went. It was a long walk, but the day was beautiful. The air was raw in the open fields, but the woods were cozy, especially in sun-warmed nooks where the first hepaticas were blooming.

"We'd better not talk from now on," I warned in a whisper as we made our way down a steep slope to the Jordan. "There's the nest! Can you see it through the trees?" Even as I pointed, the hawk stood up, spread its wings, and flapped off, squealing shrilly. By the time we reached the base of the nest tree, both hawks were circling above us.

I got busy with the cleats, nailed them on one by one until I had reached the lowest branch, then came down for the bucket, filled it loosely with moss and dead leaves, attached the twine securely to its handle, and started up in earnest. Presently I was at the nest—suspended between heaven and earth, as it were—examining the two handsome eggs. The old birds did not attack me, though occasionally one dived and squealed at the same time, making my spine tingle. Carefully, I placed the eggs in the little bucket and let it down to Father. "Just untie the string," I called. "I want to get the nest, too!"

The bulky nest was all of three feet across. Putting the coarse twine around and under it, and dislodging the great structure without breaking it apart, was almost more than I could manage, but finally I got it all free of the crotch, let it swing outward past the trunk below me, and started it on its slow journey earthward. It was surprisingly heavy, but the twine was strong.

When we got back to town, I found part of a dead tree, hauled this to the museum room on an upper floor of Oglebay Hall, nailed it in place, and installed the nest for everyone to see. By this time I must have considered myself the curator in charge of the bird collection at the college.

Youngsters the age of my sister Dorothy and me were proud of everything odd and special about the Bethany of those days, this largely because we didn't have much else to be proud of. Evie was much younger than we, so we did not include her in much that we did. The city of Wheeling, much larger than Wellsburg and seventeen miles off in another direction from Bethany, was not reachable by trolley, so we almost never went there. Bethany had no theater, no recreation center, no organized entertainment of any sort. In summer the electric lights went off throughout the whole town precisely at 11 o'clock each evening—three inexorable blinks followed by darkness that seemed to disapprove of anything aside from going to sleep.

We youngsters fell into the habit of congratulating ourselves on that which we knew we had—always the big college clock, whose bell so gravely tolled off the hours; always Main Street, which was paved, and the six other short streets, which were not; always the big, rounded stepping stones at side-street crossings; always the empty old church near the bridge at one end of Main Street, the new church at the other end, and the post office, barbershop, ice cream parlor, and two grocery stores in between.

And the people! How we loved to name the town's characters, as if they were among our choicest personal possessions! Some of the old-timers had come to this part of the world as retainers in the Campbell ménage. Some families were poor, far poorer than ourselves, even destitute. We youngsters considered ourselves objective, philosophical, tolerant, even benign, whenever we took inventory. Starting at one end of a street, we discussed the occupants of the first house, then of the second, and so on, telling each other exactly what we knew or—even more exactly—what we had heard about each and every person. The reviewing over, we agreed that, if there were only an Edgar Lee Masters, a The-

odore Dreiser, or a Sherwood Anderson amongst us, Bethany would go
down in history as one of the most interesting towns ever. Each cripple,
each moron, each ne'er-do-well had a place, an important place, in our
lives, and this was partly because every good Christian needed someone
to feel sorry for.

Moonshine stills that we heard about thrilled us and stirred our imag-
inations, convincing us that *our* families were law-abiding. The fact that
a certain well-liked, hard-working woman we often saw about town had
an illegitimate daughter who also was well liked gave the mother a sort of
halo—as if she might have been a Virgin Mary in our midst. Who could
the woman's lover have been? Might we be seeing him every day? Must
he not have been, *or be*, a fine man? And why could he not just acknowledge himself the father and be proud of his offspring? Thus, in our psy-
chospiritual explorations up the short streets and down, we named off
those whose personal history, manner, appearance, or vocabulary continued to entrance us. And thus we had ourselves a perfectly wonderful
time.

It crosses my mind, very forcibly at times, that my sisters and I
considered our family well-off. We knew we didn't have much. We
owned no automobile. We lived in a rented house, and not much of a
house at that. We did no traveling to far places in summer. We did not
have many clothes. But what we ate from day to day had been paid for
and tasted good. We enjoyed occasional extravagances to the hilt. We
had fine books to read, fine music to listen to, real conversation at meals.
Mother continued to practice on her Gabler almost daily; she always
had a few young students taking lessons; and she had in tow a chorus of
middle-aged ladies, every one of whom loved her. Our parents were
devoted to the church, especially to the Sunday School lessons. I have the
clearest memory of them discussing moot points on Saturday evenings
or on Sunday mornings before Sunday School convened. Sometimes we
children were brought into these discussions. Occasionally Father read us
verses that he had composed in explanation or dramatization of the lessons. The poems bored me dreadfully. I felt that they were a waste of
time. But Father was dedicated to writing them, and his ability to concen-
trate while at work on them won my admiration. Mother listened to
them faithfully, whether she liked them or not.

Now for one of Bethany's characters. There was a sharp-eyed old
woman, a Mrs. Clymer, who lived near the college campus. Her unpainted, one-storied wooden house looked deserted; there was no vestige

of a lawn; the front porch sagged; yet on that porch idled such comfortable-looking cats, and nearby grew such glorious clumps of bleeding heart, that people who passed saw cats and flowers rather than porch. For me, Mrs. Clymer was unfailingly interesting. Her eyes had an arresting sparkle. I do not recall much else about her appearance, save that she was a little stooped, she had a few silky whiskers on her chin, and she often wore a gray and lavender hood with a broadly scalloped edge. I sometimes heard her referred to as a witch, but it never occurred to me to be bothered by this. She did not mingle much with other folks. She rarely attended church. So essentially solitary was she that I found it hard to believe that she had a husband; yet a Mr. Clymer there undoubtedly was, for one day the Toonerville ran wild down Underwood's Hill, Mr. Clymer was killed, and the battered old house had unwonted visitors.

Mrs. Clymer liked me. Why she did so, I could not—and cannot—explain. Perhaps it was merely because, from the very first, I liked her. Whenever, that first fall, I passed her house on my way to classes on the hill, I found myself hoping that I'd see her. Occasionally I did. She had a garden of sorts, which she tended vigorously, surrounded by her adoring cats. She had a huge iron pot in which, following the custom of the countryside, she made apple butter. Her equipment included a big wooden paddle so constructed as to make possible the stirring of the hot contents at some distance back from the fire. One winter day I saw Mrs. Clymer near the pot, its top covered with heavy planks. She was poking at something in the pot with a stick, *but there was no fire*. As I approached, I heard her muttering—her words directed not at me but at the pot. "There's too many of you, that's all. Too many, and I can't keep on feeding you. That's all there is to it!" Her voice was matter-of-fact. There were no tears in her eyes as she glanced in my direction, but she wiped her nose with her apron. She was drowning all but one of her cats.

Mother, a true individualist, also liked Mrs. Clymer. Mother hated gossip. The fact that Mrs. Clymer was sometimes talked about led Mother to dig beneath the surface a bit and thus become Mrs. Clymer's friend. As I have said before, Mother was no angel. She was kind to Mrs. Clymer partly because she found her truly interesting, even entertaining. The day Mr. Clymer was killed, Mother went to the old house to see if she could help in any way. While she was there, sitting to one side of the front door, a visitor knocked. As Mrs. Clymer opened the door, Mother heard the voice of a woman she knew at once to be the wife of one of the college professors. "You needn't come in," said Mrs. Clymer, her voice hard as flint. "You never came before. There's no need to come now." As the door was closing, Mother heard a crisp comment from the rejected: "Well, you needn't be so impudent about it!"

That day Mother was to learn an extremely interesting fact. Mrs. Clymer's best dress, a heavy black one, a dress she almost never wore, was decorated with row upon row of plain black buttons, each made by sewing black cloth over a twenty-dollar gold piece. "So, you see, I will have something to go on," confided Mrs. Clymer.

In those days the post office was almost directly downslope from the Clymer house. The mail came daily on an early Toonerville run, and the postmaster usually had it sorted by nine o'clock. About mail time, most of the town was to be seen either in or near the post office. The postmaster had no assistant, and sorting the mail took time. On a certain cold morning, when the Toonerville had been late and the sorting had taken more time than seemed necessary, Mrs. Clymer's voice rang out, hard and clear above the shuffling and coughing, "Surely there's nothing slow around here except the wrath of God!" The pronouncement was dramatic. It brought on a hush, for Bethany prided itself on being nothing if not godly.

For a while I was not popular at the post office. After my trip to Waynesburg, I received packages from Sam Dickey containing dead specimens that I was to skin for him. In exchange for this taxidermic work, I was to receive a pair of iron tree-climbers. The postmaster questioned me about the many packages, some of which were not very tightly wrapped. One morning, I knew I was in for trouble the moment I opened the post office door. The whole place smelled to high heaven. The package, far the biggest one yet, contained a very dead great blue heron. I skinned the stinking bird that afternoon.

On Thanksgiving Day, 1915, Lewis Perry, Mike Taylor, and I again took a dip in the cold Buffalo; we now called ourselves the three polar bears and referred to our bravura plunge as traditional. That day Jim Lloyd, whose big, velvet-voiced hounds were the pride of the town's masculine element, and the despair of the feminine, gave me a fine barred owl that he had shot in Logan's Hollow. After skinning the specimen, I opened its stomach, which was packed with feathers. These I washed thoroughly, dried, and fluffed out, finding them all to be from a screech owl. It had never occurred to me that a free-flying, uncaged big owl might occasionally capture and eat a smaller owl, so I prepared a note titled "Owls within Owls" for *The Oölogist*. I considered myself a regular contributor to that little monthly.

On December 7, 1915, a neighbor brought me a small bird he had found alive in the snow. It had only part of its tail, but otherwise it seemed to be in fair condition, though it made no attempt to fly. Looking it up in such books as I had, I decided that it was a Cape May warbler. It lived only a day or so, but while it was alive I made a drawing of it. This I sent to Fuertes, who confirmed my identification and suggested that I prepare a note on this late fall occurrence for *The Auk*, the official organ of the American Ornithologists' Union. My contribution, eleven lines long, appeared in due season. This was, in a very real sense, my first professional publication.

In the spring of 1916, the powers of Brooke County decided that the road connecting Bethany and Wellsburg needed paving with brick. Wages offered were high for the times—$3.50 per day, if I remember correctly. I had long since decided that, once I had saved enough money for a trip to Ithaca, I would go there—to study under Fuertes.

When the semester's schoolwork was finished, I applied for a road job. For a wonder, the boss hired me. I was skinny, thin-faced, not at all the football player type. I guess they really needed help and had to take anyone available. I fed that insatiable Moloch, the stone crusher, until my hands ached; I moved bricks by the hundred; and I dug ditches and smoothed roadbeds hour after hour, day after day. For reasons beyond me then, not quite so far beyond me now, I found myself in charge of a little band of workmen—six or eight in all—one of whom was a black somewhat older and a great deal stronger than I who, without the slightest impudence, fell to calling me Chicago Town and to advising me, sotto voce, to work a little less hard. "Not so fast, Chicago Town! Not so awful fast! You like it better thataway, an' we all like it better thataway, Chicago Town!" The days passed slowly at first, then swiftly, and my pile of savings grew.

One night (by this time the Sutton family had moved to a larger house nearer the campus but still on "Intellectual Avenue"), I wakened with a start to find that I was out of bed and kneeling on the floor. I had been piling bricks in my sleep. I decided that the time had come for me to begin studying under Fuertes.

SHELDRAKE SPRINGS, NEW YORK

WHEN LOUIS AGASSIZ FUERTES, then at the very height of his career, decided that I was worth helping, his generosity went far beyond any I had experienced outside my own family circle. He did not know my parents. No one had urged him to pay attention to me. He must have liked my little roadrunner drawing in *Bird-Lore*. What I sent him for criticism must have convinced him that I deserved encouragement. I am sure of this now, for many times during the past forty years I have felt an irresistible urge to help a younger man whose work showed promise.

Every letter I had from Fuertes bespoke generosity. Opening packages from me, criticizing my drawings, and wrapping these for return took time, precious time. He may have welcomed the chance to express himself about my problems, for what he said to me may have made clearer to him what his own problems were. I can see that now. But letters to a far-removed youth were one thing: taking that youth on bodily, so to speak, was quite another.

When Fuertes suggested that I work directly under his supervision at Sheldrake Springs, where he and his family were to spend the summer of 1916, he was taking an awful chance. He did not know whether I was diligent or lazy. I might, for all he knew, be addicted to smoking cigarettes, carousing at night, lying abed mornings, talking incessantly, and whatnot. I was an unprepossessing young man, just past eighteen. My sisters and I knew something about manners. I was not grossly deficient in that field. But I had had very little worldly experience, and this lack must have been apparent in all that I did and said. I owned only a few clothes, my best (and only) suit being of a shade perilously close to park-bench green.

Sheldrake Springs was a village on the west shore of Lake Cayuga, only a mile or so from Sheldrake Springs Station on the railroad. When I

arrived by train, I carried an old suitcase packed with clothing, art mate-
rials, and a small taxidermic kit. Fuertes was not at the station to meet me.
I started walking toward the point, for someone told me that the Fuertes
house stood there. A truck drove past, slowed almost to a stop, and
off hopped a man who waved thanks to the driver and called to me,
"George, I'm glad you're here. The place is yours. Just do anything you
darn please, now, while you're here." The man was Fuertes.

Only a few yards from his house was the small tent Fuertes himself
had put up for me. On a cot was an air mattress, the first I had ever seen.
There was a campstool across from the cot, a coat hanger, a soap dish—
all the comforts of home. During that first night, I was awakened by the
sound of something being dragged across the wooden floor. A rodent of
some sort had found the soap under the cot and was making off with it. I
rescued it just in time.

I ate with the Fuertes family at a hostelry in the village. Meals were
festive. Fuertes was at work on two sets of watercolor illustrations—a big
series of mammals for the *National Geographic* and nine drawings of
common birds for a book titled *The Way to Study Birds*, by John Dryden
Kuser. When Fuertes was at work, he slaved. Nothing diverted him. But,
when mealtime came, he sought release from all that had driven him.
Release took various forms—funny stories, many of which included
quotations in dialect, frank comments about people in the public eye,
pranks meriting some such phrase as hi-jinktum-jee. Alphabet soup, welcomed with mild uproar, gave us all a chance to compose cablegrams
on lettuce leaves.

There was no telling, simply no telling, how that irrepressible streak
of fun in Fuertes would pop out. After our first four or five meals together,
I was prepared to believe the story about him and the oh-so-proper
waiter who needed to be reminded that nice people can be highly infor-
mal on occasion. According to the story, the restaurant was fancy.
Conversation at the table had ebbed. The disagreeably proper waiter was
close-by, where he could not fail to hear every word. Said Fuertes: "I'll
bet I'm the only person in this whole place who has a dead mole in his
pocket!" Everyone at the table knew full well that their beloved Louis was
capable of having precisely what he'd said he had precisely where he'd
said he had it; but the waiter, clinging desperately to the belief that such a
statement could be nothing but bluff, stood by as if transfixed. So out the
lovely little specimen came, its silken fur gleaming in the candlelight, to

be placed on the table where all could see it. Everyone laughed merrily, even a bit boisterously. Everyone but the waiter.

The Fuertes family awed me, not only the famous father but the other three as well. Mrs. Fuertes, whose first name was Margaret (shortened to Madge by husband and close friends), told stories extremely well, and her opinions on any subject were worth listening to, but her special gift was that of leading conversation toward a point at which a yarn from her husband would be appropriate. Mary, the daughter, a little girl of great charm, reminded me of flaxen-haired princesses I'd read about in fairy tales. Handsome Sumner, a bit younger than Mary, and nicknamed Shub, was elegant even as a youngster.

The small, well-lighted room in which Fuertes worked was at the northwest corner of the house. Here he had a table, drawing boards of various sizes, a vase full of watercolor brushes, and tubes of paint, little porcelain pans of paint, and paint boxes galore. Lying on the table was a beautifully prepared skin of a phoebe—the bird he was about to draw. When I looked closely at the specimen, I realized that it was no average scientific skin. Its back was not flat but rounded; its feet stuck up; its feathers had a fluffy, recently preened appearance. All this was no accident, for Fuertes had prepared the specimen himself to serve as a model.

Fuertes let me watch him at work. At the time, this did not strike me as remarkable. I was eager to learn. I had traveled a long way. What I didn't realize was that Fuertes might have been wretchedly self-conscious, even tense, as I stood there watching. The task at hand for him was finishing an acceptable drawing, one to be reproduced in color. If the original, when completed, proved to be off in any important way, it might have to be done over. Having a worshipful youngster at his elbow might have been ever so flattering to his ego, but it also divided his attention. Flowing on a watercolor wash is extremely tricky; this I now know from years of experience. I had no idea of it then. When Fuertes put the background wash on that phoebe drawing, he was working toward two ends, serving two masters. He was creating part of what was presently to be a bird portrait of immense appeal; he was also showing a pupil just what to do and, even more important perhaps, what not to do.

The lightly penciled-in drawing was firmly attached to the drawing board with thumbtacks. The bill of the bird in the drawing was slightly open. I thought at first that this was to indicate that the bird was singing. Not so. Fuertes picked his model up, looked carefully at its bill, examined his drawing, and stood up, saying, "We've got to catch a moth. Come on, help me find one!" So out we went and around we pranced until a moth of proper size and beauty had been flushed from the grass and captured. I watched Fuertes pencil in that lovely lepidopteran, held so tightly in the phoebe's bill. Who would ever know that I, not the phoebe, had caught it?

The background wash, pale grayish blue in the upper third of the picture, light grayish green in the lower two-thirds, was to go on before any part of the bird or its perch received color. Fuertes took a big brush from the vase, mixed some blue in a saucer, added water, strengthened the tone by adding more paint, tested the wash on a piece of white scratch paper, poured in more water, then rinsed the brush thoroughly before mixing the green wash. The two washes were in separate saucers. "Be sure to have plenty," he advised. "And do all the mixing and all the testing before you start."

Now, tilting the drawing board so that the wash would flow downward, he moved the paint-laden brush rapidly from left to right across the top of the paper. "Never let the lower edge get dry. You have to work fast!" I could see the color from the first stroke flowing down into the upper part of the second stroke. No edge formed. Presently the whole top third of the paper was pale grayish blue—all but the phoebe's head, up to the very edges of which the brush had moved swiftly, unerringly. Fuertes flicked the brush to rid it of blue, rinsed it, flicked it again, and started with the green, all this before the blue had had a chance to dry. This time the stroke was not strictly horizontal, for the uppermost part of it was to represent distant treetops. Nowhere did a hard edge form. The two tones flowed together smoothly, harmoniously, at treetop level. "Before you make another move," he cautioned, "that background wash has to dry. If you touch it while it's damp, its smoothness will be ruined. It's best to forget the whole thing for a while." Whereupon he led me outdoors again, this time heading toward the point, which was only a short way from the house. A dark-backed, short-tailed swallow flew past us at eye level. "Know what that bird is?" queried Fuertes. "A roughwing," I replied. "Good boy!" said he. And my day was made.

When we returned to the house, the background wash had dried. Now was Fuertes to bewilder me by putting a lot of seemingly unrelated dark lines and spots here and there within the area that was to become the phoebe. These were what he called the deepest darks, a phrase he had used in his letters to me. The brush he used was not small, but it had a fine tip. After he had put in a few very dark marks, he added less dark lines and patches, all neutral in tone. The phoebe by this time had a decidedly leprous appearance, but I could see that the wing was beginning to take shape.

Matching colors and ascertaining that these would, when completely dry, represent the bird's plumage accurately took time. I watched the test daubs of paint dry on the scratch paper. Presently the brush settled down to work. The phoebe's whole head, pulled together by deft strokes of dark paint on its upper half, became feathery. To accent a highlight, Fuertes "pointed" the brush with his lips, touched its tip to part of the fluffy crest, and lo, there came into being, all at one instant, a curved surface, a softness, an effect of light and shadow, a three-dimensional quality. I had seen it all happen—right there within touching distance.

So engrossed was the master by this time that he said little. He did not need to say anything. As the brush, now carrying an olive gray tone, moved over part of the wing area, the middle and greater coverts overlapped convincingly. An important fact became apparent: not every blessed feather needed to be painted separately; to delineate each separately in great detail would be a mistake, for such a handling might result in scaliness rather than featheriness.

A big blue fly became a nuisance. Not content with drinking from a saucer, it blundered about, at times between the artist's face and his picture. "Gosh," said Fuertes, "I wish somebody'd kill that brute!"

The fly buzzed drunkenly about, alighting on the table, ceiling, and floor, at length on Fuertes's head. In a vain attempt to snatch the unwelcome insect, Fuertes swung with his right hand, sending his brush to a corner of the room. I retrieved the brush. The fly continued its moaning. As it moved past me, I watched closely, took aim, and forgetful of everything but the need for eliminating "that brute," whacked my hands together. The noise was frightful. Fuertes jumped. Off went the brush again as the drawing board clattered to the floor. I was speechless with dismay. Fortunately the drawing was not damaged. As Fuertes resumed work he shouted, this time almost fiercely, "Good work, boy! You winged him that time, didn't you!" I'm not sure that I even grunted a reply. The fly had been more than winged; it was entirely dead.

Fuertes painted the moth with great care. I marveled that his brush could capture the intricacy of the wings' markings. After the moth came the perch, then a bit of wild morning-glory vine, finally the phoebe's eye. Suddenly the picture came to life. The eye twinkled. The soft plumage rose and sank. I had to look twice to be sure that the moth was not disappearing down the phoebe's throat.

What I have just said sounds exaggerated, I know. Remember that I am reporting on how I felt when I beheld the finished portrait. Not on how someone else might have felt or should have felt but on how *I* felt. That drawing, the drawing itself, had life: there is no more honest way to describe the effect that the picture had on me.

The brushes I had brought with me were all small; some were tiny. They would not do. To Ithaca we went, where I bought some fine new ones. Not many, for they were expensive. We visited Fuertes's real studio that day, too, a separate building in back of the Fuertes residence at the corner of Thurston and Wyckoff avenues. A double window on the north side of the big room was large; along the opposite wall were cases holding a wonderful collection of bird skins.

Most of the specimens that I looked at were of species I had never seen before. Especially exciting was a swallow-tailed kite wrapped in white tissue paper. Fuertes handled this specimen almost reverently, for he was determined not to rub the bloom from the dark plumage of its upperparts. The whip-poor-wills, chuck-will's-widows, and other night-jars fascinated me. One of these I examined too roughly. "Careful, boy!" Fuertes warned, "those birds are delicate!" I returned the specimen to its place in the drawer thoughtfully. I had learned an important lesson.

Fuertes showed me books with colorplates by Archibald Thorburn, a British artist I'd never heard of. "Some of those Europeans have done fine work. The feathers of Thorburn's birds are really soft. I like his stuff!" In the 1913 *Annual of Swedish Art*, a handsome publication, were colored reproductions of oils by Bruno Liljefors, again a name new to me. "Every Liljefors painting deserves close study," said Fuertes. "His birds and mammals are part of a habitat. He is just as deeply interested in their habitat as he is in them."

It is difficult to account for the fact that I did not draw a single bird while I was at Sheldrake Springs. Parts of birds, yes, but never a whole bird. I believe I was inhibited, afraid to face the crudeness of my efforts. I would watch Fuertes every day, often for hours at a stretch. Then I would tackle something on my own. My sketch of a kingfisher's head with bill pointed straight at me was a total flop. Drawings of weeds were better, though one that I still have is woefully tight.

I enjoyed walking along the lakeshore. The difference between a dry pebble and that same pebble as seen underwater fascinated me. I loved the way reflected sky robbed incoming wavelets of their transparency, sometimes flashing brightly enough to make me blink. Among the pebbles at the water's edge, I occasionally found fossils. Some of the prettiest of these I saved.

A spotted sandpiper that I found dead I decided to mount for my collection. This work took the greater part of a day, and Fuertes may have felt that I was misusing my time, though he voiced no objection. "When you get home," said he, "just put that bird on the ground near the creek and study it carefully. Remember what I've said about light, shadow, and reflected color. Black feathers struck by sunlight aren't really black. You know they're black, of course, but blackness is not what you see. The only really black spots on your sandpiper's underparts are those that are in deep shadow. Black spots struck by sunlight are gray, not black, and the gray may have a blue tone if the sky is blue or a green tone if there's green vegetation close-by." Never have I made a bird drawing since that day without bearing in mind these important statements.

The greatness of Fuertes came out in unexpected ways. On an automobile trip to the Montezuma Marshes at the north end of Lake Cayuga, we stopped at the home of a man named Foster Parker, who was to accompany us. Mr. Parker was rearing a penful of wood ducks. Big tubs in the yard were alive with tiny frogs, food for the growing ducklings. As we drove along the edge of the wetlands, many birds flew up from the cattails, among them an occasional marsh hawk. "Look, there's another marsh hawk, a brown one this time," said Fuertes to his daughter. "That's a bittern," corrected Mr. Parker. "Right," responded Fuertes cordially, "I should have known better." Turning to me he said, sotto voce, "Foster Parker knows these marshes and their birds better than anyone! I'd give a lot to know them half as well as he does." I have never forgotten the sincere modesty of that statement.

Mary and her father were very close. I recall the look on the little girl's face when Fuertes called her attention to the singing of a yellow-throated vireo. "Just listen to him," he said. "What he's singing is 'Mary, 'Mary, come 'ere'!" Mary would listen and smile, and the small bird, high in its tree, would wait a while before singing again its low-voiced, deliberate, ever so slightly raspy, six-syllabled song.

Mary Fuertes was gentle, friendly, and, even as a little girl, scholarly. She appealed to me deeply. It was she who told me of the Athrabrians, a secret society to which she and her brother belonged. Where they had found this impressive name I never learned. I did not expect to be invited to a meeting, for I knew that Athrabrian activities were shrouded in mystery. I was, however, to see one of their most prized possessions, a wave-washed letter found along the shore, a tragic missive, the only legible part of which read: "Dear Sadie, I told you I was happy. I am not. My God, to think of him behind them iron bars."

Day after day, I watched and learned from Fuertes. I was not with him all the time, but usually I was within calling distance. His drawing of a beaver—for the *National Geographic*—I saw him change drastically when it was almost finished. The part he didn't like, all of the animal except its head, he scrubbed out fiercely with a sponge. I was aghast when I beheld that wreck of a drawing. But Fuertes, powered by conviction, did what he felt he had to do, and he won. His new beaver was among the most effective drawings of the series.

Before I left Sheldrake Springs, Sumner Fuertes gave me a Lake Cayuga "lucky stone," a little ring of smooth gray stone about three-quarters of an inch in diameter. This I strung on my watch chain and wore for years. Fuertes himself gave me one of his old paint boxes—a treasure I was to take with me four years later down the whole of the Labrador coast, seven years later down the Abitibi River to James Bay, ten years later down the Missinaibi and the east coast of Hudson Bay, eventually time after time to the New World arctic, repeatedly to Mexico, once to Iceland. Never since the summer of 1916 have I painted a bird without having that battered old paint box close-by.

Cliff North of Cape Mugford, Labrador   Sketched on August 2, 1920, from the deck of the anchored motor yawl Northern Messenger.

Ichalook *Arctic char caught by Eskimos through a hole in six-foot-thick ice at a deep lake on Southampton Island in the winter of 1929–30. The two females (above) are* ichalookpik— *small* ichalook. *The big hook-jawed male (below) has a special name,* eeveetahgook. *The little fish, taken from the* eeveetahgook's *stomach, is a young arctic char of the very same species.*

Mittek   *Young male king eider caught by John David Ford at Seal Point,
Southampton Island, on October 17, 1929, and drawn directly from life that day. The
word* mittek, *widely used for eiders in general, may be in imitation of certain low
conversational notes given by both the king eider and the common.*

Kingalik   *Drake king eider's head drawn from a freshly shot specimen on Southampton Island on June 30, 1930.* Kingalik *is Eskimo for "it has a nose."*

Greater Scaup   Head of a fully adult drake captured at Kayuta Reservoir in upper New York state on April 23, 1932.

Oldsquaw   Head of an adult drake shot near the mouth of the Natashquan River on the north shore of the Gulf of St. Lawrence on May 22, 1928. The bird had almost completed its molt into the plumage worn in summer on its far northern breeding ground.

Eye and Head of Aiviuk This eye was removed from an adult female aiviuk, or Atlantic walrus, shot on July 27, 1930. The ponderous mammal measured seven feet, eight inches long, with girth at chest of seven feet.

WEST VIRGINIA AGAIN

WHEN I RETURNED to West Virginia from those important weeks with Fuertes, my parents and sisters were living in Pughtown, a village three miles "inland" from New Cumberland, a small manufacturing city on the Ohio River near the northern tip of the panhandle. Father was the supply preacher there for the summer, and his family were living in a building that had been the Hancock County courthouse in the town's palmier days. Finding Pughtown was an adventure. The train let me off at Weirton Junction in the middle of the night. Since there was no waiting room, I made a pillow of my suitcase and slept on the platform until the train for New Cumberland pulled in. At New Cumberland someone told me which street led to the Pughtown road, and off I went.

At the end of the first mile, I decided that I had gathered too many fossils at Sheldrake Springs. At the end of the second mile, I thought it might be sensible to cache the fossils, taxidermic kit, and box containing the mounted spotted sandpiper and come back for them later. The paint box Fuertes had given me would stay with me though I died in my tracks; all else had become impedimenta.

I spied a big rock that I knew I would see from the road, made a shelter by propping a dead branch against it, and opened the suitcase. What of all this would I leave? What could I truly spare? What if I never saw it again? Refreshed by the pause and by the thought of the excitement these new possessions would stir up in Pughtown, I decided not to cache but to carry, closed the suitcase, picked it up, and resumed my journey. Half a mile from town I heard a horse—not a neigh from a distant pasture but the clop-clop of hoofbeats. The buggy stopped and a friendly voice said, "Hey, you! Want a ride?" Was the question rhetorical? Could the voice be real? It was the first human sound I'd heard in a long while. As we rode along, the man told me that he didn't go to church himself but that he'd heard of my father.

65

Summer was almost over. Home was a two-storied brick building not far from Father's church. Next door to us lived old Mr. Yant, whose pride and joy were his bees. We Suttons did all our living on the first floor; the second floor was empty. I found a table near a window and got at a drawing of a chimney swift someone had found dead. I'd not be sending everything to Fuertes from now on; I'd work until I had something *worth* sending. Specimens that I might obtain with a shot-loaded .22 would not be badly damaged, so I would make drawings of them and mount them, too.

I started keeping notes, not mere lists but paragraphs dealing with behavior, vocalization, and molt. What I saw and heard from day to day sometimes puzzled me. Certain warblers and small flycatchers, species that I felt sure had not nested anywhere in West Virginia, showed up well before fall, causing me to wonder when migration southward actually started. A black-billed cuckoo that I shot proved to be a young bird, one that had lived the whole of its short life near Pughtown. I had never seen a black-billed cuckoo at Bethany in summer. Yellow-billed cuckoos, yes, but no blackbills. I was beginning to sense the importance of recording concise data having to do with the seasonal distribution of birds.

Father was, according to our neighbors, quite a preacher. Endowed as he was with a fine speaking voice and powered by conviction, his sermons had an almost seismic effect on the little community. We, his family, knew him to be studious, often preoccupied, on weekdays, a man of slender build, slightly stooped, devoted to his books, sermons, and kitchen garden, but on Sundays, in the pulpit, he became august, authoritative, apocalyptic, even terrifying. His voice, raised for emphasis, shook the church, even as his face reddened and his eyes turned fiery blue. In spite of ourselves, my sisters and I felt our backs stiffening as he drove home an important point.

Father may have been orthodox as a younger man. But at Pughtown he challenged the fundamentalists, hurling forth questions and answers so fiercely that his hearers were genuinely upset. They began to feel that he did not believe the Bible. I argued with him about his most heretical statements, trying to convince him that it was unkind to destroy beliefs unless these could be replaced with something equally comforting. Father replied that his hearers should be stirred up, forced to face facts. In his opinion, what people called faith was all too often mental laziness, a flat refusal to think. Callow fledgling that I was, I had long since decided that all such figments of the imagination as the virgin birth, Jesus Christ's resurrection from the dead, and His changing of water into wine at the wedding feast were part of a benign God's plan for making life interesting. What worried me was not the miracles themselves but the way in which people fought tooth and nail over them. God in His wisdom had seen to it that I got through that hollow log in Texas. He had given me His birds to study. They were what counted.

Father was a genuinely good person. He went out of his way to become acquainted with people who seemed to him to be neglected, offering these lonely souls companionship. Having no car, he walked considerable distances to reach them. He made no attempt to convert them to anything; he merely wanted them to know of his interest and concern. He had an abiding love for the soil, and the soil responded—a rapport established during boyhood on his father's farm in Illinois. At Pughtown his liking for hollyhocks became a mild obsession. He planted the flowers along the edges of empty lots, in front of cinder piles, in short, wherever ugliness could be hidden. He did this unostentatiously, almost secretly. It was rather wonderful seeing all those big bright flowers, literally hundreds of them, in places that without them would have looked shabby. By summer's end, Father had garnered shoeboxes full of hollyhock seeds for use in coming summers.

Friends drove us back to Bethany in their big Studebaker. Our not having a car of our own was proof enough that we were poor, but that proof did not gnaw at my vitals. Our house had no garage, so where would we put a car? We could walk to any part of town without trouble. If we had to go to Wellsburg, we could take the Toonerville. No, it was really better not to own a car, especially since none of us knew how to drive one. I was good at rationalizing.

I was now a sophomore in college. My enthusiasm for bird study interfered sorely with homework. As the leaves turned bright and the nights chilly, migrant warblers poured down from the north, among them two species difficult to tell apart, the blackpoll and the baybreast. These were exceedingly common at times. I collected many specimens before realizing that in each species fully adult individuals in winter feather and young birds in first winter plumage were much alike. Eventually I made a comforting discovery: blackpolls were yellow-legged no matter what their age, while baybreasts were dark-legged. The yellow was not a bright shade; it wasn't always easy to see; but it was there and if seen it settled matters. Thus, bit by bit, did I learn about birds.

A crippled red-tailed hawk, brought to town by a farmer, was so beautiful that I decided to draw its head directly from life. Wrapping the powerful creature in an old towel so it could not flap its wings or strike out with its talons, I did the best I could. The hooked beak stayed wide open, the tongue lifted and extended. My picture of the head was much better than another of the whole bird made after it had died.

I enjoyed classes at college on the hill, especially geometry and Greek. Professor Balch, who taught the former, was a handsome man, given to bringing the tip of his pointer to the end of his nose or chin while lecturing. My favorite theorem dealt with parallel lines. Explaining why I liked it so well reveals both flippancy and dishonesty. The theorem was simple. I understood it perfectly—a valid reason for liking it—but the real, the deep-down reason was that one member of the class had a wonderful way of saying it. For this young man, who could not pronounce either l or r to save his soul, the word "parallel" became "powwow"; so the theorem, fully stated, became *If each of two wines is powwow to a thud wine, the two wines ah powwow to each othah*. Rascals that we, the rest of the class, were, we led discussion toward the dark mysteries of parallelism on the chance that our champion of the twenty-four-letter alphabet would recite this theorem from start to finish in his own inimitable way.

Professor Balch was to win a spot all his own in my affections when, given the opportunity to name a youth thought by him to be worthy of (possibly in need of) appointment to the Naval Academy at Annapolis, he offered to name me. Never have I forgotten the look on his face as he talked this over with me. And often have I wondered how going to Annapolis at that early age might have affected my life and career.

Professor Gay taught us Greek. The class was not large, and there was excellent rapport between teacher and pupils. "Greetings, O pupils," he would say—in Greek, of course—each day as he went to his desk. "Greetings, O professor," we responded in unison. Whereupon, unable to move without the help of Xenophon and the great King Cyrus, we "proceeded three more parasangs into the plain," learning, as we went, amazing facts about military strategy, natural history, and techniques of camping. Xenophon was a man after my own heart.

Biology I enjoyed chiefly because it gave me a chance to draw; but watching a living amoeba, paramecium, euglena, or volvox through a microscope was exciting, and I came to regard the green freshwater alga called spirogyra as wonderfully beautiful. Drawing was much easier for me than it was for most of the other students. Professor Hover watched over me in a way that could have made the rest of the class a bit jealous. I was not popular. I was not an athlete, hence was no big man on our little hill. But I was not without friends, and always, always, I had my birds. Never did they forsake me.

Anna Ruth Bourne, a truly distinguished woman, and a lady, taught us English. Behind her sly smile and deceptive wink were an analytical mind and a moral rectitude that had us somewhat spellbound. Away from the classroom, we referred to her as Madame Bourne, but we never called her this to her face. "You need not call me Professor," she said to a young man who was obviously doing his best to create a good impression. "I am Mrs. Bourne. Please refer to me in no other way." And with that we got back to "Hail, holy light, offspring of heaven firstborn," and other Miltonian matters having to do with a lost, strayed, or stolen paradise.

By this time we Suttons had moved to a new home—a two-storied house still on "Intellectual Avenue" but considerably closer to the campus. Here I had my own room, my own table and bookcase, and a fine glassed-in wall cabinet that Father had built for me. In this case I put mounted birds as my collection grew—the hooded merganser Lewis Perry had shot along the Buffalo, the barred owl from Logan's Hollow, the black-billed cuckoo from Pughtown, the spotted sandpiper from Lake Cayuga, a belted kingfisher, and about a dozen passerines. The case was not large enough for a great blue heron that stayed downstairs in the music room and that, on one memorable occasion, served my sister Dorothy and one of her girl friends as a coatrack. What a rage I flew into when I found that precious specimen of mine sagging under girls' wraps!

The worktable in my room fascinated my sisters. I never caught them snooping, but I could tell from conversation at meals that they knew a good deal about what I had been doing there. They were not especially interested in birds, but they could not help wondering what was going on at that table. Everyone who went to the bathroom had to pass the door to my room, and the door had no lock, so what were young girls of inquiring mind to do—go by, curiosity wholly unsatisfied? Driven by the hunger pangs which beset me at all hours, I had on the table a bowl for snacks. These had a way of disappearing while I was out of the room. I sensed that parental counsel was not what I wanted. Parents might suggest that I provide not only for my sisters but for my sisters' friends as well. What I wanted was to have my worktable and its appurtenances respected—in short, let alone. A fine wild turkey, shot in the mountains of the central part of the state by a neighbor, helped in an unexpected way. On skinning the big bird, I found a double handful of dry, clean, wholly undigested chestnuts in its crop. That very afternoon the salted peanuts on my table had disappeared. I filled the bowl with the contribution from the turkey and announced at supper that what was on my table could, of course, be eaten by anyone but that it was intended not as casual refreshment for passersby but as provender for a man of purpose. I had work to do. I needed sustenance, especially in the middle of the night. I pointed out further that what I kept in the dish "sometimes came from something's stomach." Not for a long time was anything else stolen from that table.

The turkey, a hen, was a genuine wild turkey, with a deep brown tailtip. It was a species that Fuertes might need in his collection, so I wrote him about it while the unstuffed skin was still soft. On December 2, 1916, the great Fuertes wrote: "I was delighted to get your good letter, and am more delighted, if possible, to learn that you have a turkey for me. I think you better make it a skin, with the neck turned to the side, to rest on its belly. I'd love it mounted, but my room is so small, and mounted things collect so much dust. I have no wild turkey and have long been trying to get one."

I stuffed the skin, let the specimen dry for a week, and mailed it. On January 13, 1917, Fuertes wrote that the turkey was "a great and welcome addition" to his collection and "a very fine bird." The card on which I had written all the data I could assemble (locality, date, crop contents, etc.) he attached as the label. Years later, long after Fuertes's death, when I examined that specimen in the Louis Agassiz Fuertes Memorial Collection of Birds at Cornell University, my clumsy label was still attached to one of its legs.

A delightful experience in the summer of 1917 was the discovery of a ruby-throated hummingbird's nest in our front yard. Flowers near the house were visited regularly by a female hummer, recognizable as such by her grayish white throat. We had no idea that her nest was close-by. One day someone chanced to see her fly straight from the flowers to her nest, which was on a horizontal elm branch directly above the front walk. In the nest, or rather perching on its rim, were two young birds almost ready to fly. We and our friends had been passing directly under that nest for weeks without knowing it was there. Standing under it, I ascertained that it was about four feet above my head. Another hummingbird nest that I found that summer was near one end of a long dead branch that had caught on another branch high in a living sycamore and that swung back and forth in every breeze, though never enough to dislodge nest or contents.

On August 3, 1917, I received a long letter from Fuertes—five pages, all in pencil. On page 2 was a quick sketch of an eastern kingbird, this to show me how my drawing of that species was "a bit full in the neck and flat in the chest." The high point of the letter was on page 4, a paragraph that I read and reread, sensing as my eyes moved from word to word that I was transported by them: "The house wren is the best of the lot, and in itself I shall make no criticism whatever. You would have done well to get a chunk of bark & copied it just as lovingly as you did the bird. I think the attitude beyond criticism, and congratulate you on it as a piece of painting."

How many, many times have I recalled the second sentence of that paragraph as I have struggled with the problem of making ice look cold, water wet, moss soft, petals translucent! And I have passed the word along, too. As younger men have asked me to comment on their work, I have quoted every word of that sentence, verbatim.

PITTSBURGH

FATHER'S BEING WITHOUT a steady income must have distressed him deeply. A less durable man than he might have buckled from sheer despondency. He did some supply preaching from Sunday to Sunday, but this did not help much. The purely personal side of his problems did not worry me, but I became increasingly aware of the fact that family funds were being drained away for rent, clothes, and groceries. We owned no property anywhere. What hurt most was the realization that Mother was suffering, quite literally suffering, over what she had come to regard as Father's failure. He seemed unable to hold a position anywhere. He had, perhaps, been too outspoken, too impolitic. Recently he had put a sizable sum of money into an outfit called the Chemical Lime and Sand Company—an investment that had yielded no return. Mother could not forget mistakes of this sort. I suspect that she and Father had many a heated argument that my sisters and I did not hear.

Supply preaching took Father to a suburb of Pittsburgh, and on one of his trips to the great city I went along. I now suspect that it was a father's bewildered love for a nonconformist son that led him to take me to the Carnegie Museum, a big stone building full of wonders—the fossil remains of gigantic ancient reptiles, the famous Heinz Collection of ivory carvings, gallery after gallery of paintings, and hundreds of beautifully mounted birds, among them a California condor with wings fully spread, a pair of ivory-billed woodpeckers clinging to a section of tree trunk, and a family of red-shouldered hawks and their nest. Especially dramatic was a group showing a camel driver astride a dromedary whose flank had been ripped open by an attacking lion. The lion's mate lay dead just in back of the camel. The driver's hand, clutching a dagger, was raised, ready for a second killing. The lion was snarling, the poor camel bellowing or gasping. I found it hard to tear myself away from that remarkable taxidermic tour de force.

A long hallway on the third floor led from the front of the building to the back. Following this hallway, Father and I passed a big door marked Laboratory of Mammalogy, then another big door marked Laboratory of Ornithology, and I realized that on the other side of that gold lettering something very important, something truly vital, must be going on. At the end of the hallway, I paused and turned, feeling a powerful pull toward the big doors. "Father," I said, "I want to talk with the man who has charge of the bird collection. Maybe he's here right now. I have to talk with him." Father, hiding his surprise—if indeed he felt any—asked a question in reply: "Do you want me to go with you?" My answer was no.

I have many times wondered why I did not want my father to be with me on that momentous occasion. Was I trying to prove to him (and to myself) that I did not need his help? Was I afraid that he would be bored by too much talk about birds? Did I feel that his time would be more profitably spent looking at exhibits? Questions of this sort did not enter my mind as I stood there summoning strength and resolve. My ego was asserting itself. That ego—whether driven primarily by desire for independence, by eagerness to become acquainted with a top-notch ornithologist, or by fear that Father might do or say the wrong thing—was ruthless. I was not thinking of Father and his problems or about the rest of the family and their problems. I was thinking about *me*. "I'll meet you at the front of the building in about an hour—at the place where we came in," I said as I started toward the door marked Laboratory of Ornithology.

W. E. Clyde Todd, the museum's curator of birds, was seated at his desk in what he referred to as the Bird Range—a phrase I had never heard before. About him were big, unpainted metal cases arranged in long rows and in two tiers. The windows were large but high: to see anything aside from sky through them would have required climbing a ladder. The whole place was as neat as a pin, and it had a distinctive smell, a smell composed partly of carbon disulfide (used regularly as a fumigant), partly of petrels, shearwaters, and albatrosses (all of which have a wonderful aroma), partly of skunk (great horned owls that have caught skunks smell that way no matter how long the owls have been dead), and partly of the dry, well-cured dermis, epidermis, bone, marrow, and subcutaneous fat of birds.

For a wonder, Mr. Todd knew something about me. He had read my little articles in *The Oölogist*. Yes, he knew Sam S. Dickey and James B. Carter of Waynesburg: the two young men had been obtaining data for his proposed book on the birds of western Pennsylvania. No, that book would not be coming out at all soon, but parts of it were already written. The project of greatest importance was an ornithological survey of the vast Labrador Peninsula, a project on which he had been working for many years. At the moment, a detailed report on bird collections from the Santa Marta region of Colombia was claiming his attention. My head fairly spun as I learned of the numerous enterprises that were under way.

Mr. Todd sensed at once that I was callow but eager, that I had potential. I did not tell him anything about my family's financial problems. I merely said that I did not know what I'd be doing during the coming summer. Before leaving his office I told him that, no matter how small the salary might be, I wanted to become his assistant, that I would work for him if he could find a place for me. I felt no need to discuss the matter with Father. I had not intended, when I opened that imposing big door, to land a job. But, when I found Father and told him that Mr. Todd expected me to help him, I knew that I was experiencing a feeling of elation wholly new to me. Sure, I was still an undergraduate. Sure, I had worked on the Brooke County roads and mopped the floors of Oglebay Hall and mowed lawns and filled silos. But all that was now part of a dim, inglorious, rapidly fading past.

On the streetcar that took us to the old "Pennsy" railway station, I said hardly a word to Father. I was preoccupied with plans. I would learn to prepare bird skins as fine as any human had ever prepared. I would paint bird pictures that even Louis Agassiz Fuertes would consider good. As soon as possible, I would finish a report on the birds of Brooke County or perhaps enlarge it to cover the whole of West Virginia's northern panhandle. In the big gloomy station, I noticed that my eyes were burning. I blamed the smoke and steam at first, then realized that I was feeling shaky all over. On the train I said nothing about how I felt, though I suspected that I was running a fever. Home at last, I went right to bed, too miserable to discuss the big news with anyone. I would let Father do the talking.

In the morning, everybody knew that something was indeed wrong. The red spots all over my face made me look funny, but no one, not even my sisters, considered my plight quite a laughing matter. The doctor diagnosed the illness as chicken pox and commented that I was pretty old for a children's disease of that sort. The malady ran its course, the fever subsided, the spots disappeared. There was something faintly ironical, I thought, about a professional ornithologist's coming down with chicken pox after his first visit to a Bird Range. Once I had regained my usual vigor, I was ready to discuss with one and all the new job of which I was so proud. "He is to be connected *with the Carnegie Museum*," I could hear people saying.

Sister Dorothy, now seventeen years old, was teaching at a little country school on the banks of Stott's Run, two and a half miles south of Bethany. Dorothy walked back and forth each day. I did not worry about her as a rule. But one evening when she did not return at the usual hour, my imagination got the better of me. As the sun sank behind College Hill, I told Mother that I was going to find Dorothy. I started off. The evening would have been beautiful had I not been so worried. I crossed Donegal Bridge beyond Point Breeze, made my way along the far side of the Buffalo for a quarter of a mile, and entered a big open field. I realized that it was growing dark. No Dorothy. At a farmhouse I asked if anyone had seen her. Obviously concerned, and ready to accompany me, the farmer and his wife said they had not seen anyone going by—a statement that did not prove much, for Dorothy had told me that she did not always follow the same route in her comings and goings. A barred owl gave its eerie, eight-syllabled whoop in Logan's Hollow. Thin clouds veiled the stars. The white schoolhouse, ghostly in the half-light, was pathetically small and silent. No Dorothy anywhere—no note on the door, no light inside. Genuinely perturbed, I hurried home, running by spurts, wondering how we'd organize a posse. In town at last, I went straight up the slope from Main Street for home. I had lost my appetite. I was half-sick with dread.

The first person I saw as I entered the kitchen was Dorothy. The look of compassion on her face etched itself deeply into my memory. This time there was no teasing, no joking, no hilarity. She and the rest of the family knew that I had been through a trying experience, that I had done my best. Dorothy had reached town just as I had left it—she on one side of a house, I on the other.

In June of 1918, I went to Pittsburgh to live. I found a room on the second floor of a narrow frame house on Forbes Street (now Forbes Avenue), a block or so from the museum. The rent was high, but I figured that if I lived modestly I could save something each month, even though my salary was small. I had no car. I intended to dress acceptably but had no desire to be active socially. At a funny little shop across the street from the museum I bought a small apricot, peach, or apple pie each day for lunch. Someone told me of a Mrs. Reiker who served meals family-style, so I became part of her family each evening at dinner. I opened an account at a bank, came away with a checkbook, and felt very worldly.

My savings account would grow slowly enough, but I had an important plan in mind. If the right sort of house became available in Bethany, the Suttons would buy it. The Suttons badly needed property that they could call their own.

At the museum, Mr. Todd set me to adding color to the black-and-white lithographic illustrations in the *Catalogue of Birds in the British Museum*—the twenty-seven-volume bound set that he kept for reference near his desk. All the plates in the Carnegie Library's set (the Carnegie Library was in the same building with the museum) had been hand-colored long since, when the volumes had first appeared, and these beautifully colored pictures I followed as best I could. The work was tedious because the surface on which I painted was not flat (the pictures were all in books; there was no way to remove them) and because I disliked copying someone else's work. I did learn a great deal, though, about strange birds from other parts of the world, and I derived satisfaction from feeling that what I was doing might be of real assistance to those who used the books.

Mr. Todd also put me in charge of the egg collection. The eggs were kept not in the Bird Range but in one of the big exhibition halls on the first floor. Each clutch was neatly ensconced in cotton in a separate box, and the boxes were fitted into glass-topped trays. Of special interest were eggs collected along the Labrador coast by a man named W. W. Perrett. Part of the Perrett collection had been obtained by the Smithsonian Institution, but the part that had come to the Carnegie Museum included such rarities as the eggs of the pine grosbeak. Among collections received from South America were tinamou eggs so fantastically bright and so glossy that I thought they must surely have been sprayed with enamel. They looked like Christmas tree ornaments!

Many bird specimens in the museum's study collection needed remaking. Mr. Todd had reshaped some of them after softening them with live steam, but that treatment had made them extremely brittle. It became my duty to relax ill-shaped specimens by wrapping them in wet cloths and leaving them overnight in what Mr. Todd called a sweatbox. Thus softened up, many of them responded well, but others came apart badly, some losing the rhamphotheca, or horny covering of the bill, others the tarsal scales or the claws.

Remi Santens, the museum's chief taxidermist, knew that I was short of funds, so he proposed that I help him during off-hours with private work he was doing for wealthy people of the city. I skinned ducks and geese for him, spending hours, literally hours, scraping fat from between the feather rows. Presently I did some of the mounting, too. I recall in particular two spruce grouse whose skins had been crudely removed in the field and salted. The major leg and wing bones were all missing, so these I had to carve from wood. I worked in what was then the Mammal Range, the room next to Mr. Todd's. I often worked late. One night a board in one of the extra long wooden trays holding skins of pachyderms split from stem to stern, producing a loud report so utterly unexpected that I shook all over from sheer terror.

I did not meet the museum's director, the white-haired, leonine William J. Holland, author of the famous *Butterfly Book* and *Moth Book*, for some time. Putting me on the payroll must have been managed by Mr. Todd or by one of the secretaries in the front office on the ground floor. Eventually I did meet the man, and the meeting was an encounter. I had wrapped a package that was to be mailed from the front office. Dutifully I took it down, expecting to hand it to a secretary. But Dr. Holland chanced to be the first person I met, so I gave it to him. He took it with a grunt and snapped at the string as he walked toward his inner office. "Who tied up this wretched package?" he roared. Poor "Aunt Jennie" Stribling, his chief secretary, began removing hairpins and pulling at her hair—a sure sign that a storm was brewing. "Did you do it, Robert, James . . . what *is* your name anyway?" I told him it was George. "Oh," said Dr. Holland, in a wholly different tone, "so you're that George *Miksch* Sutton who's helping Mr. Todd." He had, wonder of wonders, pronounced all three names flawlessly. Then: "Where did those Miksches come from—North Carolina, Pennsylvania?" "They settled in Winston-Salem and in Bethlehem," I answered. "Well," purred the lion, "then I must have known your grandfather on your mother's side, or maybe it was your great-grandfather. The name's Moravian, isn't it? Now come in and tell me about yourself and your plans."

The subsidence of the blast was so abrupt and so dramatic that I could scarcely find my voice. But I managed to tell Dr. Holland about my eagerness to draw birds well and to become a good ornithologist. Aunt Jennie began replacing hairpins, proof that a dove of peace had been sighted or heard somewhere. Our conversation came to an end with a statement from me: "Dr. Holland, if the Bird Division can be provided with some strong twine, the packages will be well wrapped."

My encounter with the director made history in a small way, for the Laboratory of Ornithology got its twine. Furthermore, it revealed Mr. Todd's cordial dislike of Dr. Holland. This feeling, which was close to hatred, expressed itself in an unwonted raspiness of voice, reddened face, and bulging eyes; it came to the surface of the dark waters occasionally with the epithet "that Big Blow." Dr. Holland didn't like Mr. Todd either, it seemed, the Holland epithet for Todd being "dyspeptic curator." The Todd feelings for Holland were so powerful that I learned to use them to my own advantage. If criticism of my shortcomings as an assistant threatened to wear me down, I had only to mention Dr. Holland and the focus of the conversation changed at once.

Every museum has its characters. The Carnegie of those days had its charming Miss Maud Gittings, who seemed to understand everybody and who went out of her way every blessed day to be kind; the scholarly O. E. Jennings, unfailingly courteous in answering queries about plants; Hugo Kahl, an odonatologist of Norwegian descent, who often discussed with me the "beautiful dwahgonflies" that I might capture for him in far places; the Link brothers, Gustav and John, both skilled taxidermists; the incredibly shy Annie Dierdorfer, whose life was centered in making artificial leaves for habitat groups; the hale, wholehearted Mrs. Clayton, who macerated bones; the nearsighted, gracious Mrs. Courtney of the front office; the stalwart, outspoken Mr. Banks, an expert cabinetmaker who designed and made a handsome taboret for me from an extra fine piece of mahogany that Ernest Holt had given me. All these people became my friends. I believe they all liked me, and I liked them.

But I never learned to like the city. I tried walking in Schenley Park, but there was no getting away from the noise of street traffic and of the long Baltimore & Ohio trains that passed at all hours. The trees and grass were real enough, but their being where they were, between walks and pavement, always neat, always carefully trimmed, made them seem part of an evil plan to make captivity tolerable—like the dripping of water from a fake ledge into a fake pool in a tiger's cage. At the Schenley Oval, where there was a racetrack, I found a bit of true wildness that helped, a pair of horned larks. How eagerly I followed those little birds about—the female, who might lead me to a nest, and the male, whose singing in the sky was the only proof I could find anywhere that part of the world was still unmanicured, unspoiled.

The robins of Schenley Park never comforted me as the horned larks did. They too seemed part of that evil plan, except—I add in all fairness—when I heard one singing in the rain. Listening to those simple phrases, so wistful and so honest, I knew that no man-controlled, man-contrived sound could reach into me in quite that way.

A pair of robins had a nest not far from the great greenhouses of the Phipps Conservatory in the park. My friend Rudyerd Boulton and I were out one evening looking for birds. Rud squeaked noisily—kissing his hand in imitation of a young bird in distress—and a robin crashed into the back of my head hard enough to make me giddy for a split second, not to mention lost feathers floating past my face. Funny little episode that: I should have been angry at the robin, but I was furious with Rud. If his deceit was to be so all-fired effective, he might at least make clear that it was *he* who was doing the deceiving!

Mr. Todd suggested that I try my hand at preparing write-ups dealing with displays in the exhibition halls and with birds to be looked for locally. My first effort dealt with the habitat group of red-shouldered hawks. The second was a list of birds that one might see in the Pittsburgh area. This was published in such a way as to leave room on the back for suggestions to bird students. One of the suggestions, all of which I wrote, read thus: "Do not hesitate to ask questions of the Carnegie Museum's ornithologists, no matter how simple they may seem." What I had meant, of course, was simple *questions*, not simple *ornithologists*. The merry laughter caused by that suggestion taught me an important lesson about word arrangement.

WORLD WAR I, BETHANY, AND PITTSBURGH AGAIN

BACK TO COLLEGE I WENT in September of 1918. Despite all that we were reading in the newspapers, despite the rationing of sugar, butter, and meat, despite even knowing that men from our countryside were being killed in Europe, World War I seemed a long way off until Bethany College became a unit of the Students' Army Training Corps. All at once I was wearing a uniform, learning military etiquette, and going through the motions of close-order drill. I recall standing in line waiting to receive a typhoid, smallpox, or yellow fever shot. The young man in front of me, a chap I had learned to like, lost consciousness and slumped into my arms. I wasn't good at drilling or saluting; I wasn't at all the military type; yet there was something oddly satisfying about being part of it all. On one memorable occasion, the commanding officer appointed me color sergeant for the nonce, since the flag was to be flown from the tower of Old Main and I was the only person available who had climbed the tower often enough to know just how to do it.

A savage epidemic of influenza put scores of student-soldiers and about half of the town's civilians into bed. Mother and both my sisters were down with it, so visits at home were anything but jolly. So many men of the area were being called to military duty elsewhere that a labor shortage developed. When the milkman had to leave, the authorities turned to me. I had drawn diagrams of the calves at the big barn; I had helped fill the silo there; there was no reason, everyone figured, why I should not be good at delivering milk.

In addition to the cows in the college herd, there was a bull named Windflower of Waddington. This fine animal had been imported from afar, so the nameplate above his stall read "Imp. Windflower of Waddington," a singularly appropriate name, I thought. A strapping young Greek, John Kasvikis, a ministerial student, cared for the herd. John occa-

80

sionally had to jab "Imp" Windflower with a pitchfork—just to make clear who was boss. Nearly everybody in town bought milk from the college dairy. It would be up to me to bottle and deliver this milk regularly.

It all started perfunctorily enough. Charlie Poston, my predecessor, told me to come to the barn at 3:30 the next morning. That first morning I learned about the cream separator and the bottling procedure. Everything was to be kept scrupulously clean; this was the first rule . . . and the last. Most consumers wanted a quart a day. Washing the bottles, scalding them with live steam, and filling them with milk would be simple enough. Delivery would be made from a small wagon hauled by an old horse named Joe, who knew exactly which turns to make, which parts of town had disagreeable dogs, and which houses received more than the usual quart.

During my week of indoctrination as milkman, the bridge at the north end of town was being replaced. A shallow riffle several hundred yards upstream from the half-built structure held no terrors for Joe, since he had made the crossing many times, but a heavy rain one night caused the Buffalo to rise swiftly, and the following morning Joe had grave difficulty keeping his feet. Charlie Poston and I had to make ourselves as heavy as possible to keep the wagon from floating away.

I was to learn something disagreeable about human behavior soon after I was left in full charge. At a drab, small house on a side street, I picked up the bottle in the early morning twilight, noted that the green ticket in it indicated that a quart of milk was wanted, then happened to see that the ticket was not that at all but, rather, a piece of green paper cut from the top of the ticket book in exactly the same shape and size as a true ticket. I had not been warned about this sort of problem. "Keep the bottles clean" had been the parting advice. All at once I realized that the people at this house could have been tricking us a long time. Others, too, might have been tricking us. An even more demoralizing thought entered my mind: now that I, a younger person, was in charge, everybody was assuming that I would not be on the alert for such irregularities or would not be brave enough to make an issue of them.

I looked long and hard at the green bit of paper to make certain that it was not a ticket. I heard Joe and the wagon starting on, for already we had given this house far more than its allotted time. "Whoa!" I yelled at Joe, who stopped abruptly, snorting as he turned his head in my direction. He had never heard me yell in this way before.

Summoning courage of a sort I hadn't known I possessed, I knocked sharply on the door. No answer. I knocked again, more loudly. This time came a muffled "What is it ya want?"

"If you want milk, you'll have to put real tickets in the bottle," I said, quite loudly. "What's in the bottle this morning looks like a ticket, but it isn't one. There'll have to be two real tickets tomorrow morning, or there'll be no milk." As if to reinforce my words, Joe repeated his snort. He didn't approve of all this loitering.

There were two real tickets in the bottle next morning, but somehow I felt not relieved, gratified, and victorious but like a sort of accomplice. How long had this dishonesty been going on? How many nice people in town might, conceivably, have been getting away with it? My little world wasn't very lovely at the moment. The Carolina wren that usually sang *pea-deedle, pea-deedle, pea-deedle* so merrily this time of morning seemed to be singing *Which jailer? Which jailer? Which jailer?* instead.

Close-order drill, classes, homework, and the milk route had me on the run. There was little time for ornithology. Yet between scenes I made watercolor drawings of a considerable number of common birds, each picture about seven by twelve inches, for a Pittsburgh man, Charles B. Horton, who let me pay with pictures rather than money for life insurance policy premiums. I had good ideas during classes, so I took scratch paper with me and mapped out pictures while lecturing went on. Eventually I took pieces of illustration board with me, penciled in the bird figures and twigs during class, and put the colors on later.

One of Bethany's Greek-letter fraternities, Beta Theta Pi, came to view me with favor. I became a member, and, since all members and pledges were in uniform, we lived at the Beta barracks. My early rising morning after morning no one would have objected to had it not been for the alarm clock, which roused the whole establishment. Those beloved brethren of mine, wishing to make clear that they disapproved of the clock, set it an hour ahead one night after I'd gone to bed. I got up, hollow-eyed, at two o'clock, walked to the barn as if drugged, found that I was there early, realized that I had been tricked, pondered the possibility of storming back and smoking out the house, and settled for lying down on hay strewn along one side of the barn's main runway. Soon I was sound asleep. *Sound*, did I say? A wild dream wakened me. As I opened my eyes, I realized that a blunt horn was poking me in the ribs. What I was seeing, only inches away, was not shrubbery fringing a limpid pool—it was bristly eyelashes encircling a big eye, the lashes and eye of

Imp Windflower of Waddington! For a split second I argued with myself over the possibility that all this could be nothing but a nightmare. Then, with an alacrity toward which my entire life must have been building, and with a resolve to avoid offending Windflower in any way, I wriggled backward, upward, to my feet, and *over the stanchion*—to safety. John Kasvikis had arrived on schedule at *his* hour. Not knowing of my presence, he had let the cattle in as usual, and Imp was at the point of taking his long-standing dislike of humans out on me!

That fall of 1918 was chaotic. I hardly knew where I lived or whether I was really living at all. I slept at the Beta barracks, delivered milk daily, occasionally visited home, was a senior-in-uniform at college, was elected president of my class (campus politics were beyond me; I was more acceptable than anyone else to the two or three warring factions), and suddenly found myself expelled with a handful of other students who were outspoken in opposing the militarization of our beloved Bethany. I was so numb from lack of sleep, close-order drill, and the incessant runaround that it made little difference to me whether I was in or out.

Then came the armistice . . . and the slow return to what President Warren Gamaliel Harding called normalcy.

Once I was out of uniform, I returned to Pittsburgh, where I was given full-time employment as Mr. Todd's assistant. How good it was to be at work that I liked! Part of each day's activity was discussion of fieldwork to be done on the Labrador Peninsula. Mr. Todd had told me in detail of the several important expeditions he had made to that remote, wild part of the North American continent and, in equal detail, of the work that remained to be done. He was planning a trip along the coast, and he was thinking of taking me along.

By this time I had become fairly well acquainted with Mr. Todd. He was so very different from anyone I'd ever known that my attempts to find a category for him were futile. The day after I started working that summer, I learned that he had never tasted coffee. The fact itself interested me. I recalled how I had disliked coffee myself as a boy and how I had wondered why so many of my elders liked it, but it had never occurred to me that a person might develop an aversion for a drink without even tasting it. Mingled with the suspicion that Mr. Todd had, indeed, had a sip of the stuff somewhere was the slightly uncharitable hope that circumstances would oblige him to taste coffee and that I would be present at the tasting. How could Mr. Todd *know* that coffee was anything but delicious? Mr. Todd explained that his mother had told him that coffee was harmful, that he would be better off without it. Whether he had promised never to touch it he did not say, but I could not help wondering how a mother's warning could be so totally convincing. My childhood friends and I had looked with a kind of favor upon habits that we were lectured about.

Mr. Todd did not drink tea. Coca-Cola was on his blacklist. He did not travel or collect specimens or work in any way on Sundays. He did not believe in tipping. Of course, he did not smoke, and I believe he disapproved of chewing gum, though I recall his elaborating on the usefulness of chewing gum in repairing a canoe.

Mr. Todd no doubt believed in laws and ordinarily observed them, but, if they interfered too much with his plans, off they went into his special limbo. Take the case of the primers (rhymes with climbers) that were to be sent to a collector of bird specimens in South America. This collector used metal shotgun shells over and over, filling each with powder and shot neatly packed in between wadding and adding at the business end the tiny primer or cap, which had in it a fulminate that ignited when struck by the firing pin. Mr. Todd had been receiving hundreds of fine specimens from this collector, who had plenty of shell cases but no primers. So, despite federal regulations against mailing explosives, Mr. Todd figured out a plan that involved removing the stuffing from an old eagle skin, replacing it with packets of primers, sewing the skin up neatly, putting it in a box marked SCIENTIFIC SPECIMEN, and mailing it. Mr. Todd knew precisely what he was doing. He carefully explained to me how flagrant the infraction was. But the primers had to get to South America, and soon. That fact simply canceled out the postal regulations. No wonder the South American bird collections at the Carnegie Museum are among the finest anywhere today.

It was difficult to imagine Mr. Todd as a boy. What could his parents have called him? His full name—Walter Edmund Clyde Todd—was formidable. Could his mother ever have said, "Walter, come here a minute," or "Edmund, you forgot your arithmetic book," or "Clyde, don't forget about the groceries on your way home"? Might W. E. Clyde Todd ever have been called Walt, or Ed, or Eddie? No, definitely no! Not a person who came to the Bird Range ever called Mr. Todd anything but Mr. Todd. And the feeling was reciprocal. Never did Mr. Todd call me George.

Mr. Todd was remarkably well informed. What he knew about physics, mathematics, and astronomy amazed me. Yet he had no degree from any college or university. I am not sure that he had graduated from high school. His obvious interest in metaphysical phenomena almost alarmed me. On occasion he seemed to welcome the opportunity to dismiss birds from conversation and to focus upon trances, visions, and the like. He never mentioned peyote or hashish or any other hallucinogen, but he inquired quite sincerely about my own psychic experiences—as if I'd actually had any—and about my impression of him at times when he was under the influence of powers he did not understand. As a mature person, I now realize that Mr. Todd was offering me genuine friendship, an unusual sort of camaraderie, but at the time I was bewildered and a bit frightened.

Mr. Todd kept the great bird collection in excellent order. The thousands of specimens were lined up in rows on sheet cotton held in place by cardboard strips fastened at the ends of each tray with thumbtacks. It was part of my job to put the cotton in the trays and to line the specimens up. If any tray refused to move in and out smoothly, to the carpentry shop it went. No tray was allowed to go in too fast lest the bump throw the specimens out of alignment. Time after time, during my first weeks at the Carnegie Museum, the silence was broken by Mr. Todd's "No, no! You must be more careful! Don't let the tray hit that way!"

Eventually I was asked to help with the cataloging. Mr. Todd entered the scientific names and the data in huge books that he kept in his desk. His penmanship was exquisite. It was my job to read localities, dates, and the like from labels and to add the official numbers with a guillotinelike device called a numbering machine. Placing numbers on the labels in such a way as to miss the handwritten data was not easy. Occasionally, as a result of my awkwardness, a number had to be thumped on again. On one memorable morning—could I have been experiencing a trance?—I put the wrong numbers on a whole trayful of birds. Lord knows how the accident happened. Mr. Todd, to my amazement, did not scold me. He may have said something like, "Oh, dear!" Then he compared the numbers on the labels with those in the catalog, found where the trouble started, informed me that erasing what he had written would be far more satisfactory than erasing the numbers on the labels, and proceeded to spend hours, literally hours, scrubbing out and replacing that lovely handwriting. As I remember the experience, he offered no philosophical comment whatever. He must have known that through suffering I was learning.

I found Mr. Todd to be a man of remarkable determination. He lived in the town of Beaver, about thirty miles northwest of Pittsburgh, and commuted daily. Invited to his home for a weekend with him and his wife, I found that he had long since carefully ascertained that the next-to-the-last seat in the last coach in the train was the safest. Leaving the museum early enough to reach the station and this particular seat before the last-minute crush of passengers, he and I ensconced ourselves comfortably. It was a warm day. A young lady sat down in the seat in front of ours. Presently she tried to open her window. It would not budge. The young lady directed no appealing glance our way, but I thought a bit of help was in order, so I tried my hand, then both hands, then everything in the window-lifting line that I possessed—to no avail. Honestly ashamed, and somewhat desperate, I was at the point of looking for something like a crowbar when the brakeman came by. Now were we to hear a thumping and a whacking so unequivocal that it's a wonder the wood did not splinter. "Sorry, ma'am," said the brakeman. "You'd better sit over there, where the window's open."

Whereupon came Mr. Todd's sotto voce comment: "I could have told you the window wouldn't open. Cinders blow in, you know, and I decided long ago that it would be better never to open a window at or near my seat. So I put little pieces of wood in." At the moment this management of habitat did not seem so very remarkable, but since that pleasant weekend in the Raccoon Creek country that Mr. Todd loved so well, and that now bears his name, I have wondered how many little pieces of wood were put into how many window latches in how many coaches in order to keep cinders out of Mr. Todd's eyes!

This was the man who continued to show me maps of that vast *terra incognita* called the Labrador, to point out the routes he had followed in crossing the peninsula's height of land, to mention the possibility that I might be part of his four-man expedition down the fog-hung coast the following summer.

LABRADOR

DOWN THE LABRADOR I WENT in the summer of 1920. It was Mr. Todd's Expedition Number 9, my Expedition Number 1. What a summer!

I took with me two dozen or so sheets of fairly heavy drawing paper, each nine by twelve inches; the old paint box that Fuertes had given me in 1916; a taxidermic kit; a double-barreled 12-gauge shotgun with an auxiliary .32-caliber tube for the right barrel; a sleeping bag; and an assortment of clothing and toiletries, including oilskins, rubber boots, and a tube of Unguentine, the tag end of which I still squeeze from. In my outfit was also the museum's heavy, somewhat boxlike Graflex, a camera that I did not use very often.

Mr. Todd and I had several days of bird collecting at Curling, Newfoundland, a town not far from the west coast of the great island, before the expedition really started. At Curling I had two memorable experiences—one with a varying hare that happened to come my way as I was sitting on a stump watching a white-throated sparrow that I thought was nest building. The hare may have heard me and been curious. When it appeared among the sapling spruces twenty feet away, I sensed at once that it was puzzled. I was a shape, an entity, a something that demanded more than passing notice. The hare came closer, tacking back and forth as if pulled against its will. I watched closely without letting my eyes or eyelids move quickly. The hare probably was young, though it looked full-grown. Certainly it was as innocent-looking a creature as any I had ever beheld. Now only six feet away, it held its head toward me, put its ears forward, laid them back, hopped slowly closer. Not quite satisfied with what it could hear, see, or smell from that distance, it came very close indeed, stood on its hind legs, put both its front feet on my right knee, and reached its wobbling nose toward my face. What was it looking at so intently—a mouth, a nose that did not wobble, two eyes?

Obviously it was not content with a knee. What was its hare mind decid- ing as it gazed? That I was a strange sort of stump? That I was a fascinating paradox—a man with a gun who did nothing but sit?

I may, for all I could ever know, have been the first man that hare had ever seen. Almost certainly I was the first it had ever set foot upon. It must indeed have been puzzled. What puzzled *me* chiefly—my thoughts have dealt on this from time to time—was the animal's reluctance to leave. It did not dash off wildly. It took a hop or two away and looked back as if convinced that a moment more of close association with this stump would banish all doubt, solve every problem, establish an impor- tant precedent.

My other memorable experience was with a beaver. People in Cur- ling had told me of a beaver dam several miles east of the area in which I was doing my bird work. I decided to look for the dam. Beavers had, I knew, been protected throughout Newfoundland for some time, so I thought I might be lucky enough to see some of them.

I came upon a narrow arm of the beavers' pond unexpectedly and was surprised to see a large beaver standing in shallow water along the opposite shore. Believing myself unseen, I crouched, took careful note of the vegetation near the water, and decided that if I kept low I could move around the pond to a point very close to the beaver without being seen by it. I started my approach. The beaver moved a short way into deeper water but showed no alarm. Convinced that I had not been seen or heard, I advanced more rapidly, finding myself only fifty feet or so from the beaver, which by this time was swimming in slow circles. To my surprise, the animal did not slap the water with its tail. I had fully expected it to become apprehensive and to sound an alarm.

I reasoned that, since I was seeing the beaver so well, it must be seeing me. Wondering how good the animal's eyesight was, I stood up slowly. The beaver swam closer, walked toward me through shallow water, and looked straight at me—as if expecting me to say something. It dawned on me that the creature had known all the while what I was up to, that now, in its own woodsy way, it was smiling inwardly. I moved, waved my arms slowly, spoke a word or two. The beaver neither dived nor swam off. Slightly annoyed at the thought of the trouble I had gone to by keeping low (the lower I had got, the more mosquitoes had bit), I walked to an aspen sapling, broke off a sizable branch, returned to the shore, and threw the branch toward the beaver. Oblivious to the sarcastic flavor of this gesture, the beaver swam to the branch, grasped the heavy

end with its teeth, took a firmer hold, and swam grandly off with it, leaves
and all.

At Curling I was so busy preparing specimens that I had little time
for drawing. On June 29, however, I made a pencil sketch of a freshly
shot hermit thrush's head, another of a northern waterthrush in characteristic tail-up attitude, and a third of a purple finch's tongue, this one to
show how that important organ fitted into the mandible.

At Battle Harbour, a settlement and mission station on the outer
coast just north of the Strait of Belle Isle, Mr. Todd's Expedition Number 9
was eager enough to get underway on July 7, but bad weather held us
up. We did the best we could for more than a week of wind, cold rain,
and fog, collecting a few birds and small mammals. I found a worktable
near a window at the little frame hospital. There, away from fog and
drizzle, I prepared specimens. On July 7 and 8, I made several pencil
sketches too, none direct from life, all from memory. On the sheet whose
upper left-hand quarter I had filled at Curling on June 29, I dashed off a
sketch of scoters flying abreast a few feet above the sea, five sketches of a
water pipit, four of a savannah sparrow, three of a common redpoll, and
two of a horned lark.

On July 8, I happened upon a least sandpiper that was caring for
two tiny chicks. The old bird scuttled about with tail spread wide and
wings slightly lifted, making mousy squeaks. When, at length, she quit
scurrying about and stood still, the chicks ran to her, snuggled up against
the warm, featherless areas in the middle of her belly, and dried off.
What a cozy sight it was, the more so since it contrasted so sharply with
the chilly dampness of the air!

On July 9 and 10, we took a side trip to the Saint Mary's River,
where I climbed a small cliff to a rough-legged hawk's nest containing a
newly hatched chick, an egg, and part of a mouse. The old birds
squealed and dived at me, but the downy white baby eagerly swallowed
bits of the mouse that I gave it. Pencil sketches made on that trip were
chiefly of the hawks, but one was of two redpolls, another of a gray-
cheeked thrush with its bill full of insect food.

Among the best of the sketches made at Battle were two of voles
captured on July 16 in snap traps set among scrubby willows. The
ground-hugging vegetation so appealed to me that day that I drew several bits of it, even—in a sort of never-say-die mood—a chunk of moss
and a vague blob of seaweed (plate 2). The most valuable of the Battle
Harbour sketches were, however, those made on July 17 of a greater

shearwater's tarsi and toes and the underside of the same handsome creature's wing (plate 3). This specimen I did not shoot myself. A fisherman who had caught it on a hook baited with a chunk of cod liver brought it to me.

Old-timers who live along the Labrador call themselves livyers (or liveyeres), a word believed by Oliver L. Austin, Jr., author of "The Birds of Newfoundland Labrador," to be a merging of "live" and "here," a corruption aimed at distinguishing people who live all year round on the mainland coast from Newfoundlanders who sail their schooners alongshore summer after summer, fishing for cod. Livyers call Newfoundland *Noofundland*, accenting the last syllable, and they never say "up north"; it's always "down north."

I heard some rare talk from the livyers at Battle. While walking with an old salt along the outer shore, I flushed a semipalmated plover from its nest almost underfoot. The bird ran a short way, then fell on its side, whimpering and flopping its wings, feigning injury. Said my companion: "She shore is punishing something wonderful, now ain't she, sore?" I had to bear in mind that "shore" meant "sure" and the "sore" meant "sir." Not many steps farther along, I called attention to a horned lark singing its fragile, tinkling song two hundred feet overhead. This time the nicely alliterative comment was: "That's one of them little beach birds bawling."

The expedition finally started on July 17. Our vessel was the Grenfell Mission's *Northern Messenger*, a trim forty-five-foot motor yawl with an auxiliary sail. We did not refer to Mr. Todd as captain, to John E. Mitchell as mate or navigator, to Edward S. Parsons as chief engineer, or to me as bird skinner, photographer, and general flunky, though these titles came close to applying. Mitchell and Parsons, upperclassmen at two famous Ivy League colleges, knew something about sailing, whereas I didn't. They were ever so much more sophisticated than I, too, a fact of which they, as well as I, were aware. I was intensely proud of my own college, but it was painful having to explain where Bethany College was, that she had been founded long before the Civil War, while West Virginia was still part of old Virginia, that she was considerably the oldest Bethany of the several American colleges having that name, and that, though her student body had never been large, many famous men were among her alumni.

The Labrador coast is not hospitable. It is rising slowly, so even the best of charts may not make clear where the bad shoals are. The tides are incredibly large and powerful. Icebergs drift constantly southward from the west coast of Greenland, some of them as big as a city block and

Common Vegetation   Field sketches in watercolor, Battle Harbour, Labrador, July 16, 1920.

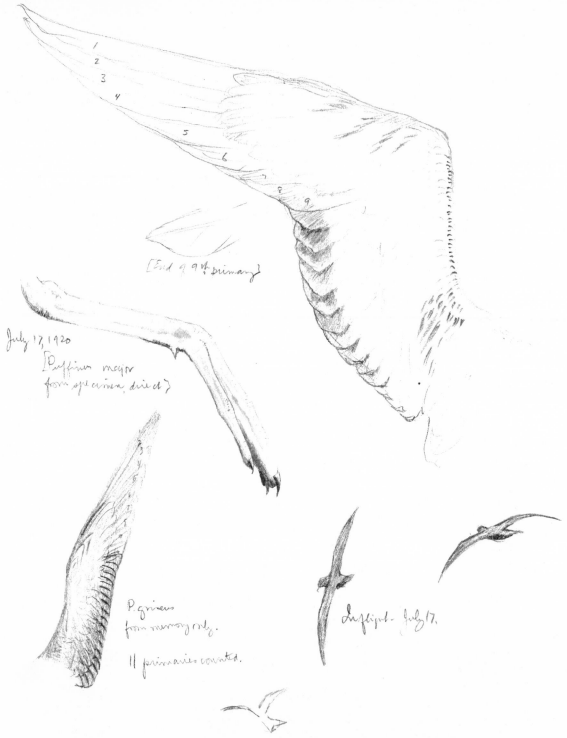

1
2
3
4
5
6
7
8
9

[End of 9th primary]

July 17, 1920
[Puffinus major
from specimen, direct]

P. griseus
from memory only.

11 primaries counted.

In flight- July 17.

Seabird Sketches   Pencil and watercolor, Battle Harbour, Labrador, July 17, 1920. In
upper half, from left: foot, tip of inner primary feather, and underside of wing of
greater shearwater. Lower half, from left: wing of sooty shearwater, flying black-
legged kittiwake, and two flying sooty shearwaters.

capable of producing a tidal wave when they break or turn over. Cold water and warm continental winds meet, producing fog that may last for days, weeks, even months. What one sees of the land from a vessel is bleak. Everywhere there is rock, most of it dark, almost black. The few narrow beaches are of dark sand or gravel.

The send-off at Battle Harbour was jolly, but the departure itself was not very auspicious. Hardly had we set sail when a "breeze of wind" swooped and we came so close to capsizing that friends ashore started for us in a motorboat. Who kept the *Northern Messenger* from keeling over I shall never know. It must have been Jack or Ed or the two of them. It was not Mr. Todd, and most certainly it was not I. Indeed, I never felt so utterly useless in my whole life as I did during the first few hours of that voyage. There seemed to be not one single thing I could do correctly.

Very rapidly did I learn a mariner's vocabulary and the niceties of a mariner's pronunciation. I had known what a rudder was, of course, and a keel. I had heard of rigging. I knew that every vessel had its foreparts and its aft, its bow and its stern, its starboard and its port. But "starbird" was the way to pronounce that word, with the accent on the first syllable, and, though a sail was properly called a sail, a mainsail was a "main-sull" and a rearsail a "rearsull." Herman Melville and Joseph Conrad had contributed "fo'c's'le" and "galley" to my vocabulary, though I had never been quite sure whether a fo'c's'le was inside a vessel or out. Bit by bit the words "bowsprit," "halyard," "hatch," "boom," "tiller," "jib," "deadeyes," and "belaying pins" became familiar. I even learned to say "mainmsst" instead of mainmast. Oh, a landlubber learns very quickly when actually at sea. It's a way to stay alive.

Our first run took us as far as Venison Tickle, where we dropped anchor at dusk. "Tickle" is a livyer word that appears often on Labrador maps. It must mean strait or little strait, though it is not to be found in this usage in most dictionaries, and it may connote a place for safe anchorage, though I am far from sure about this. Our second run ended at Spotted Island, our third at Indian Harbour, where we remained a week. North of Indian, ice was a problem.

Most of the oceanic birds that we saw were new to me. I had seen pictures of them, and skins, but never the living creatures. I marveled over the beauty of freshly shot specimens. The white parts of gulls, puffins, and murres were unbelievably free of blemish, as if there were no such thing as dirt along this cold, wild coast. As I climbed about rocky islets, I surprised noisy companies of razor-billed auks (the livyer word for them was "tinkers") swimming in the green water with bills and tails tilted upward. The guillemots, velvety greenish black save for the big white spot in each wing and the brilliant red of their feet and mouth lining, reminded me of butterflies as they flew about only a foot or so above the water. When the surface of the sea was mirror-smooth, each flying guillemot became two, twinkling along one above the other, the lower upside down.

Puffins that I caught in their nest burrows bit savagely. One bit so hard that it tore the skin of two fingers on my right hand, arsenic used as a preservative got into the wounds, and I was bothered by two small open sores for weeks. A puffin's facial expression was irresistibly droll. This was due partly to the cold grayness of the eye, whose cornea was remarkably flat, and partly to the ornate eyelids, fleshy yellow rosette at each mouth corner, and bizarre, parrotlike beak. At the Bird Islands near Hamilton Inlet, on July 20, I sketched a puffin that I had shot. My drawing of the fully webbed, three-toed, orange red foot clearly shows the slender, sharply pointed, black claws.

Most beautiful of all, in their solemn, silent way, were the shearwaters—creatures that we saw chiefly in bad weather well out from shore. Against the slaty darkness of the sky, the flying birds performed a wonderful sort of ballet—the members of the scattered company scudding along in troughs between the waves, rising enough to clear the whitecaps, describing a shallow arc above the horizon, and gliding back down to become darkness against darkness once more on set wings almost as narrow as the blades of scythes. Graceful, indescribably graceful, were the shearwaters, tireless, true farers of the sea. I wondered what all their arc describing was about. What were they finding to eat? Where were they going? There were two species—the dark-all-over sooty shearwater and the greater shearwater, whose underparts were creamy white. Both nested far away in the southern hemisphere. This season was their winter, this Labrador their winter home. They were called hagdowns by the livyers, who gave the same name to jaegers and fulmars.

Somewhat to my surprise, I was never lonely. This was partly because I was busy, but it was also because the bleakness of what I saw and experienced every hour was in some inexplicable way companionable. I did not expect Mr. Todd to discuss confidential matters. I did not want Jack Mitchell and Ed Parsons to become my close friends. I was glad the two young men knew each other so well. They had so much to talk about, so many ideas to compare, so many experiences to relate. I enjoyed hearing them discuss the socially prominent young ladies we had met at Battle Harbour. Occasionally they used the unfamiliar and aristocratic word *effete* or the phrase *thé dansant*, both very French and rather wicked-sounding. Theirs was a world I felt I would never know anything about.

At Hopedale, we became acquainted with the Reverend W. W. Perrett, the very man whose egg collection I had worked with at the museum. Mr. Perrett had continued to obtain eggs as opportunity offered and had built up another collection. At Hopedale, there were a few glaucous gulls, the most truly arctic birds I had ever seen. These were quite as large as great black-backed gulls, or even larger, and their cry of annoyance—a sullen-sounding, deep-voiced *kah-kah-kah*—was much like that of the blackback. We were to see blackbacks and glaucous gulls along the entire coast, but north of Hopedale the glaucous was much the commoner of the two.

Beyond Hopedale, the *Northern Messenger* proved her seaworthiness many times over. One unforgettable day, a snow squall struck us. The morning had been hostile. Ice was everywhere—great bergs, the largest well out from shore; smaller, brown-stained ones that were grounded when the tide was out; and rotten pans that broke up as we passed them. All sails were up. I was forward, motioning with my arms and calling out "Port hard!" and "Starboard hard!" as necessity dictated. A steady wind from the east shoved us forward. Since we dared not run too rapidly through the ice, Ed stopped the engine. Unexpectedly we found ourselves in an iceless stretch where the waves were big, each with a foamy whitecap. The wind had stopped. A dark cloud swept across the sky to the northeast as a weird light turned the sea to grayish olive and the ice to sulfur yellow. Before we had time to think of lowering the sail, a gust pounced, swirling snow enveloped us, and the main boom swung with a hideous creak, knocking the stovepipe away and almost sweeping three of us overboard. We got the mainsail down, but as we tackled the rearsail the jib flapped violently and began to rip. I rushed forward to loosen the halyard but was too late. With a screech the rent ran the full length of the canvas, from top to bottom. The torn strips flapped and snapped, threatening to blow off. I crawled out onto the bowsprit, determined to save what I could. The wet, torn sail was obstinate.

Realizing that we were nosing into a wave, I hung on hard, gasping as the icy water covered me. *Gather that sail in!* I told myself. *Gather it*

in, you fool landlubber, gather it in! Another wave rose. Again I hung on
hard and gasped. By this time we were lunging wildly. I wondered if
anyone was at the wheel. But on I went, reaching for sail and tying it
down. The waves blinded me, took my breath. Between lunges I heard
myself saying—out loud and clearly enunciated—"Oh, Lord! Oh, Lord!
Oh, Lord!" And the Lord must have heard that simple, fervent prayer, for
I got the ripped sail tied up at last—if not properly, at least tied up—and
the squall did not make an end of us.

About this time we began saying grace at meals. In unison we quoted
Coventry Patmore's *Magna est veritas*, lines long familiar to Ed and Jack
but unknown to me. I became very fond of the poem:

> Here, in this little Bay
> Full of tumultuous life and great repose,
> Where, twice a day,
> The purposeless glad ocean comes and goes,
> Under high cliffs, and far from the huge town
> I sit me down.
> For want of me the world's course will not fail!
> When all its work is done, the lie shall rot;
> The truth is great, and shall prevail,
> When none cares whether it prevail or not.

I came to consider the pale blue that suffused translucent parts of big
icebergs as among the most exquisite colors I had ever seen, but I found
it impossible to contemplate this color—or, for that matter, anything else
about an iceberg—objectively. Rapt in admiration, fascinated, I could not
forget the hidden ice lying in wait beneath the waterline. I could not
forget the *Titanic*. I could not forget the treacherous swiftness with which
the whole mass might break in two or roll over. An iceberg could be
ever so lovely to look at, but first of all it was sinister.

At Port Manvers—not a town, not a mission station, but a harbor of
sorts—the skipper of a fishing schooner piloted us to a good spot fifteen
miles south of Cape Mugford. The weather was worsening, but on we
went the following day. When, on July 30, we dropped anchor in Mugford Tickle, close to the precipitous cape of the same name, the fog shut
down. We could not move for several days. There was little to do but
wait. Great chunks of ice drifted slowly past us, carried by the inexorable
tidal current. Between tides all motion stopped, all motion and all noise.
The scattered chunks now reminded me of huge alabaster urns on display

in a vast gallery with a glass floor—or of toadstools, hourglasses, crouching animals, and nude human figures in grotesque attitudes. Awed by a stillness that seemed ominous, I found myself listening for the little sounds of lapping, creaking, swishing, rustling, rubbing, and crunching, none of them very clearly audible, that signaled the changing of the tide.

Using our little white tender, I rowed along the base of a high cliff, hoping that guillemots would fly out from the rock-rubble talus, revealing their nest sites, or that I would spy young gulls on a shelf that I could reach without too risky a climb. So thick was the fog that I could not see more than the bottom half of the cliff when I looked up at it, yet in the water between me and the shore the reflection of the whole rock face, even of its very top, was wonderfully clear.

On August 1, the weather improved a little. Mr. Todd climbed the hill on Ogualik, a small island just south of our tickle. The view from the summit was, in his own words, "a panorama of bays and inlets and lakes, with mountains rising in peak after peak to the farthest of vision," but he saw very few birds.

On August 2, the weather continued to improve, though not enough to warrant departure. That day I became acquainted with a bird I had long wanted to see-—the purple sandpiper. Several facts about the species impressed me: it was dull-colored, plump, and short-legged, and it moved deliberately except when flying. To my surprise, it seemed capable of standing or walking on any slope, whether of ice or rock, no matter how steep, as if its soles were adhesive. I managed to shoot one of the two that I saw. On picking the dead bird up, I was struck by the brownness of the basal third of its bill, the brownish flesh color of its tarsi, and the faint purplish shine on the dark parts of its back plumage. As I flexed the stubby legs and stroked the soft, thick plumage, a real thrill went through me. In a very special sense of the word, that most exciting of shorebirds had become mine, really mine, at last!

The air was almost soft that day, the sunlight actually warm. My hands were dry and comfortable. Perched atop the *Northern Messenger*'s cabin, with the Fuertes paint box beside me, I drew the sandpiper's head and one of its feet and sketched from memory the living bird. On the same sheet, I did a swimming guillemot that I had watched, plus some circling gulls (see plate 4). Then, sensing that I was quite alone— for the others were off in the tender—I found another sheet of paper and tackled a direct-from-life portrait of the huge, somber rock face off to the north of our anchorage. Never had I done a drawing in quite this way. The experience was memorable. Overhead, back and forth, passed glaucous gulls, by this time so used to our vessel that they voiced no annoyance. So cooperative was the tidal stream that the *Northern Messenger* was virtually motionless. What I drew must have been close to, perhaps even part of, the Bishop's Mitre, a well-known landmark that we passed while journeying northward the following day.

The mountains of northern Labrador, the Kiglapait and Torngat ranges, have an austere, formidable, black-and-white majesty all their own. The highest of their peaks are not to be compared with the Matterhorn or with Aconcagua, of course, but they have a unique grandeur deriving in part from the grave difficulties attendant upon seeing them at all. They are back a way from the coast. Not by any means are they always visible, for fog hides them much of the time, especially in summer, and in winter no one goes that way.

Occasionally, when the moon was bright and the wind favorable, the *Northern Messenger* traveled at night. If the ocean was free of ice and we were well out from shore, the helmsman had only to steer for a distant headland and let his thoughts wander as they might. When my turn came, I marveled at the beauty of it all—the softness that moonlight gave to even the hardest of substances, the comforting presence of the land mass off to port, the obsidian blackness of the seawater, spangled at its surface with reflected stars and, farther down, with thousands of phosphorescent jellyfish that lit up when disturbed. Especially wonderful was the sky. The brightest planets were so large and so close that one played with the idea that they were part of some earthly power system, that, if one only knew where the proper switches were, one could turn them off and on at will.

A subject that tangled my thoughts was what I had come to call the *importance of representation* in human life. Why all our novels and plays and paintings? Why all the writers and composers, the short courses in journalism, the schools of drama? The cliff sketch that I had made at Mugford Tickle: why had I made it, and why might it be of value? The cliff that I had drawn—not the drawing but the cliff itself—was infinitely more beautiful than my little sketch could ever be. *Or was it*? Did my *representation* have beauty that the cliff itself could never possess? And, if the representation had beauty all its own, whence had that beauty come?

Why had I made the sketch? Did I have in mind the people who would never see the cliff itself? Perhaps. Did there lurk in my con-

Field Sketches   Pencil, Mugford Tickle, Labrador, August 2, 1920. At top, center: black guillemot swimming. In upper half otherwise: five sketches of purple sandpipers, including one foot. In lower half: eight glaucous gulls.

sciousness the possibility that my record might someday be important—
that a seismic disturbance might destroy the cliff but not the sketch? The
answer this time was an unequivocal *no*. I had made the sketch mostly
because i had wanted to. Reason enough, let us say. But why had I
wanted to? Was this not a permissible question, deserving of a thoughtful
answer?

Those drawings made by prehistoric man on the walls of caves in
Spain and southern France: why had they been put there? They were
crude—mere outlines. Yet they were wonderfully authentic. And soul-
stirring. We of today love them. We consider them great art—primitive
but great. Why do they stir the soul? Why are they great?

Those who made the drawings knew their subject matter well. To
keep themselves alive, they had to chase, kill, skin, and eat the creatures
whose shapes they limned. Pursuit and killing were a serious business, for
life itself depended on it, but pursuit and killing could not have been the
only activity of those early times. The drawings themselves stand as proof
that someone found time for drawing. That someone may, for all we
know, have been elected or appointed. He may have worked only when
the weather was very, very bad. But he worked. And he did it because
some inner force impelled him to declare: This I have seen. This I have
chased, killed, and eaten. This that I now draw has helped keep me alive.
For this that I now draw I am grateful. This, my drawing, is a testament.

Here, then, was the point, here that which has given every work of
art, every painting, every play, every piece of sculpture, every musical
composition, every poem its raison d'être: the desire to tell, the need to
be on record, the will to communicate. Thus, I reasoned, does anything
autobiographical become important—the representation of what has
been seen, felt, or experienced, no matter what the subject matter, a
representation brought into being by the conviction that a statement must
be made.

Another phrase, one that had bothered me throughout my childhood, had continued to perplex me whenever I had taken the time to
think about it—the phrase *eternal life*. I had found it impossible to believe that what we called life could continue after death. The idea of a
soul's retaining any sort of entity "for ever and ever" had been too much
for me. I had sensed without losing faith that what I continued to hear in
church about heaven, streets of gold, and angels sitting at the right hand
of God was all figurative language. My wondering why all that fancy talk
was necessary had bordered on cynicism, but it had not made me feel

wretched. I had, even when very young, found comfort in realizing that some of the most obvious facts were beyond all explanation, all logic, all reason. The fact that I *was*, that I existed at all, had confounded me utterly whenever I really thought about it. Yet never had the bewilderment prevented me from enjoying meals, the sound of music, or hours afield with my beloved birds. Perhaps, I had reasoned, life after death was no more impossible, no farther beyond explanation, than one day, one hour, one moment of life.

What had hurt, and hurt deeply, was what I had heard from many a pulpit about the rewards in heaven for those who behaved themselves on earth. I hadn't thought of such promises as a form of blackmail; indeed, I had never known quite what blackmail was. In effect the clergy had said, "You be good and you'll be rewarded. You do as I say, and you'll live forever. You do otherwise, and you'll go to hell." And hell was an awful place, awful beyond description. The trouble for me had been that the very poor people that I knew—people far poorer than my own family— were being told that all they needed to do was be good, find "salvation," and believe in God, and all their misery would be made up for in heaven. They were being advised to accept poverty, ignorance, disease, and whatnot as their earthly lot and to find comfort in believing that all would be well in life after death if only they "kept the faith, fought the good fight," and so on. This idea of meek acceptance of earthly lot as a sort of religious tenet had become abhorrent to me. I had begun to feel that the clergy were asking their congregations to believe that which they themselves did not believe at all. Worse, I found myself wondering to what extent part of the human race *profited* by keeping great numbers of their followers in religious subjugation of this sort. Gradually it had come to seem perfectly possible that great church buildings all over Christen- dom had come into being simply because the clergy had been able to frighten people into paying something like premiums for life-after-death insurance policies.

Never had I given up my belief in eternal life. Not at all. The very sound of the words had always been comforting. But that word "eternal" had, I decided, been grossly misunderstood. Perhaps the translators had not been able to find an English equivalent. Perhaps "eternal" did not represent a temporal concept at all. Perhaps it represented not a some- thing that would go on forever but a something so all-powerful, so all- pervasive, that it obviated the need for considering such trivia as begin- nings and endings, gave beauty and glory and a feeling of fitness to every passing moment, and saw through human error to the underlying human desire to be good, to do the right thing, to improve. That sort of eternal life was worth preaching about, worth working for. A man living that sort of eternal life would not need to worry about where he had come from or what would happen to his soul when he died.

The vast darkness behind the stars; the thin curtain of the aurora, heaviest and brightest at the bottom and waving slowly as if blown by wind that no mortal could hope to hear or feel; the sharp coldness of the air; the organ point strummed by the vessel's prow as it forged ahead through the water—all these were conducive to a searching of the soul. Death could not be very far away. But I was alive, *eternally* alive, not because I had become a member of some church, not because my sins had been "washed away," but because I knew that I was sound of mind and body. It was a glorious way to feel.

By degrees I discovered that I enjoyed hauling up the anchor by myself. The chain was big, cold, and wet, but it responded when I lifted and pulled hard enough. I gloried in this newfound brawn. No one objected in the least to my regarding the chore as peculiarly mine. All bosun or mate needed to call out was "Strong George," and up the anchor would come, if not on the double, at least in its own time.

In calm weather I liked to climb to what there was of a crow's nest—to see the sights from there. The ascent necessitated a certain amount of hanging on, for even in calm weather there was a ground swell, hence a swinging from side to side that became more noticeable the farther I was from deck. On one occasion while aloft I saw a big dark something pass beneath the ship, several fathoms down, then quickly surface and bolt upward, revealing the whole of its sleek, torpedo-shaped, twenty-five-foot-long, black-and-white body. Never in my wildest imaginings had I seen anything to equal the dramatic beauty of that adult killer whale as, with mouth slightly open and thickset teeth gleaming, it cleared the water completely, hung in the bright air the merest fraction of a second, and fell back into the sea.

We saw very little of the Eskimos, though we heard wonderful things about them. The story that dug deepest was of a man named Morgan of the mission station at Okak. When an epidemic of Spanish influenza struck the Labrador two years before, it had taken a terrible toll along the whole coast, especially where the Eskimos had forsaken their time-honored custom of moving from place to place in family groups and had come together in tight communities. The good missionary, desperately short of medicine and help, knew how lethal the disease was but was powerless to stop its spread. Able-bodied men who were helping him put corpses on platforms high enough to be out of reach of the dogs fell ill and died in their tracks. Morgan himself did not contract the malady. After the worst of the epidemic had passed, he remembered a family who had been living on an island not far from the village. No member of this family had come for help, nor had one of them offered to assist him. Traveling by dog sledge across the rough sea ice, Morgan reached the shack in which the family lived. There, against a wall, watched intently by crouching dogs kept at bay by two lighted candle stubs, was a little girl—still alive. On the floor were the bones of the rest of the family—all that the dogs had left.

The tidal streams at the northeastern tip of continental North America are tricky and dangerous. In McLelan and Gray straits, they make up to seven or eight knots, perhaps more, behooving the mariner to wait until the tide is truly in or truly out before proceeding, unless he is sure that he wants to travel with it. When we reached the southeastern end of McLelan Strait in early August, that channel was packed with ice—not frozen over solid but filled with chunks that moved in and out with the saltwater river. Fascinating it was to watch and listen as the chunks slid past. And frightening.

I sometimes wonder whether the *Northern Messenger* would ever have reached Port Burwell without the help of the powered schooner *Dorothy G. Snow* of the Revillon Frères Trading Company. At any rate, we were fortunate in being able to follow that large vessel around Cape Chidley and through Gray Strait. Part of the trip was made on August 14, the day on which we saw our first fulmar petrels. These were of two color phases—white-bellied birds whose backs and wings were soft gray and birds that were a slightly deeper shade of gray all over. Remarkably fearless, they flew about us gracefully, rising just in front of our advancing prow, picking up bits of food tossed to them, and sitting in small companies in the water or on an ice pan. They could not stand on their toes. When they alighted on the ice, they sank immediately to their bellies, and in taking off they shuffled forward awkwardly before becoming airborne. They must have been nesting somewhere not far away, perhaps on Resolution Island or the Buttons.

At Port Burwell we were welcomed by Benjamin Lenz and his wife,

Moravian missionaries. The kind couple made it possible for each of us to enjoy a hot bath, our first in weeks, and a home-cooked meal of seal liver patties and other delicacies. Since my mother was a Moravian, I could not help mentioning her maiden name and the Ohio town of Gnadenhutten, her birthplace. That strange name Miksch was familiar to the Lenzes. A man named Miksch had been a tobacconist in the early Moravian colony at Winston-Salem. His little shop was still there. I could not resist the impulse to tell of my mother's great dislike for tobacco and of her arch disapproval of that ancestor of hers who had sold the "wretched weed."

After our refreshing visit with the Lenzes, we could not find our tender. We had tied the rowboat securely to a great rock, of that every one of us was sure. At length, hardly believing our eyes, we realized that a white object hanging from a little cliff well back from the water's edge was what we were looking for. While we had been luxuriating indoors, the tide had gone out, leaving the tender dangling at the end of its line.

At Port Burwell, Mr. Todd decided to cast his fortunes with the schooner *Dorothy G. Snow*, whose next port of call would be Fort Chimo, at the head of Ungava Bay. This would give him a look at a coast he had wanted to see. In a private and rather serious conversation, he informed me that I was now in charge of the *Northern Messenger* and responsible for her safe return. Certainly I felt no sudden access of power or authority. I knew only that we three, John E. Mitchell, Edward S. Parsons, and I, would do the best we could.

We three had a memorable evening on the *Dorothy G. Snow* before starting south. Invited by the skipper to come aboard, we listened to many a marvelous tale. Never had I seen such an assortment of bottles as stood on the table in that dimly lighted saloon. Some of the glass was beautifully colored. I did not touch a drop, but no one made me feel ill at ease. Jack and Ed, the sophisticates, took it all in their stride. Dubbed the "Three Wee Darlings," we were informed at evening's end that we were now "Argonauts of the North." I have never received a finer honor.

At Burwell there was so much ice that Jack, Ed, and I decided to take aboard as pilot an Eskimo named Thomas, a good sort who amused us with his "too many wind, by damn" and other English pronouncements and with his incredible appetite. He consumed, without urging from anyone, virtually the whole of a little jar of mustard, after which his comment was, "Pah-lenty me! Pah-lenty me!" Not far south of Chidley, we dismissed him.

At Ryan's Bay, we anchored not far from a big schooner. The wind blew savagely that night. Our anchor dragged badly, entangling itself with the schooner's anchor chain. Before we could get away, we had to hoist not only our own anchor but also a great length of the schooner's anchor chain. Our bow sank lower, lower, lower, as the heavy chain rose inch by inch. Finally we got a line around the big chain, made the line fast, and let our own little anchor fall free.

At Hopedale, Mr. Perrett showed me a bit of the countryside back from the coast. At a pond half-hidden by shrubbery and stunted trees, we came upon a small flock of black ducks, one of which I shot. The bird's legs and feet were a wonderfully bright shade of red, its bill yellowish olive.

On August 27, just after our chart had blown overboard (I can see that big piece of white paper now, sinking slowly, very slowly, not far out of reach), just after we had passed a bluff island on which a pair of rough-legged hawks had their nest, we ran onto a reef. We did not know where we were—except that we were south of Morse's Harbour and Black Island and somewhere near Nain. We did our best to back off. The waves rocked us gently from side to side but did not lift us forward or backward. We were not perched on a single boulder. We were aground. The tide, an unusually full one, was running out fast. Presently we were down on our side, sprawling miserably in the midst of a vast, seaweed-strewn flat.

We knew that whatever was done would have to be done soon. The returning tide might not be as full as that which had just gone out, unless a strong east wind arose. We hauled the anchors far aft, made certain that their teeth were gripping firmly, lightened our load by putting things in the tender, and stuck a cheesecloth flag on top of a low island nearby. The "purposeless glad ocean" returned. The *Northern Messenger* rose to upright position, but the tautening of the anchor chain did not pull us off the reef. Once more the propellor churned the water in vain. Once more we shoved with our ineffectual boathooks. We did not budge.

It was now that I began to recognize the stuff of which my two companions were made. Not once did they become edgy or difficult. They might, I now realize, have blamed me to some extent for the predicament we were in, simply because Mr. Todd had placed me in charge or because I knew less than they did about navigation, engines, and the like. But they said not one disagreeable word. No, the three of us had gone through enough together to have lost those first misgivings. Jack and Ed were dependable.

Again the tide went out. Again it returned. We hoped that heavier waves might lift us free. No heavier waves arose.

The roar of shotgun and rifle had failed to draw anyone. The smoke from our galley had failed. The cheesecloth flag on the flat island had failed. We decided that two of us would have to go for help. We drew lots. It was a solemn occasion.

My lot was with the vessel. Wondering whether I'd ever see Jack and Ed again, wondering whether the *Northern Messenger* and I would be there on my friends' return, wondering especially how I would manage sails, anchors, and engine in case they did not return, I said good-bye. I did not envy my crewmates as they rowed away. But I did envy their being together. The screaming of the gulls that flew by accentuated the fact that I was now alone.

Alone but, oddly enough, not lonely and not really frightened. I took a perfunctory inventory: guns, ammunition, food, all were there in the vessel. I felt that somehow things would work out. Not because God was on my side or I on His. Not for any special reason.

That night, while the tide was out and the *Northern Messenger* on her side, I walked across the flats to the island where our flag was hanging. I wondered where Jack and Ed were. I wondered if they were safe. I did not worry about them, but my wondering was a sort of prayer. When I returned to my ship, a short-eared owl visited me. Flying silently about the leaning masts and perching unsteadily on the rigging, it stared at me with eyes that I knew were golden though I could not see them. The owl was hunting. Its self-sufficiency gave me courage. To this day I wonder why I shot it. Probably I felt that Mr. Todd would consider the record important. When I fired the right barrel, I was far too close. The specimen was so riddled that I did not even try to skin it. I did, however, make some sketches of the poor dead thing's head.

It is a matter of sober record that the hours I spent alone with the *Northern Messenger* were exceptional. No fog drifted in. No gale rose. No rain, sleet, or snow fell. Bearing in mind that I might need fresh meat, I shot a seal. As I walked to the little island, I discovered that many a rock underfoot glowed with the peacock colors of labradorite. I caught and sketched from life an immature glaucous gull. But I was in no mood for ornithology.

Almost exactly twenty-four hours after Jack and Ed had departed, I heard the low putt-putt of an engine in the distance. What a welcome sound! Rowing a long way along shores unfamiliar to them, following what had seemed to them to be the deepest channel, the two young men had found Nain, fine human beings, and two motorboats.

There were brief, cheerful words of greeting. The tide was high. All hands fell to, attaching the motorboats with long lines to the stern, shoving with boathooks at the bow, urging the engine on to its best in reverse. Waves rose with the wind. As the three engines sputtered, coughed, bent their necks to the task, and pulled, we moved—ever so little at first; then, with a sound of scraping, a foot or so backward; at last, with a bound, out into the channel.

Piloted by the motorboats, we made our way to Nain, where handsome spruce trees stood not far from the water's edge. Here lived the friendly Moravian missionaries Dr. and Mrs. Hettasch, who welcomed us warmly, took us in, and made us comfortable. We had salmon and blueberries for supper.

I do not recall asking Jack and Ed whether they had worn blisters on their hands. I do recall the sweet Hettasch children, a small dog they had, and two beautiful little birds in separate cages—a redpoll and a whitecrowned sparrow. How delightful those Hettasches were!

We made Battle Harbour without further serious delay or mishap. By this time, the nights were cold and leather ice covered the tidal pools each morning.

PITTSBURGH ONCE MORE

IN MID SEPTEMBER, once again in Pittsburgh, I had to explain why I did not know where Mr. Todd was. His going to Fort Chimo was not, of course, part of his original plan. For all I knew, he was still on the *Dorothy G. Snow*. Actually, he had gone no farther than Chimo on that schooner. There he had remained until September 2, when he had started a difficult five-day return trip by motorboat to Port Burwell. Even as I, safe, warm, and dry in Pittsburgh, was guessing where he might be, he was at Burwell. There, quartered with the Hudson's Bay Company, he would remain until September 25, when he would board a Canadian government steamer, the *Grib*, and start south. Within a week, vile weather would strike. On October 5, the *Grib* would come close to capsizing just before reaching sheltered water at Battle Harbour. And Mr. Todd would be obliged to continue by sea from Battle to Curling, New-foundland, and from Port-aux-Basques, at the southwestern corner of that island, to North Sydney, Nova Scotia, before boarding the train for home in late October.

My first job was unpacking and fumigating the specimens that had come back with me. Many of these had not dried out thoroughly and some needed reshaping, but not one was moldy. I was so short of funds that I gave up all thought of a visit with my parents and sisters, who had moved from West Virginia to Akron, Ohio, where Father was employed at one of the big rubber factories. Father never told me what he did at the factory, but it meant an income, and this kept the family together. I greatly admired him for his refusal to grumble over what must have been mere hackwork, and I admired my mother and sisters, too, for staying cheerful. They were wonderful people, all four of them: they could not have liked the way things were going, but Father kept to his work schedule, Mother taught piano, Dorothy taught at a normal school in the city, and Evie never peeped in complaint.

I decided to live less expensively, so I moved to a third-floor room in a tall, narrow, frame house perched at the edge of a steep bank close to the great Forbes Street bridge under which the Baltimore & Ohio trains ran. There was only a wisp of yard in front and none at all in back. The only window affording a view from my room looked down on railroad tracks. More than once, I rationalized about the beauty of flying pigeons seen against smoke and freight cars. More than once, I wakened in the middle of the night to find the room filled with smoke and train roar. Bothered by the thought of fire, I decided that I could let myself down from a hall window to the flat roof of the two-storied rear third of the house and from there jump across to the flat roof of the house next door, *if I had to*.

Since I had no way of knowing when Mr. Todd would return or what he wanted me to do while he was away, I consulted my field notes and prepared a species-by-species account of the birds I had seen on the Labrador. Then I tackled four watercolor drawings—a large one of a glaucous gull, based on sketches made at Cape Mugford, and three small ones of little-known South American birds, colorplates of which Mr. Todd had said he might need for his Santa Marta report. The gull drawing was displayed later that fall, along with the work of other bird artists, at the Library of Congress in Washington, D.C., in connection with a meeting of the American Ornithologists' Union. In making the three small drawings—of the Bangs's antpitta, the Santa Marta ground-tyrant (a flycatcher), and the Santa Marta warbler, the last a full species described by Mr. Todd—I used as models specimens collected by M. A. Carriker, Jr., whose name would stand as coauthor when "The Birds of the Santa Marta Region of Colombia: A Study in Altitudinal Distribution" appeared in 1922.

As for my paper on Labrador birds, Mr. Todd persuaded me to give it to him "for possible use later." When his monumental *Birds of the Labrador Peninsula* was finally published in 1963, I was to find myself quoted on many a page. How I wish he had let me chop down and reword some of those overwritten paragraphs!

I reduced expenses by taking a roommate from time to time. One of these was Rudyerd Boulton, another a young Belgian named Hubert Mathot, who worked at the museum and helped me with my pronunciation of French in return for my coaching him in English. My chief extravagance was the movies, but occasionally I went to a baseball game at Forbes Field, a vaudeville show in the heart of the city, or, prompted

by Mr. Todd's interest in psychic phenomena, a spiritualist séance. The
behavior of a medium, sitting there solemnly with arms reaching out as if
in supplication, roused my cynicism, but I was genuinely appalled when
I realized that some of her "messages from the other world" were making
people cry.

I made a point of visiting several churches, this partly because I
wanted to hear what various preachers had to say and partly because I
was puzzled by what it was that kept denominations apart. Some of these
so-called Christians seemed to be at each others' throats. I enjoyed the
drama of Roman Catholic services. At a mass I watched and listened,
somewhat hypnotized perhaps but not feeling in the least worshipful. The
things that did make me feel worshipful were the faint cries of migrating
birds overhead at night, the strength and perfection of a spider web
sagging with raindrops, or the unbelievable entirety of a freshly shed
snakeskin.

My social life was not utterly neglected. Members of the museum
staff often invited me to their homes. Meetings of the Audubon Society of
Western Pennsylvania were convivial. Rud Boulton introduced me to a
young lady named Ruthanna Anderson, who lived with her younger
sister Eloise and her widowed mother at 4626 Fifth Avenue, a house that
was to become a kind of second home. At 4626 things that mattered
were talked about, the music was fine, and meals were celebrations. The
Uncle Jared mentioned in conversations was none other than Dr. Jared
P. Kirtland, for whom the Kirtland's warbler had been named. "Oh, yes,"
said Mrs. Anderson, "Uncle Jared lived in a big white house in Poland,
Ohio. We'll show it to you if you'll come with us the next time we drive
over to Youngstown!" So it went. Had it not been for those three charming Anderson ladies, I might never have learned to drive a car. But I
wasn't well enough off to buy one!

One day, there at the museum, I was surprised and pleased by a visit
from Thomas D. Burleigh, a young man I had heard much about but
never met. A professor in the Division of Forestry (now the School of
Forestry) at the University of Georgia in Athens, he had become deeply
interested in Georgia's birdlife. His father (a prominent physician),
mother, and sister lived in Pittsburgh, and he was visiting them over the
holidays. To my delight he proposed that we go for a walk in the country,
one "long enough to stretch our legs and get us away from it all." On
that walk we talked about almost nothing aside from the birds of
Georgia, the book that Tom was writing about them, and the pictures of

them that he wanted me to draw. It was a fine walk. A day or so after our return, I made a little mock-up of the much discussed opus, complete with a cover sketch in watercolor of a male painted bunting. Tom's sister, amused by all this wild enthusiasm for ornithology, gave the mock-up her own title: *What General Sherman Missed*. The handsome volume itself, complete with thirty-five full-page colorplates made by me at Herbert Stoddard's Sherwood Plantation near Thomasville, southwestern Georgia, in the spring and early summer of 1952, was to appear—at long last—in 1958.

Through Mr. Todd I became acquainted with two interesting men, both residents of Sewickley, a suburb of Pittsburgh, both keen observers of birds, and both considerably older than I—Bayard H. Christy, a patent attorney, and John B. Semple, an inventor and manufacturer of tracers and fuses used widely in World War I. The two had known each other a long time and were good friends despite vast differences in temperament. Christy was taller, gentler, more scholarly and urbane. Semple was fond of practical jokes, was used to having his own way, was not above being tyrannical at times, and often poked fun at his friend Bayard.

The two men took me under their wing, and a wonderful time we had weekends, visiting wild spots known to them. Christy, who edited *The Cardinal*, the distinguished quarterly of the Audubon Society of the Sewickley Valley, asked me to draw a new cover design for his journal and suggested that I prepare articles for publication there. Semple, a crack shot with revolver, rifle, and shotgun, instructed me in the care and use of firearms and in the loading of ammunition. Soon I was calling the learned editor Bayard and the ebullient inventor JB, and JB was reminding me, almost paternally, that a new suit I had bought recently was "just a trifle too loud" to be acceptable.

Christmas of 1920 was more than I could bear with equanimity. There was nothing indecent about the family's inexpensive, overcrowded living quarters in Akron, but the resigned look on Father's face and the defiant optimism in Mother's voice made clear the family's need for a home. It was quite all right for me to be living third floor back, but it was not all right for the family. Father needed at least a garden and a library, Mother a music room and a properly equipped kitchen. The plight of these loved ones was depressing; it gnawed at my pride.

My friend JB Semple was a confirmed sportsman. He loved shooting. I sometimes felt that he enjoyed noise per se. He had a shooting range in the basement of his home in Sewickley. He belonged to the famous

Winous Point Club in Ohio and enjoyed telling me how many mallards he had shot with the limited number of shells each member was permitted to use per day. Bayard Christy did not approve of killing birds, so JB elaborated for Bayard's benefit on how the great Audubon himself had shot birds galore, made drawings of a few of them, and thrown the carcasses away. For Bayard's benefit, too, he pronounced the word "Audubon" as clumsily as possible, making it sound like "Aw-jee-bon." Bayard's pronunciation of the word was, needless to say, impeccable.

In March 1921, I went by train with Sam Dickey to central Pennsylvania to visit places at which he had found ravens and peregrine falcons nesting. Our headquarters were a hotel in the little city of Huntingdon. Near the village of Spruce Creek, at high cliffs along the beautiful Juniata River, a peregrine flew out to meet us. Its shrill, rapidly repeated cry had a hard, grating quality that sent the echoes flying and the shivers up and down my spine. It flew so close that I could see its bold facial markings and the fine barring on its underparts, but it did not stoop at us, nor did we locate its aerie. Near Mapleton we climbed one side of a steep ridge and let ourselves carefully down the other side, made our way along a narrow ledge, and had a magnificent glimpse of a female falcon as she gave us a knowing glance, bobbed her head, and swept out over the valley. Above Saddler's Run near the village of Mill Creek, we climbed to a raven's nest. The cliff was not high, but the nest itself was not easy to reach. The birds circled above us, croaking their annoyance as we clambered about. The five eggs were light green in ground color, heavily speckled with dark browns and grays.

Later that spring Bayard Christy took me on a walking trip around a waterworks impoundment near McDonald, a small city not far southwest of Pittsburgh. In a shady stand of hemlocks, we happened upon a sharp-shinned hawk's nest. The hawk flew out, circled once or twice, and sped off silently without being joined by its mate. I climbed to the nest, found six eggs—they were handsomely marked with big dark blotches—and brought them down in my hat. "Of course you'll put them back," said Bayard, as he examined them. "Yes," I replied, but without much conviction. Holding the hatful in my teeth, I ascended the tree, branch by branch. While I was putting the eggs back, Bayard called, "Do you think Mr. Todd would consider those eggs important as confirmation of a breeding record?" To which I replied, this time with enthusiasm: "Yes, indeed, specimens are really needed in cases of this sort!" So into the hat went the eggs again and down I came with them.

I made one more colorplate for the Santa Marta report, this one of an adult male Santa Marta seedeater and an individual of the same species in juvenal feather. The latter figure was much the better. Its eye was lifelike, and its toes gripped the twig convincingly.

The pictures that I passed every day in the Fine Arts Department's several galleries roused my interest in oil painting. Knowing that my room on Forbes Street would not do as a studio, for the light there was very poor, I borrowed an easel, bought two stretched canvases, brushes, and paint, and set to work in off-hours at the museum. What I did convinced Remi Santens, the chief taxidermist, that I should try painting backgrounds for habitat groups. Someone had recently brought an exceptionally fine great horned owl to the museum. Mr. Santens, Mr. Todd, the Link brothers, and I discussed the proposed group, decided that it might show the owl about to capture a skunk, and proceeded to map out the arrangement. The carpenters built the case, the Link brothers mounted the owl and skunk beautifully, and I painted a background showing bright sky and a bit of brushy woodland. The season represented was fall, so not many green leaves were needed. The vegetation included part of a tree with its roots and a lot of brambles, one sprig of which was an iron rod that supported the flying owl. So cleverly bent was this rod that its connection with the owl could not be seen from any point in the glass front of the case. A delight of my life was watching people as they tried to figure out what held the owl up. Word went round that the wires were invisible, but this was too much for the skeptics. Even grown men, driven by curiosity and sometimes annoyance, would drop to their hands and knees and creep along the case's front, doing their best to solve the mystery. Some of these truth seekers cared not a whit whether they were being watched; others glanced about furtively to make sure that no one was looking.

The Fine Arts Department put on an international show each year. The glamorous previews, to which I was invited, were exciting, though I knew only a few of the people who attended. At one show, Bruno Liljefors was represented by his famous work, *The Hunter*. This oil I made a point of looking at every day as long as it was in Pittsburgh. One portrait by an artist whose name I forget had me gasping when I found that a jeweled stickpin in the man's tie had not been painted there at all: what looked like a stickpin *was* a stickpin, fastened to the canvas.

In 1921 I became an active member of the Wilson Ornithological Society (then called the Wilson Ornithological Club), a national organization devoted to "field ornithology"—that is, the study of living birds in their habitat in contradistinction to that of skins, skeletons, and alcoholic specimens in museums. I did not attend the organization's annual meeting in Chicago that year, but in 1922 my "Notes on the Roadrunner at Fort Worth, Texas" appeared as the lead article in the first issue of volume 34 of the society's official quarterly, *The Wilson Bulletin*, and in 1926 my somewhat stylized pen-and-ink drawing of a male Wilson's warbler appeared on the quarterly's cover. That drawing was to be used continuously through volume 74 (1962). In 1963 a new cover design (also by me), a more "open" drawing depicting two Wilson's warblers, rather than one, would be used. By that year I would have served the organization variously—as its president for two stretches (1942, 1946–47).

Early in the spring of 1922, Mr. Todd asked me to collect material for a habitat group of Pennsylvania ravens. I knew just where the Saddler's Run nest was, of course, and I suspected that it was still in use.

Taking with me a double-barreled shotgun and a sleeping bag, I went by train to Mill Creek and walked several miles to the mountain. The closer I drew to the nesting cliff, the more I wondered whether the ravens were still there. Determined not to rouse their suspicions, I made camp without building a fire and ate supper early. As the evening grew cooler, I had grave misgivings. Perhaps all this effort was for naught. Perhaps I should first have made certain that the birds were here, then, after a few days' wait, come after them. Even as I pondered these possibilities, I heard a bell-like call in the distance. When I looked up, I saw a big black bird circling above the shoulder of the mountain. The ravens had not moved!

That night I was miserably cold. In the half-light just before dawn, I decided to quit thrashing about trying to find a warm spot and to get up instead. The sleeping bag was white with frost. My back was so sore I could hardly stand. In short circles I stomped around, thawing out. Breakfast was dry and tasteless, for I built no fire—lest I disturb the ravens. After caching the sleeping bag, I picked up the shotgun and the cotton-filled egg bucket and started for the cliff. As the stiffness left my legs, I enjoyed the new day. In the woods below me, a pileated woodpecker pounded at a stub and cackled. No wonder people called the big woodpeckers Indian hens. Farther away, several hundred yards apart, two ruffed grouse drummed. Occasionally I passed a patch of old snow. Nowhere did I see a flower blooming, not even a hepatica, but the moss was wonderfully green.

At the base of the cliff, I made certain that my right thumb was limber enough to move the gun's safety device quickly, then strung the egg bucket on my belt so as to have one hand free. I could not see the raven nest, though I knew just where it had been the year before. At a ledge a third of the way up, I realized that ice was a hazard. I would have to be careful, very careful.

Knowing that the snapping of a branch or the falling of a pebble might rouse the brooding bird, I moved not upward but sidewise along a ledge in such a way as to bring the big nest barely into view. I wanted to be sure that it was there. The sun's rays were brightening the ridge crest above me by this time. A troupe of small birds, chickadees chiefly, moved upslope through the treetops. They may not have known that I was there, for they voiced no alarm.

Even as I watched the chickadees, I realized that a flying raven was overhead, almost within range and circling lower. The great bird took me by surprise. Suddenly it croaked, and I knew it had seen me. Bracing my hip against the rock and kicking to make certain that my footing was solid, I lifted the gun, took aim, realized that I was not leading properly, further realized that, unless I kept in mind where I was, I might fall. I aimed again, doing my best to hold the gun firmly and to lead properly. This time the raven passed in back of a point of rock just as I was about to pull the trigger.

Now the other bird appeared, dropping past me from the nest on half-folded wings, down, down, its glossy plumage reflecting the sky. Bewildered, beside myself with excitement, I fired twice, missing badly. Untouched, the bird twisted, almost flip-flopped, leveled off, and towered. Alas, there had been no time for reloading while the raven was within range. Alas, I had not really aimed. I had pointed the gun in the general direction of the flying bird and blazed away. No wonder I had missed!

By this time the first raven was a mere speck in the sky, and the other was not far below it. Both were calling. The oddly human syllables sounded sad rather than angry. Utterly chagrined, I watched the circling pair. For a time I hoped they would dive at me, thus giving me another chance. But no—off they circled over the mountaintop and out of sight.

Reaching the nest required climbing above it and inching along a narrow ledge that angled downward. The five eggs I wrapped carefully in cotton, one by one, and placed in the bucket. The nest, beautifully lined with deer hair and grapevine bark, did not come away easily, for its largest twigs were frozen to the rock. Finally I got it loose, tied it together with binder twine, hung the bundle over my back, and made my way to the top of the cliff and downslope back to camp.

Loaded with sleeping bag, nest, egg bucket, and gun, I found the road that led out of the woods. In the valley the going was easy, though I knew I was in need of food and sleep. Not for a long time did I pass a house. Halfway to Mill Creek, I noticed that a grass fire was moving toward a big barn and a haystack. Thinking that the farmer must surely have started the fire and be watching it, I dismissed it from my mind, but the nearer I got the surer I became that unless something were done both haystack and barn were doomed. I ran a few steps, stopped long enough to put my "luggage" down, and ran on, reaching the house just as the people there poured out, some with wet gunnysacks, others with pails of water. Knowing that prompt action was mandatory, I ran to the fire, yanked off my hunting coat, and started beating out the flames with it. The efforts of the five of us stopped the fire in time. My hunting coat was just about done for. I was pretty well done for myself. The women gave me some sandwiches, a dish of pickled beets, and coffee. Never had anything tasted better. But as I sat there I became so drowsy that I had to force myself to rise and say good-bye. Had I stayed, I would surely have gone to sleep in my chair.

The raven nest was to become part of a habitat group in the museum's main exhibition hall. From memory I would paint as background the cliff up which I had climbed. Two ravens from Maine would be used instead of the pair that I had failed so miserably to shoot. The label for the group would be informative, possibly mentioning Poe's famous poem but saying nothing of frost-covered sleeping bag, chagrin, or ruined hunting jacket.

Later that spring I undertook a study of a fascinating part of northwestern Pennsylvania, a twenty-five-mile area of boggy lakes, cattail marshes, tamaracks, hemlocks, pitcher plants, royal ferns, lady's slippers, sundew, and poison sumac, an untamed wilderness known as Pymatuning Swamp. Jack Thomas, of Buffalo, New York, a young man I had met on the Labrador, volunteered to assist me. Our headquarters were at Hartstown, a village on the Bessemer & Lake Erie Railroad. Here we were so close to the south end of the great swamp that a fifteen-minute walk would take us to the very heart of a red-winged blackbird colony if we followed the railway roadbed northward or to Crystal Lake and mature beech woods close-by if we took the dirt road eastward.

At the old Century Inn, where we stayed, we were regaled with accounts of trains that had sunk, cars, rails, roadbed, and all, into the bog; of the Erie's decision to build two roadbeds so that one would always be there for use; of mystery streams that flowed now northward, now southward, depending on wind and rainfall; of vain attempts to reach the bottom of one of the lakes. On good authority, we were informed that spliced piling had been driven to a depth of two hundred feet before solid ground had been reached for the Erie's roadbed. With an odd sort of pride, the proprietor of the inn showed us photographs of several freight cars half-submerged. How many cars or trains had been lost in this way we never learned, but rumor made the number properly impressive, and the photographs were convincing.

The passing of a heavy freight at night never failed to be exciting. Trains from the north set the waves of bog rolling in such a way as to make the inn shudder before we could hear the sound of wheels. Locomotives whistled as they approached, but north of town there was little whistling since there were no crossings between Hartstown and Shermansville, six miles away. A northbound train caused very little disturbance until the locomotive and first cars had passed the station. Once the train started across the swamp, however, pictures on the inn's walls swung back and forth, windows rattled, and furniture walked around as if alive. In my room in Pittsburgh, I had become used to the noise of trains at night, but this rhythmic swaying of the whole building was something new. At times I wondered whether a limit of endurance were not being reached, but no picture ever fell and no windowpane ever broke.

As we studied the Hartstown countryside we soon learned that, where we found certain bird species, we could be confident of finding certain others also. Thus, where red-winged blackbirds were nesting among cattails, there would also be yellowthroats, Virginia rails, bitterns, and marsh hawks; where there were yellow warblers among willow saplings and poison sumac, there were likely to be alder flycatchers, too; and, where there were Acadian flycatchers in beech woodland, we might expect to find ruffed grouse, red-shouldered hawks, hooded warblers, cerulean warblers, and scarlet tanagers. I had been aware of this dependence on habitat for a long time, but at Hartstown the abrupt ending of one habitat and the beginning of another was dramatic. In the woods we could hear a scarlet tanager or a red-eyed vireo singing overhead and, almost exactly the same distance away but at body or foot level, yellow warblers singing or Virginia rails grunting. We were surprised to find that the two marsh wrens did not occupy the same habitat—the longbills liked cattails and bulrushes, the shortbills, sedge.

One morning, after a hearty breakfast, Jack Thomas and I found a red-headed woodpecker's nest. I decided to climb to it, for I wanted a set of fresh eggs. The dead stub had no branches, so I had to shinny up. Not far below the nest was a crotch, and just below this was a barkless stretch so smooth that I had to grip hard with arms and legs in order to proceed at all. I knew that I was feeling light-headed as I negotiated this smooth, slippery part, but I held on grimly, inched upward, finally swung a leg up over and into the crotch, and hung there as I came close to fainting. When vigor returned, I said to Jack that I had been feeling mighty strange. His reply was: "You looked that way, all right. I could see you getting whiter and whiter. I was all set to catch you." That time I slid to the ground—without the woodpecker's eggs.

In a big, low-lying meadow we found bobolinks and Henslow's sparrows. The unmusical song of the droll little sparrows—a species I had never seen before—quite entranced me. The birds were given to singing in a sort of chorus, each bird pouring out that funny little *chis-lick* as if it were every bit as fine as the rhapsodizing of the bobolinks. The two species nested, as far as we could see, in exactly the same sort of place. Their food preferences probably differed enough to reduce competition, so neither made the slightest attempt to drive the other off. If a Henslow's ever chased another bird, that other bird was a Henslow's. Aside from the Henslow's and bobolinks, the only birds that visited the meadow regularly were barn swallows, mere passers-over. The meadowlarks lived on higher ground.

A Cooper's hawk nest that we found well up in a huge beech was only about twenty feet above a half-finished cerulean warbler's nest in the very same tree. From the hawks' broad, shallow basin of sticks, I looked down on the female warbler as she worked away with shredded bark and bits of cobweb. As far as I could see, the hawks paid not the slightest attention to the warblers—and vice versa. The big birds swept up to and down from their nest with considerable speed, so they had to pay close attention lest they collide with a branch.

Among the most interesting birds that we found were the snipes—a species widely known in those days as the Wilson's snipe or jacksnipe. We had heard the birds hooting above the marshlands the first evening we had been afield, but we had assumed that they were displaying, or perhaps even pairing, while migrating northward. We had been fascinated by the odd windy sound and by the behavior of the performing birds. Day after day, night after night, their hooting continued. It was especially noticeable when we waded out among the cattails. Now the birds seemed to swoop toward us as if trying to attract our attention or to frighten us off. Some that we flushed flew rapidly skyward and began hooting almost at once; others stayed low, moving off horizontally in a series of bounds, each bound starting with a flutter and ending with a smooth coasting downward on partly spread wings. On May 4 we found a nest. Knowing that this evidence of breeding was important, I took the four eggs, finding them to be heavily incubated. Egg laying had obviously started long before we arrived.

Some birds that we knew were nesting in and near the swamp continued to baffle us. We found several freshly built short-billed marsh wren nests, each tightly woven into the sedge, but not a single one held eggs or young. We saw and heard brown creepers occasionally in dense woods, yet not a creeper led us to a nest.

Every walk that I took, no matter how short or long, no matter what time of day or night, was exciting. Courting marsh hawks, looping the loop and uttering cries that reminded me of a flicker, held me spellbound. It seemed incredible that these fierce raptorial birds, so wondrously designed for killing, could let themselves go in this way, as if beside themselves with nothing but joy. One marsh hawk that I watched flew to a stub, nibbled perfunctorily at what it held in its talons, and flew off, *leaving its prey*. Reaching the stub necessitated a long wade through waist-deep water. What I found there, belly-down, for all the world like a well-prepared museum specimen, was a star-nosed mole. The hawk conceivably had found the mole dead, for I saw no evidence that its skin had been torn in the slightest. Woodcocks also delighted me. Only occasionally did I flush one of those strange birds, but in the evening dusk along the road near Crystal Lake I sometimes heard the whistling wings or odd twittering of a performing bird overhead. Once I actually saw the moving silhouette against the sky.

Eventually I was to learn some of the great swamp's secrets. At a sequestered spot, I found an islet covered with showy lady's slipper in full bloom. So sheltered was this habitat that neither sun nor wind reached it. I never walked among the flowers lest some stem or leaf be broken. Never was I tempted to pick them, though I examined one carefully, marveling at the shape and structure of the strange petals. They were as perfectly lovely as anything I had ever seen. Selfishly, perhaps very selfishly, I told no one of finding them. I felt that there was no one I could trust.

In early June, I returned to Pittsburgh with my collection. Mr. Todd was pleased, especially with the eggs, since these were evidence that would make possible plotting the breeding distribution of certain species whose status had been in doubt.

Now began a lengthy correspondence with Harold H. Bailey, who had published a book on the birds of Virginia and who now, having moved to Florida, was planning a lavish volume on the birds of that state. I was bewildered by the prospect of making some seventy plates, for I knew that I could not finish them at all promptly, and I also knew that many of the species to be drawn were wholly unfamiliar to me. I did, however, have the museum's fine collection at my elbow, I was eager to show everyone what I could do, and I needed the money. My very first plate, of a flamingo colony, put my imagination to work. The drawing turned out fairly well. Of the seventy-six plates eventually made, it was the only one showing a single species. Most of them showed several. As a whole, they were shamelessly imitative of Fuertes—especially plate 16 (showing the three scoters and a ruddy duck) and plate 53 (two red-winged blackbirds, two yellow-headed blackbirds, and two cowbirds). I made some bad mistakes. Thus, never having handled a living or freshly shot red-necked grebe, I showed that brown-eyed species with a red eye, I made the bill and legs of the adult laughing gull black rather than reddish, and I showed the drake common merganser with a red rather than a dark brown eye.

The letters I received from Mr. Bailey as the work progressed were sometimes amusing. Plate 35, which showed two turkey vultures, two black vultures, two caracaras, and a partly eaten pig carcass, he liked especially, though his wife didn't care for it at all and advised against using it. Plate 57 was a badly crowded picture showing a male and a female white-eyed towhee, four other species of the finch family, and—in the upper right-hand corner—a pair of house sparrows perched on a board. Above these last two was a bit of space. Mr. Bailey, enthusiastic about the plate as a whole, wondered if it would be possible to add in this space "a little shack, with smoke coming out of the chimney, and a cottonfield with a darkie or two working there." I do not recall how I disposed of this outrageous suggestion.

I worked on the Florida plates as opportunity offered. The last of the lot, plate 2—showing a great auk, a greater shearwater, an arctic tern, two common loons, and two red-throated loons—was such an impossible assortment that I hated doing it, but Mr. Bailey had ordered it and I made it. He was guilty of kindhearted hyperbole when, in the introduction to his book, he mentioned the "marvelous accuracy" of my work.

In the winter of 1922–23, I worked out a plan with Bethany College whereby I would be reinstated as a student, take a special course in English literature with Mrs. Bourne, and receive my bachelor of science degree in June. Bethany was about sixty miles from Pittsburgh. Sessions with Mrs. Bourne would come every weekend. I bought a small car, made the trips, and was awarded the degree. The sessions with Mrs. Bourne were inspiring—not alone her comments on what we read together from the great authors, not alone the belief in me that shone from her fine eyes, but the serene beauty of the campus itself with its Old Main, its sloping walks and lawn, and its stately elms. On those Bethany weekends, I stayed with Professor H. Newton Miller and his family. How kind they were to me!

JAMES BAY

IN MID AUGUST OF 1923, John Semple, Mr. Todd, and I traveled by train from Pittsburgh to Cochrane, Ontario, where we met our two Ojibway Indian guides, Joe Stevens and Angus Beaucage, purchased a nineteen-foot Peterborough freight canoe and supplies, and undertook Mr. Todd's Expedition Number 10 down the Abitibi and Moose rivers to the Partridge creeks at the south end of James Bay. Mr. Todd wanted to revisit certain parts of the North Country, but some of the route to be followed this time would be new to him. The area to be covered was west of the Labrador Peninsula, the part of the continent in which he was especially interested, but all of it would be wilderness of a very fine sort. Since we planned to obtain blue goose specimens for a habitat group at the Carnegie Museum, the newspapers called us the Blue Goose Expedition. I was to assist with collecting and preparing specimens, but I had paper, pencils, brushes, and the old Fuertes paint box with me.

The blue goose was, in those days, considered a full species. Ornithologists agreed that in many important ways it was like the snow goose. Some believed it and the snow goose to be color phases or "morphs" of one and the same species—a concept that is widely held today. Blues and snows were known to migrate together regularly. In Canada the two were often called wavies, and "wavy" was said to be an onomatopoeic Indian word, the spelling of which was a matter of opinion or guess. Mixed populations of the two wavies wintered in great numbers on the Gulf of Mexico coast. On their way south, they stopped for a while at the south end of James Bay, then again at such midway points as Devils Lake in North Dakota, Sand Lake in South Dakota, and Lake Traverse along the Dakota-Minnesota line before moving on to Louisiana and Texas. The blue had long been one of my special birds. As a youngster, I had pored over accounts of its migrations. What I had read had made clear that its distribution in summer was not well known.

122

No one had found its nest. It was a bird of mystery, almost of myth. *You might be the one to find the blue goose's nest*, I'd say to myself. *It's got to be up there somewhere!* And my finger would trace a migration route down one coast of Hudson Bay and up the other to such remote islands as Southampton, Coats, Mansel, and Baffin or to such little-known peninsulas as Melville and Boothia. The blue goose had haunted my boyhood dreams.

Cochrane was a sorry sight, for it had recently been ravaged by fire. I do not recall meeting the guides there or buying supplies, but I well remember breakfast at the little Chinese restaurant near the railway station. While we were eating, word came that a train long overdue from the east would soon arrive. On it would be men from the Maritime Provinces headed for Manitoba, Saskatchewan, and Alberta to help with the harvest. To say that we at table were neglected when that word came is to understate grossly. Restaurant personnel, all three of them, rushed outdoors, yanked down the CAFE sign, slapped boards across the windows, returned breathing noisily, locked the front door from the inside, and stood at the windows peering out through the cracks. When the train stopped, out poured the men, scores of them, hungry as wolves. Wondering what under heaven to do, and feeling worse than useless, we heard the sound of wood cracking and glass breaking. Every showcase and vending machine in the station was more or less demolished. The men were famished. Had we not been boarded-in, it's hard to say what would have happened to what we were eating—to say nothing of us. Fortunately, the train pulled out shortly.

The first forty-three miles of our downriver trip were by rail. Our party was to travel with canoe and camp gear in one of the construction train's boxcars, but I, being young and adventurous, rode with the engineer and fireman in the locomotive. That first lap took us to the "end of steel," a point at which a bridge was being built just above the Abitibi's Island Falls. The roadbed was bumpy, very bumpy, noticeably bumpier as we moved northward. Apprehensive, if not genuinely alarmed, I yelled at the fireman, "Awfully rough here, isn't it?" "It *is* that!" he yelled back, even as I caught a blurred glimpse of a dead locomotive lying half-underwater alongside the tracks. I have never seen a more forlorn-looking object. It was so huge, so helpless, so wretchedly out of place. It had jumped the tracks.

The weather during that laborious descent of the Abitibi was cold, wet, dreary, the several portage trails slippery and treacherous, the camping anything but idyllic. We all paddled. On the portages the guides carried the big canoe upside down on their shoulders. Swinging it up into place took real brawn. This I know, for I tried it—once. Following a slippery trail with head inside an overturned freight canoe is hard work. For those of us with other gear to carry, tumplines helped. There was precious little time for collecting specimens and almost none for drawing, though Mr. Todd and I made a point of writing notes each evening.

On August 23, at the start of a portage around the white water of Abitibi Canyon, we decided to make camp, for the day was waning. Though the weather was disagreeable, I decided to take a turn for birds. After walking upslope half a mile, I entered a stand of tall burned spruces on a sort of plateau. Suddenly, as if from nowhere, a sharp-shinned hawk darted down, cackling shrilly, barely missing my head. As I turned to watch it, another swooped, coming so close that a wing brushed my ear. I had invaded the pair's breeding territory, there could be no doubt of that. Among the trees was a brood of six young sharpshins, all fledged and flying fairly well but still dependent on their parents for food. I decided against collecting a specimen, since skinning it by firelight would be difficult and we would have heavy portaging to do on the morrow. I also decided to back off, not because I felt sorry for the hawks but because I didn't want to be scratched up by them. When I came to my senses after dodging and beating off attacks, I realized that I did not know which direction I had come from. No bright spot in the gray sky helped. I knew where the river was, of course, for I could hear its roar.

After going what seemed to be downslope a considerable distance, I sensed that the sound of the water was considerably louder than it had been at camp, but this did not perturb me for I knew that I was paying extraspecial attention to such things as sounds. At length I reached a point above the river where, in the fading light, I saw below me a gorge with spectacular rapids. For a long instant I was terrified, simply terrified, for I knew I was lost. Could this be a wholly different river? Was it actually the Abitibi? Then, thinking straight, I realized that camp had to be upstream and that between me and the river there would almost certainly be a portage trail. Hoping that I'd be heard, I fired a shot to tell those in camp where I was. Shots fired in return I did not hear because of the water's roar. Failing to find the trail, which was very close to the river at that point, I picked my way upstream through the semidarkness, finally reaching camp. Never had beans, bannock, bacon, and the famed Todd stewed prunes and dried apricots tasted so good. A remarkably confiding white-footed mouse that darted in and out of the firelight entertained me as I ate. Standing on its haunches well back from the coals, nibbling at a bean held in its front feet, it was wonderfully pretty.

One memorable portage, seven miles long, was known as Long Portage, a flagrantly deceptive name in a way, since all the portages were long, some simply longer than others. Long Portage, that seven-mile one, we did by halves. Parts of the trail were under water inches deep. There were, of course, mosquitoes, deerflies, blackflies, and "no-see-ums," but these were not troublesome since the weather was bad and fly season past. A delight of dry stretches of trail were the fool hens or spruce grouse, family groups of which walked complacently out of the way or alighted on branches a few feet up when put to flight.

One of these family groups that we saw near New Post on August 24 I drew from memory in pencil that evening (plate 5). Having no table to work on, I decided against watercolor. Finding the Fuertes paint box in the depths of my gear would, in any event, have been a side expedition of its own.

Abitibi mail service was a phenomenon I had never heard of. At the beginning and end of certain portage trails, dangling at about eye level so as to attract attention, were oilcloth-wrapped packets of letters that were to be taken upriver or down by any traveler going that way. All the packets that we examined were marked "up," so we left them dangling. Some packets contained sizable items, but nothing as bulky as raw furs.

The Abitibi was far more than a series of rapids, cataracts, and portage trails. There were beautiful quiet stretches down which, aided by the strong current, we must have made up to five knots or more. A notable feature of the birdlife were the broods of half-grown common mergansers, each brood with its mother, all of them, mother and young alike, flightless, she in her late summer molt, they with their first major wing feathers only partly developed. The close-knit companies dived when they saw the distant canoe approaching; when hard-pressed, however, they did not dive but rushed off half-standing, churning the water furiously, bodies weaving from side to side, wings not flailing the air but folded in tightly, thus protecting the stubby blood quills. The noise of their sudden departure was startling, for it contrasted so sharply with the silence of the sequestered spots the birds so obviously enjoyed. One fact about this truly common species, which the guides called the sawbill, impressed me greatly: not a single adult drake did we see during our descent of that mighty wild river!

Birds were not the only creatures that claimed our attention. Not far from one camp, I surprised a bull moose that crashed off through the second growth, riding down saplings twice as tall as himself. A flat nest to which I climbed in a big hemlock held a brood of young red squirrels whose mother bit several knuckles of my hand before I could yank it away. Along one quiet stretch of river, our canoe was remarkably close to a full-grown mink that bounded along the base of an earthen bank, moving downstream almost as rapidly as we. At another point two half-grown black bear cubs ran from the water's edge back into the forest.

We reached the Moose River on August 29. The expanse of water where the two great rivers merged was broad and peaceful. From that point on there were no portage trails. The following day we made Moose Factory (known today as Moosonee), an important Hudson's Bay Company trading post. Our guides set up camp not far from the company's buildings, while the rest of us went after birds. The weather continued to be disagreeable, but stretching our legs did us good.

On August 30, I made a life-size watercolor sketch of the head of a black-bellied plover that I had collected along the shore not far from the post buildings. On the same sheet of paper, I sketched in pencil three of the handsome birds.

Supplies were to be bought. Mr. Todd, who had dealt with the company for years, had a visit with the chief trader and his family. On September 3, another dour day, we set off again, this time staying close to the river's west bank to keep out of the wind. We camped that afternoon on Sandy Island, where we were obliged to stay put a while because of the vile weather. The wind was so bad that night that it blew down the larger of the tents, the one in which we three who were not Ojibway slept. The wet canvas was more than over us, it was *on* us. There was something wonderfully amusing about the way in which the outspoken Semple and the sometimes querulous Todd accepted the situation. Not a word, not a single word, was spoken by anyone. Emerging from sleeping bags and floundering about in the darkness would have been utterly futile, and all three of us knew this. As we settled down, we heard the subdued gabbling of Canada geese flying over low. How good it was to be able to hear *anything* aside from the yawing and flapping of that wind-battered tent!

On September 5, at high tide, we took to the canoe again, this time heading southeastward. Thankful that the drizzle had stopped and the wind died, we moved forward hopefully. Presently we were out of the river's mouth, in salt water instead of fresh, in James Bay at last. The hours passed uneventfully as the tide started to go out. We had no way of knowing how rapidly it was going. What we did know was that the wind might rise, that waves in shallow water would be bad, that big waves in James Bay could be merciless.

Spruce Grouse   Sketched in pencil at camp on August 24, 1923, from memory of birds seen at close range that day along the Abitibi River, Ontario, portage trail.

Suddenly we touched bottom. Our paddles told us that we were in water little more than a foot deep. We bumped along, afloat part of the time, dragging through mud. Came the moment when we bumped no more. We were stranded. Knowing full well that the weather might change, we decided to get to land somehow. So out we all climbed, pulled the lightened canoe a considerable distance toward what looked like shore, and began carrying. The bay's bottom was so very flat that between canoe and land were lord knows how many furlongs of mud and very shallow water. As the canoe became more buoyant, it could be pulled forward, but presently the water was only a few inches deep, and the canoe had to stay where it was until fully unloaded. The edge of the water now was not the shore; indeed, there seemed to be no shore anywhere, for the vast stretches of mud flat were exceedingly wet. How we longed for something like a good old portage trail! Carrying that precious gear to some sort of campsite along what we believed to be one of the Partridge creeks was as irksome a task as I've ever helped with. The mud was slippery, the footing insecure, the wetness of it all discouraging. But carry we did. We carried it all—even the canoe. By this time night was half-over.

Came daylight and we realized that what we had thought to be one of the Partridge creeks was only a saltwater tidal stream. So, after a bit of rest, and again at high tide, it was move again, my hearties, pick things up and move again! At length—and not very far away, fortunately—we found a real Partridge Creek, a fine stream of coffee-brown muskeg water, not very wide but good and deep, with a strong current. At a high spot along the west bank, a foot or so above water level and several hundred yards inland from the mud flats, we made camp.

A fine camp it was. The creek itself, its water potable, was almost literally within arm's reach. Joe and Angus had no trouble finding wood for the fire. We were disappointed at seeing no wavies, but there were other birds to find and collect—among them the first Le Conte's sparrows to have been reported from that part of Canada.

Our guides, good men both, were not talkative. They were obviously amused by our interest in small birds, and they could hardly hide their disdain when we brought in a freshly trapped mouse. Occasionally they caught a varying hare in a wire noose set along a runway. Their surnames interested me, but my questions about lineage educed no edifying or entertaining comments. Indeed, I gathered from the expression on their faces that what I wanted to know was none of my business. This was not because they disliked me; it was because they were by nature self-contained and uncommunicative. I came close to opening them up when I chanced to mention the mud-and-stick goose decoys the Cree Indians were said to make. The word "Cree" kindled a small flame of jealousy. When I told them of *my* decoys, made of mud and a stick around one end of which cotton was wrapped (in imitation of a blue goose's white head), they smiled broadly, commenting that a decoy of that sort was "Better than Cree! Good! Ojibway!"

A whiskey jack or gray jay (the species then widely known as the Canada jay) with a malformed bill became a camp pet. We enjoyed the bird's visits at mealtime. It became extremely bold while we were eating, for it learned that we would give it beans or chunks of meat and bannock. Eventually it took to coming into the tent where Mr. Todd and I were skinning specimens. Here, not hungry but curious, it found small objects that it could carry off despite the crookedness of its lower mandible. We didn't shoot the jay, but we had to frighten it off lest it steal some really important item. Not one spool of thread or taxidermic tool could we spare!

JB Semple, good sport that he was, offered to help with skinning large specimens. He worked slowly but carefully and was especially successful with such tough birds as hawks, owls, and ravens. The smallest birds that he tackled were a bit bigger than robins. He would remove the bird's skin, scrape the fat off it, and turn it over to me for stuffing. One fairly large shorebird that I asked him to help me with gave him trouble as he was skinning over the tail. This was, admittedly, a tricky part of the job. With his sharp scalpel, he cut not through the small subterminal caudal vertebrae, thus keeping intact the tail and pygostyle supporting it, but right through the basal quills of the major tail feathers, so that they all fell apart. Genuinely contrite, but playing the part of the innocent nonprofessional, as was his wont on occasions of this sort, he said: "George, you're well known to be an expert. Everyone says this. I believe, I really do believe, it's time for you to take over with this one!" If, on the label for that specimen, I did not write "tail glued in; do not measure," I certainly should have.

Our collection grew slowly. JB shot an adult male merlin that flew past camp on the other side of the creek. He carefully noted the spot at which it fell and I, using the canoe, crossed over, followed his signals, and found the fine specimen. In a willow half a mile west of camp, I happened upon a bulky, deeply cupped, feather-lined nest in which a brood of northern shrikes had been reared the preceding summer. Some of my hunting I did in the grassy belt between the willows and the mud flats. Here waterfowl abounded, chiefly pintails and black ducks. The absence of mallards surprised me. We must have been a bit too far north and east for that species. Quartering over the grass and flats were several marsh hawks, most of them young birds with light reddish brown underparts. One that I flushed at close range had been eating a black duck, but I had no way of knowing that the hawk had indeed killed the duck. Among the interesting specimens that I obtained was a short-billed dowitcher. This I came close to losing even after I had shot it, for while looking for the dead bird in the grass I stepped right on it, pushing all but its toes out of sight in the mud.

On September 16, I sketched in watercolor the head of an immature drake pintail that I had collected along a tidal stream. The ducks that I saw that day included a few green-winged teal.

On the flats were thousands of shorebirds, most of them of the small species known collectively as peeps. The flocks had to be watched, for there was no telling when some rarity would show up. Well out from shore were scattered boulders, on one of which I sometimes sat, hopeful that a flock of wavies would arrive. Well protected against the wind by dark oilskin hat and coat, I was so motionless that I must have looked like a rock. On one occasion, a peregrine falcon almost alighted on me. It flew swiftly downwind just past me, circled sharply, extended its feet for a landing as it swung into the wind, and shot off to one side when I moved my head. I had not known that it was coming, for I had been facing downwind.

Peregrines were usually wary. There could not have been many of them near our camp, but there were at least two—an adult and a young one. They must have done their hunting quite separately, for I never saw more than one at a time. I learned to watch for one whenever the peeps became suddenly restless, flew up bunched tightly together, then, instead of staying low and finding a fresh feeding spot, rushed higher and higher, eventually mingling with other agitated flocks, all of which milled about the peregrine. Sometimes I did not see the falcon at first, but I could feel its presence as I watched the shorebirds. Presently, sure enough, there it was, moving leisurely along, headed for some perch on which it could watch for prey or rest. The shorebirds seemed to know that, as long as the falcon was flying steadily forward, there would be no sudden stoop and capture. I came to suspect that whenever a peregrine flew slowly past in this way, paying no attention at all to its fussy escort, it had already made its kill and dined well.

Every day I repaired my Ojibway goose decoys and made blinds by sticking leafy willow branches into the mud in rows. The tides had no respect for the decoys, so the mud bodies had to be built up and patted into shape repeatedly. The weather was surprisingly good on the whole, though the nights gradually grew colder. We continued to see small flocks of Canada geese—probably pairs that had nested thereabouts and their offspring—but the wavies failed to appear. We began to fear that we had come to the wrong place. Joe and Angus, not given to admitting that there might be a brighter side to anything, offered no encouragement. The thought of the ignominy, the utter ignominy, of returning to Pittsburgh without one single specimen of blue goose was depressing.

Then came September 29 with its leaden sky, knife-sharp north wind, and hordes of wavies white and blue. When we first heard the birds, they must have been miles off, but the wind brought their wonderful jangling clangor to us, almost turning camp upside down. We three Americans were so excited that we were hardly coherent. Joe and Angus took it all in their placid Ojibway stride.

Out to the flats I went, farther this time than ever before, well past the blinds and the big boulder on which I had sat so many times. Soon I found another good boulder, scooped mud away to make room for my feet on the south side, sat down with my back to the wind, and listened. A squall struck: hard snow hissed as it hit the mud and bounced. Alas, the sound of the wavies seemed no closer than it had been back at camp.

I knew that any attempt to stalk the newcomers would be futile, for there was nothing—no mound, no embankment, no big boulder, no tuft of willows—behind which to make an approach. All I could do was wait. Presently I heard a shot off to the southeast. I looked in that direction and saw a man standing, then sitting down or kneeling, I couldn't be sure which. It was JB Semple. A small flock of wavies was flying toward him only a few feet above the ground.

I decided to go back to the willow blind farthest from shore. Glad to be on the move, I stumbled at first, for my legs were stiff, then ran. The blind was in fair shape, though the decoys needed attention. The wet cushion of grass, gathered long since, had to be kicked into a heap. On this I sat, sheltered a little from the wind by the willow branches.

The musical, slightly falsetto clamor to the north grew louder. Something had stirred the geese up. Perhaps they were coming closer. Soon a flock of six flew directly over me—two adult snows and four young birds. Calling excitedly, they circled the blind once, well within shotgun range, and alighted about two hundred yards away. From where I was, low in the blind, they now appeared to be at the very edge of the grass. The young birds had their heads down, as if feeding. The old birds, suspicious, kept their heads up. Watching them, I wondered why I hadn't made one good blind at the edge of the grass. I also wondered what had kept me from shooting when the six birds had flown by. I hadn't even lifted my gun.

Now there was a wild chorus of calling to the north. I got to my knees for a brief look, then lay on my side, peering out through the willow branches. The hundreds of silvery flecks above the horizon whirled and eddied: wavies, some well aboveground and drifting eastward, some coming straight and low in my direction.

The shrill, sometimes rough cronking became louder, more distinct, much louder, earsplitting. A flock of eight birds passed over, so close that I could see their dark eyes clearly. Again I did not shoot. Other flocks came and passed, alighting between my blind and the grass a long way off. Again I rose to my knees for a look. The wind was fierce, but the snow had stopped. The sound of wind and wavies mingled in a kind of roar. I got down again as companies of up to twenty birds went by, some so low that I could have touched them with the gun's muzzle. I wasn't sure that they had been aware of me. There was something bewildering about the sound of their wings, the closeness of their big bodies moving so resolutely downwind. I must have been hypnotized. If not, why hadn't I shot?

As I lay there on my side, watching, listening, I slowly became aware of coldness at my hip. Focusing attention on the ground within the blind, I saw water trickling in between the willow branches. At first merely puzzled, I peered out to behold James Bay gleaming all about me. The water was far brighter than the sky, and it had a disquieting propensity for *looking* deep. I was on a tiny island that was fast being inundated. The tide, helped by Captain Henry Hudson's great bay and the strong north wind, was returning. Knowing that there were channels that I might have to swim to reach camp, I was momentarily impelled to flee. Then I remembered the wavies and realized with a sense of shame that I hadn't so much as a feather to show for the hours I had just experienced.

A fair-size flock, a few of them adult blues, flew past, alighting in shallow water just the other side of another of my blinds. Keeping low, I started to stalk them. It was cold, slow business, creeping forward on one hand and two knees, making certain that the gun stayed dry, and watching those blues. The old birds kept their heads up, as if expecting trouble. I did my best to be inconspicuous.

At last I figured I was close enough for a shot. Rising on my knees even as the outcry of the startled birds sounded, I found to my disgust that I could not throw the gun's safety forward with my thumb. Push as I did, and hard, that little piece of metal would not move. Everything about me was wet, of course, and muddy. My hands were so cold that I tried pushing with both thumbs. Alas, the safety would not move. I had missed my chance.

Never had I experienced anything like this. Looking toward camp, I perceived that much of the grass was now underwater. I rose, shivering, stiff in the legs, discouraged. Fording the tidal streams meant wading up to the waist and a bit more, though nowhere was I obliged to swim. It was while I was in deep water—where I must have looked about three feet tall—that I shot my first blue goose. As I stood there, wondering whether to go ahead or try for a shallower crossing, I looked up to see several wavies passing just within range. The gun was ready this time, for I had tapped the safety bar forward with a pocketknife and left it that way. I aimed, pulled the trigger, and a gray young bird fell. Again, and a white-headed adult went down with a broken wing. The gun was a double-barrel, so there was no more firing. Every unfired shell that I had with me was wet by this time anyway. The crippled adult disappeared completely underwater, bobbed up, dived again. In retrieving it I got soaking wet, all but my head.

I was so elated that I did not feel either the wetness or the cold. I hurried campward, slogging the whole way through water knee-deep. I arrived to find one exasperated sportsman, one unexasperated ornithologist, and two slightly amused Ojibways putting gear into the canoe. Virtually the whole campsite was under *inches* of water. "Look what I've got!" had been on the tip of my tongue for half an hour. I'd practiced the words over and over, but not one of them got spoken. "Where the devil have you been all this time?" almost certainly was on the tip of JB's tongue, but the question never came out. Mr. Todd had not a word to say. As I perceived the look on his face, I could not keep from thinking of what that remarkable man had said to me about trances, hallucinations, and other metaphysical phenomena. I helped as best I could by putting things into the canoe. Including my geese.

The important fact was that we had our blues. JB, a far better shot than I, had obtained several. Where and how the specimens got skinned I do not remember, but it was not at the Partridge Creek camp. Where I made my pencil sketches of the curiously piebald wavies that I had seen, I simply do not know. The sketches were not made directly from life and they are not very good, but they were an honest attempt to put down what I had seen out on the flats.

We ascended the Moose and the Abitibi expeditiously, for the weather was cooperative. At the Carnegie Museum, Gustave Link and his brother John mounted our blue geese beautifully. I painted a background for the habitat group.

Alas, I had opened the Fuertes paint box very infrequently during that busy, eventful expedition. I had fully intended to make a detailed sketch in watercolor of every blue goose that we collected, but where could I have done any sketching during those last frenzied hours at the south end of James Bay?

FLORIDA

IRONICALLY ENOUGH, it was not until I had finished all but two of the seventy-six colorplates for Harold H. Bailey's *Birds of Florida* that I actually saw that part of the world. At the invitation of JB Semple, whom I knew pretty well by this time, I spent about a month in the southernmost part of Florida, collecting birds with him for the Carnegie Museum. JB's winter home was in Coconut Grove, a suburb of Miami. From Coconut Grove, using a car with a canoe lashed on top, we worked out into the wild country. The outing was memorable, not alone because Florida was so different from anything I had ever experienced but also because JB was such a fine companion. He and I were afield almost continuously from March 10 to April 3, 1924.

JB was a born outdoorsman. He enjoyed getting away from his elegant house in Coconut Grove and roughing it. Not that he and I suffered at all from privation, for we had plenty to eat, each of us had a pup tent in which to sleep, the weather was good most of the time, and such minor difficulties as mosquitoes, ticks, mud, and saw grass were to be expected. I had one brush with an alligator, but the only snake we saw was a dead one being carried by a flying red-shouldered hawk. We built up an acceptable, though not large, bird collection.

To give me time for preparing specimens, JB did all the driving, cooking, and camp work. The driving was easy most of the time, but along the canal road far from garages and filling stations there were bad spots, and in one of these the car got stuck. The redoubtable JB insisted that we could charge fiercely forward or backward and get out, but the more fiercely we charged the deeper we went, so the pursuit of birds became a pursuit of rocks, dead branches, and armfuls of grass. After about three hours of carrying, we had a neat, more or less dry, snugly packed pavement in front of each rear tire and at last, with fine flourish and fanning of muddy water, out we roared. The delay did not dampen JB's spirits. "We'll not get stuck in *that* sort of place again, I can tell you!" he announced.

As we drove southwestward, we kept a constant lookout for birds, but most of the species that we saw were not needed at the museum, so JB could lecture me on the boiling of equipment down to a minimum. "Now take that skinning kit of yours," he would begin. "Most of what you have in there you don't really need. There's no sense in lugging it all around." He was quite right about one item, a heavy pair of wire cutters that I used not for cutting wire but for breaking large bones. With camp work done, JB busied himself filing down the jaws of a small pair of wire cutters until they were only about an eighth of an inch thick and serrate along the cutting edges. "Here's what you need for that bone breaking," he said, as he handed me a neat, lightweight tool that would serve me well the rest of my life.

JB enjoyed driving. Especially did he enjoy putting the car to work collecting specimens. We wanted to obtain at least one example of the small, brightly colored race of the American kestrel, a race endemic to the southeastern United States. The handsome little falcons were common in the open pinelands. Without the car we could have obtained one without much trouble, but in certain areas where the ground was flat and dry, the grass thin, and the trees widely scattered, JB perceived that we could get a bird by combining the car's talents with ours. Said he, using a voice just unctuous enough to hint of pulpit, "Now you just sit up there nice and comfortable on the hood or front fender with your gun, and I'll drive you right under the bird. If it flies off, you can get it with a wing shot. They don't fly very fast. And remember that they're often within range even though they look small." For a moment I took him seriously and was about to expostulate; then I realized that he was joking. The car, a four-door Franklin, had running boards. On a running board I stood, gun in right hand, left hand gripping the frame of the closed front door, and off we went—at times in a straight line toward a perching bird, more often in a wide circle intended to head the flying quarry off. JB, ever the director, would shout, "We're almost close enough now. Get ready! I'm about to stop! That bird's closer than it looks! It's in range right now! You'll have to move fast!" And I, excited, bothered by knowing that I was being watched, would hop off, lift the gun, lead my moving target, and blaze away, usually missing. When I finally did get a bird, JB applauded hilariously, as if our side had won an important victory. When

I missed, he took the failure in stride, saying that he had stopped the car too abruptly.

The one swallow-tailed kite of our collection I got without the help of the car. It was one of two birds circling overhead, barely within my double-barreled 12-gauge shotgun's range. With specimen in hand, I noted the deep red eye and the exquisite bloom on the dark plumage of the upperparts and recalled the day, eight years before, when Louis Fuertes had shown me the specimen in his collection. A surprising feature of the bird just collected was the dried blood and dirty stains on the feathers of its lower belly, these from prey carried in the small, not very powerful feet.

We saw this handsome kite at Royal Palm Hammock, along the canal road at Bear Lake, near the old, long-since-abandoned building at Flamingo, and at Gator Lake, but nowhere was it common. The largest number that we saw at any one time was seven—at Flamingo. We watched these seven as they circled, with wings set and tails spread wide, the very picture of elegance and effortlessness. On other occasions, we saw a single kite diving playfully at a flying brown pelican and two kites in hot pursuit of a barred owl that had made the mistake of flying from one hammock to another in broad daylight.

Barred owls were common. We heard their eight-noted whooping almost every night. Occasionally one whooped during the brightest part of the day. In the evening, we could call them up with a crude imitation of their cry, and sometimes they came very close. "What we really need for this," said JB, "is an old rubber boot. The smell of a burning boot brings owls from all directions." If I wanted a good look at a barred owl by day, all I had to do was hide under some vines, keep still for a minute or two, then squeak loudly, kissing the back of my hand in imitation of a mouse in distress. As a rule only a little loud squeaking sufficed: in the beautiful owl would come, alighting not far away, gazing straight at me with a puzzled look in its big dark eyes.

JB's culinary prowess was impressive. By our third day afield, he had a neat set of serviceable containers made from grapefruit rinds whose pulpy inner lining had been eaten away at night by cotton rats or other rodents. When we finished with our grapefruit, we put the empty halves off in the brush where the rodents did *their* finishing. It struck me as odd that they never so much as nibbled at the outermost part of the rind. A JB salad made from small pieces of boiled or fried bird meat mixed with chunks of fresh tomato, croutons, and mayonnaise was delicious. The croutons were bits of well-dried, not toasted, bread. The bird meat was, of course, from specimens we had collected.

A bird not represented in the museum's collection was the Cape Sable seaside sparrow, a little-known form discovered and named only five years before. Cape Sable was this bird's type locality, so specimens obtained there would be topotypical and as such of special value to taxonomists. We realized that the few specimens then known to science had all been taken in salt marsh, so when we reached the famous cape our first job was finding the marsh where the water was brackish. We did not have far to go, for the vast switch grass "prairie" just north of the cape was all brackish. We pushed through the head-high grass, surprised to find the underfooting comparatively dry. Not for hours did we find a sparrow. Genuinely puzzled over the fact that we had heard no singing, I began to feel that we had not found the right place, that the habitat was for some reason no longer suitable, that the sparrows had moved from the switch grass into some other sort of vegetation.

Just as the tide of our enthusiasm was ebbing badly, a gray-looking little bird flushed, flew above the grasstops for several rods, and dropped back into cover. I weighed the brief glimpse in the balance of personal experience, decided that a swamp sparrow or a Lincoln's sparrow would surely have looked dark brown rather than gray, and shouted to JB, "Maybe that was our bird!" All at once the sun's heat was no longer merciless, the mosquitoes no longer unbearable, and presently we had a specimen—the first either of us had ever handled. We decided that the yellow above and in front of the eye should be a good field mark.

We found surprisingly few species of birds in the uniform stand of switch grass, among them the common yellowthroat, palm warbler, and long-billed marsh wren but not the savannah sparrow, grasshopper sparrow, and eastern meadowlark, all three of which were common in lower vegetation on slightly higher ground above the brackish area. The fact that neither JB nor I flushed a rail in the switch grass was fair proof that rails required water as well as grass.

On the evening of March 15, we camped along the canal road close to East Fox Lake. Here we were in the midst of a vast prairie that only a few years before had been underwater—an arm of the Everglades. We were so close to the tall grass that some of the sounds of the marsh seemed to come from inside our tents. Scarcely had we settled down when two big black-and-white birds circled silently above us. I had never seen their like before but knew at once from their long, decurved bills and naked heads that they were wood storks. Said JB: "The crackers call them flintheads. We'll probably see a good many of them here." Their flight was wonderfully sustained and graceful. I could not help marveling that such ponderous creatures could handle themselves so well in the air. Without flapping their wings at all, they continued circling as they drifted eastward. Soon three more appeared, then others, singly and in pairs, all coming from west of us. Some flew in a straight line, but most of them circled once or twice, as if curious. With my binoculars I could see their heads turning as they looked downward at us. Occasionally I heard a throaty cry from one of them.

As evening gathered, a muffled bellowing issued from the dark hammock west of us. JB did no explaining. He knew full well what the sound was but enjoyed seeing me puzzled. I decided that great numbers of bullfrogs, or possibly alligators, must be producing the sound. I could not believe that birds of any sort were responsible for it. During our four days at the East Fox Lake camp, we did not see a single human being aside from ourselves.

On March 19, we drove to the hammock from which the flintheads had been flying, finding it to be the mangrove fringe of Gator Lake. The canal road took us close to the south shore. After the car had stopped and I had had a chance to watch and listen a while, I realized that the weird sound we had been hearing was that of a big flinthead colony. Separate squawks, grunts, and squeals now sounded distinctly above the mumble—reminding me of dark figures seen clearly against murky fog.

We unlashed the canoe, put it into the water, and paddled quietly about among the mangroves, looking for a campsite. At length, not far from shore, we found a little island that seemed an adequate spot, for it was flat and dry, there was plenty of room for two pup tents and a fire, and along one edge there was a thick horizontal root to which could be fastened a board that would serve as my skinning table.

With one canoe trip, we moved our gear to the island. The day was hot so, using my new table, I got at specimens that needed attention. JB built a fire, cleaned and put into the pot the bird bodies that I handed him, and set up the tents. Whether the bird bodies ever got thoroughly cooked or not, the broth was delicious; the grapefruit from JB's yard was refreshing; and the baked beans from a can and dry bread all hit the proper spot. Dry bread was a JB specialty. It was not toast. Noisy when chewed, it was never moldy, and its flavor, though sometimes suggestive of salt marsh, was beyond reproach.

The most noticeable bird at our camp was a catbird. The pretty creature obviously regarded our little island as its home. So friendly was it that we fell to calling it Tommy. The other camp birds were common grackles, which seemed to be finding food at the water's edge; the larger boat-tailed grackles, whose shrill *keep-keep, keep, keep, keep* sounded almost continuously from the tops of the mangroves; and the Carolina wrens, several of which seemed to be in full song. Herons, pelicans, white ibis, spoonbills, cormorants, anhingas, red-shouldered hawks, and blue-winged teal flew past from time to time. The place teemed with birdlife. Most of the herons were little blues, but there were many Louisianas and snowy egrets and a few great blues. The only great white herons that we saw in the area were finding food in marshy places outside the mangroves that edged the lake.

The flinthead colony, which occupied several small islandlike clumps of mangrove close to the lake's north shore, we visited that afternoon. All the young birds had fledged, though some were not yet flying strongly. As we paddled from clump to clump, the parent birds and the oldest young flew off. The young that remained stood on the nests and heavily whitewashed branches, staring blankly in our direction with mandibles slightly parted. Their incessant muttering reminded me of a busy barnyard. Even the youngest birds looked like the adults, except for their shorter bills and the patches of white down on their heads. Many white ibis and herons of several species roosted with the flintheads. As the motley company gathered that evening, the dull roar produced by their mingling voices was hard to believe.

While we were eating late supper, JB announced that a trip to Coconut Grove was in order, for our food supply was running low—especially grapefruit. In the morning, off he went in the Franklin, leaving me in charge of camp. He was gone for a bit more than a day.

I treasure the memories of the hours spent alone at Gator Lake. The whole world there was so serene! Never did the flintheads seem to be in a hurry. As the great birds circled higher, ever higher, I felt that I had never seen color so intense—not bright exactly, certainly not gaudy, but intense—as the blue above them. While paddling among the mangroves, I happened upon a raccoon sound asleep in an old flinthead nest. The sunlight, stabbing through the leafage, struck the fur in such a way as to make it look like spider webbing. I had to look twice to make sure that what I was looking at was curled-up raccoon and not a web-covered mass of dead leaves. I could not resist the thought that life would be easy indeed for any raccoon living near a big flinthead colony: eggs to eat, tender young flintheads to eat, old nests to sleep in—all easily reachable with a bit of a climb.

A flash of white from the spread tail of a bird flying only a few yards ahead of the canoe reminded me that the branches, leaves, and roots about me might well be the habitat of the mangrove cuckoo, a bird I had never seen. Shoving the canoe's nose into the saw grass, I stepped out, sank down, down, into the mud, and decided not to wade after the cuckoo but to stay abovewater on the mangrove roots. This sort of stalking was tricky, for some roots did not bear my weight properly. While clambering along, paying more attention to what was ahead than to what I was stepping on, I frightened a big alligator, whose tail thrashed fiercely as the reptile shot off, covering me from head to foot with mud. Convinced that the commotion had frightened the cuckoo (to say nothing of the way I felt), I got back to the canoe, paddled in the direction I thought the bird had taken, and found it again. To my surprise, it was not wary. It was much like a yellow-billed cuckoo in behavior, but its underparts were rich tawny buff rather than white.

At camp once more, Tommy the catbird welcomed me. I had no idea what the sex of the winsome bird was, but Tommy sounded right so Tommy he continued to be. When I opened my skinning kit, he came closer and closer, fluffing his plumage, spreading his tail, obviously much interested in what I was doing. When I had removed the skin from the first of my specimens, I cut off a little chunk of meat and tossed it to him. Tommy flew directly to the bit, picked it up, gulped it down, and looked at me as if expecting more. More I gave him. His companionship was delightful.

After giving Tommy several bits, including bone as well as meat, I realized that he was scrambling headlong after them, as if determined to get them before something else did. His behavior seemed a bit ridiculous, for there was no other catbird around. His haste was not silly. Something *was* taking the bits of meat, though the culprit was not another bird but a tiny, full-grown, silken-furred shrew, quite possibly the smallest mammal I had ever seen and certainly one of the prettiest. It was lightning-quick. Suddenly it was there, in plain sight, then as suddenly gone. Bits of meat that I saw as they reached the ground were not there when I looked again a split second later. No wonder Tommy had been obliged to move fast!

To make sure that Tommy would get his share, I tossed some bits well away from the table. These the bird went after without delay. Bits for the shrew I put closer and closer to my feet, eventually on the toe of a shoe. There the shrew found them. The swiftness of the little mammal and its ability to disappear among the dead leaves reminded me of a magician's tricks.

That evening the sky darkened long before sunset. I hauled the canoe out of the water and turned it over, put loose camp gear and the boxes of dried specimens into JB's tent, and closed that tent's front carefully. Recently prepared specimens I stowed alongside of the spot where I would lie in my sleeping bag. If odors from them were to attract raccoons, I wanted to be sure that I would be there to protect them in person.

The noise of the downpour, which lasted for hours, was not soothing. A gentle rain would have put me to sleep, but this one made me apprehensive. When it stopped and I dozed off, I was wakened by a wild dream.

As I lay there wondering what it was that brought dreams on, I realized that my attention was focusing on a sound that was not part of any dream. It was an actual, not an imagined, sound within inches of my face—a sound of wet leafage moving, of scraping, pushing, and snuffling—perhaps all three. Was it an otter, a skunk, a raccoon, possibly a bobcat? As if in reply to my unspoken question came an explosive cry, a sort of cough, that made my hair stand on end. There was another sound, too, a sort of thump or heavy footfall. Then silence.

The following morning, wakened by Tommy's loud mewing near the front of my pup tent, I did my best to find footprints. I decided that my visitor must have been a mammal of some sort, perhaps a marsh rabbit. Whatever it had been, it had swum to the island and away from it.

JB was his ebullient self. My first question had to do with bad spots in the canal road. He had somehow avoided them. I told him about Tommy and the shrew.

We devoted that day and the next largely to obtaining some adult flinthead specimens. Getting them was easy enough, but skinning them was not. My table was far too small for birds of this size. Each specimen had to be cut at the nape before I could pull the skin over the head and remove eyes and brain. The work had to be done promptly because of the heat and dampness. Skinning was only part of the job: unless I opened fleshy parts of the feet and wings and applied preservative, decomposition would set in.

An unexpected problem was the turkey vultures, those sharp-eyed scavengers that must have watched from the sky as we brought the dead flintheads back to camp. Soon after I started skinning, two or three vultures circled closely, finally alighting above camp. The mangroves were not high, so the perching vultures were not very far away. JB, busy cleaning the guns, waved the unwelcome visitors off, but they soon returned, more vultures with them, sending down leaves, bits of bark, and an occasional dropping as they alighted. JB was obliged to frighten them off again, this time with clapping of hands and shouting. The vultures were persistent, continuing to annoy us until JB fired his shotgun—not directly at them but close enough to let them know what we had in mind. If the skinning of flintheads is to be mentioned in the history of mankind's endeavors, JB's name must be mentioned along with mine.

When I returned to Pittsburgh from Florida, one matter needed attention above all others—a display of bird art that I had promised Mr. Todd to assemble for an American Ornithologists' Union meeting scheduled for Pittsburgh in mid November. The display would include works by contemporary bird artists of the United States and Canada. The union had never met in Pittsburgh before, nor had a formal gallery showing such as I had in mind ever been part of a meeting. Having been assured by the Department of Fine Arts that a gallery would be available and that the hanging would be done by their professional staff, I wrote about forty artists, asking each to send up to six examples of work. The response was gratifying. The names of thirty-one artists appeared in the printed catalog (the work of one Canadian artist was held up at the border by customs officials), and about 140 works were shown. The one oil from me was of a great white heron, a study based partly on what I had just seen in Florida and partly on a photograph by Norman McClintock, a friend of Bayard Christy. T. S. Palmer, the highly articulate secretary of the union, was lavish in his praise of the display. In his formal report, published in *The Auk*, he called it "the chief feature of the meeting."

Another matter also demanded my attention. The Board of Game Commissioners of Pennsylvania wanted me to move to Harrisburg to head their Bureau of Research and Information. To make the offer more attractive, they added the words "state ornithologist" to the title. The offer was so good that I, at twenty-six, could not turn it down.

HARRISBURG

THE MOVE TO HARRISBURG was easy, for I had been living in a furnished room in Pittsburgh and had few belongings aside from clothes. The move was not entirely joyful, for I had not completed my study of the birdlife of Pymatuning Swamp, my formal description of a new swift that I had discovered had not been published, and, worst of all, I felt that, had my performance at the Carnegie Museum pleased Mr. Todd, he would have managed somehow to keep me there. Taxonomic work that I had done at his request on a collection of birds from Venezuela had disappointed him. In that collection I had found the swift, but my report as a whole had not measured up to Mr. Todd's expectations. This he had said to me in almost those very words, though he had not spelled out what I had done wrong or failed to do. He had seemed to like my style as a writer; he had encouraged me to go on with bird drawing; and he had found my fieldwork so acceptable that he was to continue to ask me to help him with his expeditions for years.

My salary as state ornithologist of Pennsylvania and as chief of the Bureau of Research and Information of that state's Board of Game Commissioners was much the largest I had ever received, so, partly as a result of a word in my behalf from W. Gard. Conklin, chief of the commission's Bureau of Refuges and Lands, I found myself living at the Engineers' Club on Front Street in Harrisburg. This old part of the city charmed me, for the houses there, many of them narrow, three stories high, close against each other, and rather prim-looking, reminded me of pictures I had seen of cities in Europe. Without a vestige of lawn between house and sidewalk or between sidewalk and street, they were separated from the Susquehanna River by a lovely expanse of wooded park. It was my good fortune to become well acquainted with some of these very houses later, but, when I first saw them while walking to my office in a new building near the state capitol, they looked like Ambassador's Row. One

144

house in particular fascinated me. There the glass in a certain first-floor
transom window was thick, of a curious green shade, and lumpy. I
couldn't help wondering when and by whom that house had been built.

From my quarters at the Engineers' Club, I could not see the Susquehanna, but I was soon to learn that flocks of whistling swans often
stopped on the river during migration or even wintered there, and I was
told of a big wooded island on which fish crows and black-crowned night
herons nested. When I inquired about spots at which birds might be
looked for near the city, I was told of Wildwood Lake, where woodcocks
performed their strange sky dances in early spring.

My assistant was a wiry, vivacious, extremely able young Pennsylvania German named Leo A. Luttringer, Jr., whose father, Colonel
Luttringer, was in charge of the state arsenal. A veteran of World War I,
young Leo was to become as loyal a friend as I have ever had. Whether
he believed in all that I argued for or not, he always gave me to understand that he was in back of me. He was a daily blessing, for he had
been with the game commission for some time, he knew the field force
well, and he was politician enough to realize the importance of keeping
in touch with key men whose views were worth bearing in mind.

Everyone knew that my special interest was birds, so I was asked to
prepare a brochure titled "A Year's Program for Bird Protection," a com-
pilation of material pertaining to birdhouses, birdbaths, winter bird
feeders, trees and shrubs whose berries might attract birds, etc. Nothing
about the publication was especially original, though Witmer Stone, who
reviewed it in *The Auk*, liked the following sentence well enough to
quote it: "Are we never to realize and admit that our most sincere reason
for protecting birds is simply that we want them as they are about us,
whether they are each saving our State so many cents apiece annually or
not?" That sentence I had worked at hard; I had rearranged its words a
dozen times; it had become a sort of credo. Of the several drawings that
I had made for the forty-seven-page opus, the most noteworthy was a
direct-from-life watercolor of a gray-phase screech owl someone had
brought in. Having no studio, I had made the drawing in my office. The
little owl had been a perfect model, for it had hardly even blinked while I
was drawing it.

An article that I published about this time was titled "How Can the
Bird-Lover Help to Save the Hawks and Owls?" This was aimed chiefly at
fanatics so violently opposed to the killing of birds of prey that they
called all hunters bad, without making the slightest effort to learn what

many of these same men were doing—either as concerned individuals or through their hunter's license money—to improve laws and law enforcement, to preserve wildlife habitat through the setting aside of game refuges, and to educate the public. I was now in a position to see the hunter's side of things as well as the bird lover's. I knew that hawks were widely known as chicken hawks and bird hawks and were shot accordingly. I knew that this wanton killing would have to stop. But I also knew that many a sportsman of my acquaintance was ecologist enough to sense that the presence of predators in a given area was proof *not* that songbirds and small game were being wiped out but that these prey species were thriving *partly as a result of the predators' policing of habitat*. The predators could not survive without prey; it was the predators' job to keep that prey reproducing itself; the predators accomplished this not alone through capturing sick and crippled individuals but also through forcing every grouse, quail, rabbit, and squirrel to stay alert, endlessly alert, during every waking moment. The shrill-voiced "down with the hunters" fanatics, with their closed minds, annoyed, even angered me. Most of them knew nothing, nothing at all, about the game commission's varied activities; about the commission's continuing fight to keep the hunter's license money out of the general fund, where it would be used for highways, bridges, dams, and whatnot; about the commission's determined effort to educate the public concerning basic facts having to do with wildlife management. In my article I urged bird lovers to see both sides of the problem, to bear in mind that many a confirmed hunter was also the very best kind of conservationist. I'd not have been fully aware of this myself had not my work with the commission brought me into direct contact with many truly broad-minded sportsmen.

Aware of the fact that no book dealing with Pennsylvania's birdlife as a whole had been published since 1890, the year in which the enlarged and revised edition of Dr. B. H. Warren's *Report on the Birds of Pennsylvania* had appeared, I planned an ambitious work that would bring the state's ornithology up to date, but as time passed I found that fieldwork of the sort required was out of the question. I was now first of all a mouthpiece for the game commission, more newspaperman than bird student, more shaper of conservation policies than bird artist. I was not unhappy with my work. I did not feel that I was being forced to do what I did. But my plans for an exhaustive treatise on Pennsylvania's birds changed and narrowed, finally restricting themselves to studies of species that seemed to need attention. Thus, when snowy owls or goshawks moved into the state in unusual numbers in winter, I plotted the sightings, found out what I could about the birds' food habits, and reported on these. For a time I paid special attention to the breeding distribution of the two geographical races of the common grackle that occurred in the state—the so-called purple grackle of the east and the bronzed grackle of the west. Game protectors and others sent me many specimens, and the skins of some of these I preserved, but this work I regarded as personal rather than official, and I never prepared a report on my findings. The book I finally decided to bring out was a small one, not intended to be the last word. The manuscript for this I wrote piecemeal as I visited various parts of the state. Its title: "An Introduction to the Birds of Pennsylvania" (1928).

The close attention that I paid to writing obviously interested Leo Luttringer. He typed away at my longhand manuscripts, never complaining even when he had to redo page after page. One somewhat effusive sentence that I wrote about a flock of purple finches, each male of which was "singing its own version of the song of life," so intrigued him that he memorized it. This I could not help knowing, for now and then he quoted it—the whole thing verbatim, grinning mischievously.

In off-hours I corrected proofs of the colorplates I had made in Pittsburgh for Bailey's *Birds of Florida*, an opulent volume published in 1925. The more I looked at the pictures, the worse they seemed. If only I could have done them *in* Florida! I was, however, inordinately proud of the fact that I had illustrated a major work.

Another order for illustrations had come my way by 1925. The John C. Winston Company of Philadelphia needed a colorplate of birds for a dictionary. The picture I did for them, a miscellany of twenty-four species, from a hummingbird at upper left (one-sixth actual size) to an ostrich at lower right (one-thirtieth actual size), was a monstrosity of sorts, though it did show a variety of bird shapes and color patterns. Winston used it not only in their dictionary but also as the frontispiece for William Atherton DuPuy's *Our Bird Friends and Foes*, a little book for which I made several pen-and-ink drawings. Many of these were poor, especially that of a mockingbird. In this drawing, as in that of a robin, the line work is downright offensive. The inaccuracy of the wood duck drawing is pardonable: when I made the drawing, many bird students believed that the mother duck helped her brood out of the nest cavity. We know better now.

Wanting to be afield more, and knowing that my study of Pymatun-

ing needed to be completed, I arranged to visit the swamp in late
February of 1925. This was my first winter visit to the area. I asked my
sister Evie, then sixteen years old, to accompany me. We put up at the
Century Inn in Hartstown, where passing trains made the old frame
building shake, convincing Evie that I had not been overdescribing the
place. Dressed warmly, we tramped through the snow to spots with
which I had become well acquainted. Birds that we saw and heard were
in no way exceptional, but in an old woodpecker hole not far from the
ground in a dead stub we found a white-footed mouse in its thistledown
nest. The "wee, sleekit, cow'rin', tim'rous beastie" was surprisingly gentle. Instead of fleeing, it ran up my arm, paused long enough with big
eyes sparkling and vibrissae quivering to give us a thrill, then whisked
back to its nest, some of which I had to stuff back in on top of it.

That same day we followed the footprints of a big raccoon to a forty-
foot pine. I had supposed that the tracks would lead on from the tree,
but there above us, not more than fifteen feet up, was the raccoon. Evie
was beside herself with excitement, for she had never before seen a
raccoon in the wilds. When I started up the tree, she confessed to misgivings. "Will it bite you? If it comes down while you're up there, will it get
after me?" I had to say that I didn't know what a raccoon might do under
the circumstances but that it would probably climb to the top of the tree
before doing anything else. In this I was wrong.

As I climbed higher, so did the raccoon. As the trunk became more
slender and I closer, the handsome animal made its way out on a long
branch that became horizontal with sagging. There, looking first at me,
then at the ground, the raccoon sized up the situation. I fully expected it
to let itself down to the next lower branch, then perhaps to the next,
then back to the trunk, and so on to the ground, but this it did not do. It
stayed where it was, looking neither angry nor frightened.

I clung to the trunk with my left hand and reached as far as I could
with my right. When my fingers touched that beautifully ringed tail, the
raccoon jumped. No snapping of jaws. No snarling. Just a clean, graceful
leap outward from the bouncing branch, a spread-eagle descent, a
thump on hitting the ground belly first, a matter-of-fact return to all
fours—as if jumps from trees were in no way extraordinary—and a
scamper off into a wet part of the swamp. "Watch it," I called to Evie,
who had managed to get herself aboveground on some roots. "See how it
runs. It doesn't trot, the way a dog does. It paces!" Never before had I
lectured from a tree.

Not long after my visit to Pymatuning, word reached me that Ernest Hunsinger, of the commission's field force, had found a goshawk's nest in Potter County, northern Pennsylvania. This was wonderful news, for I had had very little experience with goshawks. The nest had held three eggs when first climbed to on March 31. On April 27, it had held two recently hatched downy white young and one egg. When I climbed to it myself on May 19, the two young were almost fledged, the smaller still in the nest, the larger on a branch several feet above it.

The nest was about thirty-five feet up in a slender beech. I climbed to it twice that day. Each time I went up, the powerful mother attacked savagely. Had I not worn hat and hunting coat, my head and back would have been scratched badly. On my first climb, the young bird in the nest tried to fly but, failing miserably, flapped heavily to the ground. In the nest I found a dead chipmunk, a hairy woodpecker's wing feather, and the hindquarters of a black squirrel. The unhatched egg was buried beneath debris and fresh sprigs of hemlock.

While the men who had driven me to the woods were walking to their car, escorted by the belligerent mother hawk, I made a crude blind from dead branches. When the hawk returned, she did not see me at first, but when she did discover me her attack was fiercer than ever. She even struck at my feet, which protruded from the blind. Her shy mate, a considerably smaller bird, I saw only occasionally. In pellets of un-digested matter that I took from the nest on my second climb, I was surprised to find little evidence that ruffed grouse—or, for that matter, birds of any sort—had been preyed on.

What I experienced at that goshawk nest convinced me that I should examine the stomachs of all hawks and owls sent in for bounty. Pay-ment of bounty for certain predatory mammals and birds was traditional in Pennsylvania, though when I started examining stomachs the only birds for which bounty was paid were goshawks and great horned owls. Many of these continued to be sent in. In the stomachs I found a great variety of remains, with enough poultry and small game to make clear why many farmers and hunters considered the bounty system a good thing. I argued as persuasively as I could against it, not because of the wretched dishonesty and ignorance that were known to be part of it but because I was convinced that the predators were valuable and deserving of protection. Those who championed the bounty system pointed to areas in which both predators and small game abounded and clamored loudly for more predator control there, not realizing that in many such areas the game throve not in spite of the predators but *because of them*. This paradox was more than most hunters, poultry raisers, and game protectors could accept—despite the all-too-obvious fact that, without predators to control their numbers, deer had become a formidable problem.

The dishonesty mentioned above included sending pelts across state lines; the ignorance, gross misidentification of carcasses and parts thereof. It would be impossible to say how much bounty had been paid in earlier years for such wholly innocent creatures as nighthawks, which are not even birds of prey but whose names bespeak villainy, and for the feet of barnyard chickens because these resemble to some extent the feet of hawks.

It soon became clear that there were many ways in which I was expected to keep the public informed about the game commission's work and problems. I enjoyed giving talks about matters on which I was well informed, so I made a point of learning many important facts about the commission's history, about the work of its several bureaus, in particular about such very real problems as the overabundance of deer. Parts of Pennsylvania were far wilder than most people of the larger cities realized. In these wild parts deer throve, chiefly because such large predators as timber wolves and cougars had long since been extirpated. So abundant had the deer become that they had destroyed their own food supply, being forced to eat the toxic foliage of such plants as the mountain laurel, to invade orchards and truck gardens, where they became a serious pest, and to cross highways in such numbers as to cause accidents. In the so-called South Mountain District, where apple growing was an important industry, orchards had to be protected from deer with fencing at least nine feet high. As an ornithologist, I was especially interested in the way in which the numbers of turkey vultures increased as a result of the availability of carcasses of deer that had died of starvation.

The solemn fact that everyone had to face was that deer had been overprotected. So long had sportsmen and nature lovers worked toward saving them that the problem of *unsaving* them was sticky. Full-grown bucks with spreading antlers were recognized as legal. Young male animals, known as spike bucks, were also legal, though shooting them was frowned upon. But when an "antlerless deer" or doe season was so much as mentioned, many an organization protested loudly. Too long had people been caring for the "soft-eyed mother deer," some of whose spotted progeny would grow up into proper venison. Seasons in which both sexes might be declared legal were unthinkable since too many trigger-happy hunters would be shooting at anything that moved—including fellow hunters.

So for a time my principal job was lining up facts in support of an antlerless deer season and proclaiming these facts from the housetops. One part of the job was building up a film dealing with the deer problem, another preparing a bulletin titled "The White-tailed Deer in Pennsylvania." I had never been a big game hunter or much of a mammalogist, but I did the best I could.

Since everyone knew that I liked giving talks, I soon found myself traveling widely, often holding forth several times a day—one talk at a high school in the morning, another before a service club at noon, another before a women's club in the afternoon, and another before a general audience in the evening, frequently after a banquet. The many sportsmen's clubs vied with each other in putting on spreads, and I found myself part of these on many an occasion.

Though I had never been much of a photographer, the commission furnished me with a lightweight motion-picture camera, and I proceeded to build up a wildlife film. Refuge keepers, game protectors, and professional photographers all helped. I showed the film all over the state.

Public appearances were sometimes demanding, sometimes truly difficult. Just before that first doe season, the commission was very unpopular in some areas. Defending the board's position required fortitude on my part as well as a certain amount of political know-how. On one occasion a disgruntled chairman introduced me without giving my name, saying, in effect, "Those people in Harrisburg have sent someone to explain what they're doing, so he's here now." Then, turning to me: "All right, go ahead!" That time, thoroughly annoyed, I lashed out with verbal whip, hoping that it would crack loudly enough to be heard by everyone, including men of the press, and fiercely enough to nick someone's ear.

Talks in defense of the doe season often involved heated arguments. I took the whole thing so seriously that I found myself tense and irascible. At evening banquets, I went through the motions of eating, got through with my talks as best I could, answered questions, some of which were snarled, then—along toward midnight—found myself so wildly hungry that I begged the local game protector to take me to an all-night restaurant for whatever we might find there. Doe season talks came so frequently that I began to suffer from indigestion, partly as a result of irregular eating. Finally I sensed that the situation was getting out of hand and told myself to quit worrying. The obvious fact was that, even after the worst of evening confrontations, I felt better in the morning.

Some of those evening affairs were memorable—not the talks themselves but what happened in connection with them. On one occasion the sportsmen's club in Erie, northwestern Pennsylvania, asked me to present my film. The dinner was excellent, the auditorium spacious and comfortable, the stage nicely decorated with corn shocks and autumn foliage, much of which was still attached to branches fastened above the front of the stage in such a way as to leave the screen in plain sight for everyone. I was introduced cordially, for the people of that area had seen the light with regard to the doe season. I said a few things about the game commission's history, made clear what the film was intended to prove, and asked that the lights be turned out. Within seconds after the darkening of the room, snickering started. I had not said anything intended to be funny so presumed that something amusing had happened in some other part of the room. As I went on, explaining certain difficulties the commission had had in making clear its position concerning the doe season, the laughter started again, grew louder, and spread in waves around the room. I fell to wondering whether I had mispronounced some word or forgotten to tuck my shirttail in.

The trouble was that the loudest laughter seemed to come when it was least appropriate. It accompanied my most serious statements. And it became steadily stronger, much stronger, turning my performance into farce. I was close to desperation, even misery, when I felt a smooth something gently brushing my forehead. Ducking from sheer fright, I glanced up, realized at once what all the fun had been about, and laughed. The applause was utterly hilarious. A pet raccoon that I had thought was a mounted specimen attached to a branch had come to life when the lights went out, had started moving toward me while I was talking, had finally arrived at a point directly above me, and had been reaching, reaching, reaching downward with its paw, doing its best to touch me.

I added to my wildlife film as opportunity offered. Most of the scenes were of an unexciting sort—hunters getting into their car, that same car bumping along a mountain road, hunters putting their guns down before crossing fences, hunters shaking hands with farmers and uniformed game protectors, etc. At a zoo I tried to get a convincing shot of a gray fox eating a cottontail. The dead rabbit played its part admirably, but the fox, a bit shopworn from months of captivity, looked frightened and miserable. In getting a close-up of a black bear, I entered the tame creature's cage, took the footage needed, and was vastly surprised when the five-hundred-pound animal stood up facing me, put its paws on my shoulders, looked straight into my eyes for an instant, and turned its head up and away with mouth slightly open, as if hopelessly disenchanted. Harry Van Cleve, in charge of the game commission's traveling wildlife show, was close-by, armed with a club, ready to whack the bear if necessary. I have often wondered what whacking would have accomplished. Annoyed, the bear would probably have knocked me senseless.

Word came from a mountainous part of the state that a hibernating black bear and her two cubs had been found. This was great news, for it meant another trip into the wilds. The den was under the roots of a great tree. Snow covered the ground, except at the den's edge, where warm air had been rising continuously. The two tiny cubs were fairly active, though it appeared to me that their eyes were not yet open. The mother was not sound asleep, but she was extremely drowsy. She raised her head while we were looking down at her, opened her small brown eyes briefly, gave a prodigious yawn, and let her head fall back heavily. Spring was not yet calling loudly enough to waken her. Needless to say, we moved off without disturbing her.

On May 12, 1926, I received from Lansdale, southeastern Pennsylvania, a live common loon in elegant breeding feather. The bird had mistaken wet pavement for a stream and grounded itself. No bones had been broken but, being a loon, it could not walk. It was truly dangerous: had I not kept a proper distance between it and my face, it might easily have stabbed one of my eyes with a sudden thrust of its powerful bill. After I had photographed, sketched, and banded it, Leo Luttringer and I liberated it at Wildwood Lake on May 15. That evening it flew from the lake to the Susquehanna River. Over a year later, on July 31, 1927, it was found freshly dead on the north shore of Lake Ontario near the town of Brighton. The man who happened upon it believed it "had been killed by a skunk, as the approach and attack were all clearly indicated in the sand." Who could say how far south that bird had traveled to its 1926–27 wintering ground?

THE EAST COAST
OF HUDSON BAY

IN THE SPRING OF 1926, Mr. Todd asked me to assist him with his Expedition Number 11, this time to a part of the Labrador Peninsula that he had not yet visited, the northern half of the east coast of Hudson Bay. Knowing that I had long been interested in the blue goose—at that time still believed by some taxonomists to be a full species, and one whose nest had not been discovered—he stressed the possibility of our finding the bird breeding at Payne Lake, a little-known body of water situated midway between Hudson and Ungava bays at about latitude 60° north. Maps told us that the Kogaluk River flowed from the general vicinity of this lake westward to a point near a trading post called Povungnituk, so Mr. Todd assured me that if we could get to Povungnituk early enough in the season we might travel inland in our canoe as far as the Kogaluk was navigable, then *walk* the rest of the way to Payne Lake. On detailed maps the Kogaluk was represented by a dotted line connecting a vaguely de-lineated chain of small lakes, but through what wonderfully fine wild country did it flow: not a settlement or a trading post worthy of the tiniest dot or circle within miles of its headwaters! As far as Mr. Todd knew, no ornithologist had ever set foot upon that part of the Labrador Peninsula, and there our bird of mystery might be! What we ourselves had seen of blue geese at the south end of James Bay in the fall of 1923 had con-vinced us that their breeding ground was in the northeasternmost part of the continent or on one of the eastern islands of the Canadian arctic archipelago.

As an employee of the Board of Game Commissioners of Pennsyl-vania, I had to be borrowed. The board, a fine group of sportsmen, knew that I'd be miserable were I obliged to remain in Harrisburg while an-other Blue Goose Expedition was going on elsewhere, so they lent me willingly enough; our eight-man party forgathered at Mattice, Ontario, on May 19; and down the Missinaibi, a major tributary to the Moose, we arranged to go—four of us in one big freight canoe (JB Semple, who was financing the trip; Mr. Todd; Paul Commanda, a full-blooded Ojibway Indian, who had helped Mr. Todd on several of his earlier expeditions; and myself) and two Indians and two French Canadians in another. Two canoes would be needed, for with us were tents and other camping gear, a big outboard motor, about one hundred gallons of gasoline and oil, and enough food for the whole trip. At Moose Factory, equipment and provisions would be loaded into the larger canoe, the smaller canoe and its four men would return to Mattice, and the expedition proper would proceed to the east coast of Hudson Bay and northward as planned.

On our way downriver, we did not need the outboard motor. All went surprisingly well, except for a brush with tragedy above Hell Gate Rapids. Advised to carry around this stretch of white water, we were on the lookout for the upper end of the portage trail. As we quit paddling, we noticed a small canoe moving slowly against the current on the opposite side of the river. In the canoe were two men who, to our surprise, failed to wave or acknowledge in any other way our shouts of greeting. The poor chaps had reason enough to be silent. They and two others had been prospecting, the party of four in two canoes. Believing that they could run the rapids, thus saving time, they had lost one canoe with its two men the day before. The grieving two who were still alive were utterly done in from hours of futile searching. How sobering was their request that we proceed with proper burial if we happened upon the bodies! Not for days did the drawn, weathered faces of those two men leave my thoughts, nor could I see any floating object without wondering whether it might be a corpse.

The weather was good, save for an unseasonably warm afternoon followed by a snowstorm that held us up for a day and a half. There were, of course, the carries, notably the one called Long Portage, several miles south of which I happened to see a hen common goldeneye fly from the top of a dead tree stub not far from shore. Certain that the duck had left a nest, I convinced Mr. Todd that we should stop long enough to investigate. I was good at tree climbing, but the twenty-five-foot stub was large and without branches, so shinnying up would have been difficult and tiring, to say nothing of the problem of hanging on while examining the nest. The stub stood in a thick grove of aspen saplings, one of which I climbed to a height of about twenty feet. There I pulled two other saplings toward me and tied them to the one I was in, thus making a tripod on which to stand. In the half-light at the bottom of a four-foot cavity, in a bed of gray down, were seven pale blue eggs, the first goldeneye eggs I had ever seen. Getting to them required tearing away rotted parts of the stub. Placed carefully in cap and pockets, they reached the ground safely. The date was May 31.

At Moose Factory, four days later, we learned that the ice had not yet gone out of Hannah Bay, so crossing over to the east coast was out of the question. The two Indians and two French Canadians set off upriver. Comfortable in camp, we proceeded to collect specimens; Mr. Todd had a visit with the chief trader and his family at the Hudson's Bay Company post; and each of us did his share of grumbling. Grumbling in the North Country is not a sign of weakness or unhappiness or poor sportsmanship; it is just a traditional and acceptable way of passing time.

The easy life at Moose Factory was, in a special sense of the phrase, calm before storm. Had I, while there, foreseen all that lay ahead, I might have asked Mr. Todd to let me go upriver with the Indians and French Canadians. The first of the journey northward along the coast was to be thrilling; I was to love it all, even the hard parts. But when real trouble was to strike at Richmond Gulf and the canoe would be unable to go farther, when Mr. Todd was to decide that he and Paul Commanda would return to civilization in one way, while JB Semple and I would return in another, when, in short, the expedition as such would come to an end, I would enter a part of my life that, viewed in retrospect, was traumatic. I was to wonder, very seriously wonder, as the last of those weeks passed, what to do were my friend and companion John Semple to die, whether it would be up to me to decide for or against burial at sea, what means I would use in getting word to his relatives. Those days of worrying and wondering were a sort of long-drawn-out nightmare. No doubt I was oversensitive, overimaginative. Alas, I am also far ahead of my story.

When the expedition departed from Moose Factory on June 14, we four were completely on our own. As for the weeks that we and the big canoe were to experience together, let Mr. Todd, a man not given to overstatement, do the telling: In his *Birds of the Labrador Peninsula*, he states:

> In such fashion [after leaving Moose Factory] we skirted Hannah Bay, and finally got over to its eastern shore, and camped for the night on a sandy shoal at East Point. Here our real troubles began. The weather, which had been calm and clear, now changed; the sky became overcast and threatening; and a heavy wind and rainstorm developed. June 18 was one of the stormiest and coldest days I have ever seen in the north country in

summer. It rained and blew hard from the east through the night, until at three o'clock the next morning the wind jumped suddenly to the west, and increased in force until it was hard to face. And with the wind came a fine stinging snow. The tide came in early, with tremendous force, and brought with it the offshore ice. Our empty canoe, left bottom-side up, was turned completely over, but fortunately without breakage. To avoid further trouble we had to move our camp to the shelter of the trees. We had now to wait until the wind and tide should move the ice, which had packed against the shore. When at length we did attempt to move we made only a few miles, to Mesakonan Point, and were then again brought to a halt by foul weather and impossible ice conditions. The full story of our trip, indeed, would contain many repetitions of this statement.

We had counted on being able to travel half of the time on an average, and on making forty miles a day when we did go. As it turned out, there was only one day (July 1) when we succeeded in making the full forty miles, and we were laid up in camp the greater part of the time. The season was abnormal; there was scarcely any summer weather at all; and the prevailing westerly winds banked the broken ice against the east coast to such an extent as seriously to impede our progress. Foul weather, heavy winds and rain, and dense fog added their quota of danger, discomfort, and delay. Sometimes there would be a long stretch of clear water, where we could make time, and then again we would come to an ice-field, and have to pick our way through it, with many twistings and turnings, before we could find another open lead. Always there is the danger, when sailing through moving ice, of being cut off from the shore. Several times we came to places where we had to push the ice-cakes aside in order to open a channel, or even to get out and chop off projecting ice-edges with the ax, before we could get through. Our guide complained that he had not suffered from the cold all last winter as he had this summer. There were two redeeming features of the situation: the first, that we were spared the annoyance of mosquitoes and black flies; the second, that we had more time and opportunity for bird work than otherwise we would have had. We visited several colonies of sea birds on the outlying islands, and made an unusually fine collection of eggs.

The above-quoted summary makes no mention of one precious day lost while backtracking for a sackful of powdered arsenic put out in the sun to dry and, in our haste to break camp and get away, forgotten. That hateful poison we used as a preservative in preparing bird skins. Fearing that the Cree Indians would mistake the innocent-looking stuff for flour, sugar, or baking powder, we muttered, gave each other dark looks, and went back for it. Nor does the account include a word about the severe shoulder injury sustained by JB Semple when he slipped on a wet rock and fell while helping to load the canoe. Good sport that he was, he never complained, but he winced occasionally, and we knew he was suffering because he no longer teased anyone. Mr. Todd was, I must add, very teasable: he had brought along for his own use a folded-up rubber bathtub, an item that JB considered worse than superfluous. I, too, was teasable. My taxidermic kit was too full of unnecessary junk, according to JB, and some of my pronunciation was faulty. "You should say *boo-kay*, not *bo-kay*," pontificated JB, probably repeating exactly what his wife had said to him once upon a time and making me wonder why I had brought the handful of little flowers back to camp for everyone to admire. Paul, the taciturn Ojibway, JB did not tease.

My most remarkable experience on the long stretch between Hannah Bay and Richmond Gulf was of a wholly unexpected sort. The date was July 12. Held up on the eleventh by ice and dense fog at camp near Kakachischuan Point, we were socked in and miserable. We were not by any means as far north as we'd planned to be. Much of the summer was gone. We were discouraged. Everything we had was wet, even, it seemed, that which was inside the tents, all this despite the fire that the faithful Paul kept going. When, to our disgust, the fog continued on the second day, I decided that any kind of jaunt, even a perfunctory one, was preferable to moping, so off I went, first up a straight stretch of trail to the top of a hill near camp, then, following a faint trail that led off to the right and gently downward for a mile or so, again to the water's edge. Puzzled by the fact that I could see no chunks of floating ice in this water, I tasted it. No, it was not fresh; it was part of the sea; the west wind had blown the ice away from shore; our camp was on an island and this was the island's eastern side. The fog was so dense that I decided to keep to the water's edge, for the trail had ended. I propped a dead branch against a tree as a marker and went on. As long as I stayed within sight of the water, I would not get lost, no matter how big the island or how dense the fog.

Within an hour I had shot three specimens—two drake goldeneyes, one fully adult, the other subadult, and a hen red-breasted merganser. All had fallen well out from shore and I had got pretty wet retrieving them, but I felt good as I started back to camp. I had no trouble finding the lesser trail, for the marker was easy to see.

When I reached the straight stretch of trail leading downslope to camp, a sudden puff of east wind cleared the fog. Wind from the east— from the right direction at last! A shore lead would be opening up! We'd be moving! I saw Paul carrying a rolled-up tent. Though I knew I was needed at camp, I could not resist the impulse to stop, to shout, to hold the two goldeneyes up with one hand for Paul to see, and to wave with the other hand, merganser, gun, and all. Paul waved back, though he did not shout. I knew he was glad to see the ducks, for they would be meat for the pot. Ordinarily he would turn his nose up at a merganser—"one of them fishy sawbills"—but not this time!

Before taking another step, I had a strange feeling, a feeling so strong that it promptly became conviction, that Paul had done more than wave, that he had pointed at something, something important, something needing investigation. Without in the least knowing why, I decided that he had pointed to a small spruce tree off to the left, about twenty feet from the trail. As if drawn by a magnet, and not quite knowing what I was doing, I walked to the spruce, looked carefully in and under it, and to my amazement found a dead duck at the edge of her nest—a pintail. In the nest were eight eggs. The discovery was a prize of the trip. Mr. Todd would be delighted. Kakachischuan Point might well prove to be among the northernmost spots at which the pintail had been found nesting along that entire coast.

Elated, I fairly danced downhill to camp. All hands were busy, for the wind had risen and the ice was moving away from the shore. "Paul, you scoundrel," I said, "how did you happen to find that nest?" His reply mystified me. It mystified me then and it has mystified me a thousand times since then. His two words were: *What* nest?" He had never even walked along that trail. There had been wood aplenty at camp level.

The above-reported discovery, under what Mr. Todd himself called unusual circumstances, can hardly be dismissed as mere coincidence. The closest I can come to an explanation of it all is this: I had seen part of the dead duck, or possibly the down at the edge of the nest, as I had walked along the trail earlier in the day. The image of what I had seen had stayed in my mind, not quite in focus. When, out of the corner of my eye, I saw that same part of duck or nest again, my subconscious forced me to find some excuse for looking under the little tree.

Another unforgettable experience was a climb above camp in Manitounuk Sound. Much of the shore there rose steeply, even vertically. Attracted by the cries of a pair of rough-legged hawks, I tried to ascertain from their behavior where the nest might be. Some birds stop their noisy protest almost immediately when an observer who is approaching their nest turns to walk away, but let him about-face and take one step again toward the nest, and the alarum begins again—a game of hot and cold, as it were. The squealing continued no matter which direction I took. I climbed higher and higher, eventually being able to look down on the circling hawks. Watching them was exhilarating: through the binoculars I could see their outermost wing feathers moving upward on the down-stroke, back to horizontal on the upstroke. The nest, atop a great hexagonal basaltic column, was in a difficult place. I doubt that anyone could have got to it without the help of a helicopter. As far as I could tell, it was empty; the young had probably flown and by this time were scattered widely. At camp I sketched in pencil one of the old birds as I had seen it from above. The date: July 24.

Held up by ice near the mouth of the Little Whale River, we did not reach Richmond Gulf until July 28. The channel connecting this large saltwater lake with Hudson Bay is so narrow and the tide so powerful that the rushing water forms a whirlpool, at times a veritable maelstrom, a real threat to navigation. Over and over we had been advised to be careful when entering Richmond Gulf with the canoe, to be sure that we went through the narrows only when the tide was fully in or fully out. We had been told of an oceangoing vessel that had tried going through at the wrong time, been caught in the giant eddy, and spun slowly round and round with bow down, unable to escape until the tidal river had ceased to flow.

We were cautious enough in our approach. The trouble that struck us in those narrows had nothing to do with tides or whirlpools. The metal in our outboard motor's main shaft crystallized, the shaft snapped, and we were obliged to paddle. Fortunately we did not have far to go, and there was neither ice nor wind to contend with. At the trading posts, we were welcomed warmly—the Hudson's Bay Company and the Revillon Frères Trading Company had each recently established a post on the same large island—but nobody had spare parts for outboard motors and, try though all hands did to repair that main shaft, it refused to be repaired. The important part of our expedition, indeed the expedition's chief raison d'être, was over before it had even started. There would be no Povungnituk, no Kogaluk River, no Payne Lake, no blue geese.

A Revillon Frères emergency boat would, however, take us north-ward to Port Harrison in about two weeks. There we would board a much larger vessel, the powered schooner *Albert Revillon*, on which all four of us would go as far as Eric Cove, near Cape Wolstenholme, at the west end of Hudson Strait. At Eric Cove, Mr. Todd and Paul Commanda would wait for the Hudson's Bay Company's supply ship, the *Bayrupert*, on which they would return to Montreal. JB Semple and I, on the other hand, would remain on the *Albert Revillon*, going round the whole of the Labrador Peninsula, eventually to the railroad town of Rimouski, Quebec, on the south shore of the Gulf of St. Lawrence.

So we had two weeks for fieldwork at Richmond Gulf. Here, though at about the northern limit of trees, we found extensive stands of spruce on certain sheltered slopes, not large trees, to be sure, but healthy and well shaped. Where they grew close together, the lower branches of all save those along the outer edges of the forest were dead and covered with lichen. The shaggy epiphytes grew on living branches, too, often hiding the bark completely. Under the trees was a carpet of moss, a sphagnum probably, soft, resilient, inches deep.

Many of the specimens that we collected at Richmond Gulf were water birds, notably three black scoters, all females, taken July 30. We covered the wooded areas quite thoroughly, finding Wilson's, blackpoll, and orange-crowned warblers, northern waterthrushes, ruby-crowned kinglets, white-crowned and tree sparrows, common redpolls, dark-eyed juncos, and gray-cheeked thrushes. More exciting than any of these for me were a northern three-toed woodpecker that I saw on August 9 (plate 6) and four pine grosbeaks and three brown-capped chickadees that I saw on August 10, the very day of our departure. The grosbeaks were in a loose flock, an adult female and three young birds, the latter all flying well. To my surprise, I failed to see a gray jay, though Mr. Todd collected an immature specimen of the species on August 4.

The voyage to Port Harrison was something of a holiday. We were in no way responsible for the boat; Paul had no fire to tend, no meals to cook; there were no specimens to prepare. For a wonder we were not held up by wind, ice, or fog. Just before entering Nastapoka Sound, we had a distant look at Nastapoka Falls. So white was the great cataract that it looked like sky seen through a hole in the black cliff.

At Port Harrison, from August 14 to 16, we were definitely beyond tree limit, a fact confirmed by the presence of such tundra-loving birds as Lapland longspurs, horned larks, and snow buntings, all of which were fairly common. A savannah sparrow that I obtained on August 16 surprised me: I hadn't expected to find that species so far north. Not far from the post, a famous man was buried—the hero of *Nanook of the North*, Robert Flaherty's splendid documentary dealing with the daily life of the Inuit. A wooden cross on the top of a rocky hill marked Nanook's grave.

Aboard the *Albert Revillon*, we were comfortable enough, though there was not room for all of us in the cabins. Being considerably the youngest of our party, I was asked to sleep on the bench at one end of the long built-in table at which we ate. Not far from the opposite end were stairs up to the deck. At the side of these was an iron cookstove, fuel for which was obtained by lifting the hinged third step from the bottom of the stairs, a detail mentioned here because it figures later in a memorable episode. The table was edged with molding to keep the dishes from sliding off. When the sea was rough, the dishes stayed on fairly well, though their contents sometimes didn't. To our surprise, the vessel did not

Black-backed Three-toed Woodpecker   Sketched in pencil and watercolor at camp along the Abitibi River, Ontario, on August 22 and 24, 1923. The head and foot were drawn directly from a young female specimen collected that day.

head directly northward along the coast but westward, then northward, around the Ottawas and Mansel Island. Several miles out from the Ottawas, and nowhere near ice of any sort, we ran close to a polar bear. How golden white and broad the head was, how little the black eyes, how bottle green the great body as seen through the clear water!

At Eric Cove, where there was an important Hudson's Bay Company post, all four of us had a few hours ashore. JB and I climbed the hill in back of the company buildings, finding on its far side steep cliffs inhabited by the largest bird colony I had ever seen—thousands upon thousands of thick-billed murres. JB's shoulder was hurting him, but he felled four murres with four wing shots, shaming me badly. I had to shoot several times to get my four. Each of us also obtained a bird that was wholly new to us—Kumlien's gull. In these the dark parts of the wingtips were pale ashy gray, not black, and the bold pattern there was beautiful. I made a watercolor drawing of the head of my specimen, whose eyes were light greenish yellow, flecked so minutely with silvery gray as to call to mind a fish's eyes. Mr. Todd was greatly pleased with the gulls, for each was an adult in breeding feather.

Farewells at Eric Cove were anything but flippant. There was no backslapping. Each of us knew that, to a very considerable extent, the expedition had failed. We had accomplished a little, to be sure, but only that. At Eric Cove, Mr. Todd hoped to make significant observations while waiting for the *Bayrupert*. JB and I would do what bird work we could on our way southward with the *Albert Revillon*. But that northern half of the east coast of Hudson Bay would still be a vast *terra incognita*, ornithologically speaking.

The *Albert Revillon* had little more than left Eric Cove when she suffered a solar plexus blow. JB and I were at the table, finishing a meal with the others, when the ship shuddered, lurched suddenly upward, and settled back as the throbbing purr of the engine ceased. Utterly dumbfounded, we all stared at each other as the schooner lost momentum, stopped, started to wallow. Rattling sounds that had been muffled by the engine's hum became noticeable. The effect was disturbing. Word came to Captain Murray from the chief engineer: "We're stopped, sir. The propeller's gone."

I did not know how to take news of this sort. Neither, it seemed, did anyone else. Did powered schooners actually lose propellers? Well, hardly. Ram icebergs? Yes. Run aground? Of course. Break rudders? Sometimes. But lose propellers? No, certainly not. Captain Murray's face

showed surprise but no distress. His eyes narrowed, as if to see more
clearly what manner of plight we were in.

JB and I did nothing and said nothing, which was just as well.
Auxiliary sails, though not used for some time and in need of repair,
would be run up. Perhaps there'd be another propeller at Fort Chimo, at
the head of Ungava Bay. Going to Chimo would take time and change
plans drastically, but Chimo would be much more likely to have a propeller than Eric Cove or Port Harrison. Fortunately, indeed very fortunately, there was almost no ice in Hudson Strait.

I had the murre and gull specimens to prepare. My workroom was
the hold, my table the top of a box, my chair one of the scores of big
stones that served as ballast. The light was poor and the place chilly, but I
didn't mind the cold while I was at work. JB did not offer to help with
the skinning. For this I was glad: the shooting at Eric Cove had not done
his shoulder any good.

The sea was rough in Ungava Bay, but there wasn't much ice. JB was
so seasick that he gave up coming to meals. Since he and I were extra
baggage, we were not exactly welcome aboard. Captain Murray was
genial enough, especially when we played whist with him after the evening meal, but the rest of the crew merely endured us. Not one of them
went out of his way to engage us in conversation or to be friendly.
Someone drew footprints with chalk where we walked back and forth
on deck watching for birds. This may have been a mere prank, but it
seemed impolite, if not hostile. We were to learn that the chief engineer
and the mate did not like each other at all. A continuing feud of this sort
might have been ever so much fun to read about, but it was not pleasant
to live with day after day, hour after hour.

Recalling that the Labrador livyers often caught fulmars, jaegers, and
shearwaters on hooks baited with seal liver, I tried fishing for them from
the stern. There weren't many birds, and those that did fly around the
vessel paid not the slightest attention to the floating bait, as far as I could
see. At one unforgettable moment, a following wave swamped the aft
third of the schooner, carrying off sundry loose items and leaving me,
soaking wet but grateful to heaven at finding myself still aboard, holding
fast to the rigging.

The following morning the valiant JB, looking so gaunt that he frightened me, came to the deck, announcing that he was there to give me a
shooting lesson. I wondered whether he should be up and about and said
so, but he replied that the activity would do both of us good. "Now," he

lectured, "there are lots of things to remember in a situation like this. The ship is moving forward. It's also pitching from front to back as well as rolling from side to side. The wind's blowing. The bird's moving. You have to remember all of these things and do your best to average them. Remember first of all to lead your bird. If it's going fast, you have to lead a lot. I don't really need to tell you that, for you've shot ducks. Try to wait until the ship stops seesawing and bucking before you shoot."

There was a long pause. "Now take that bird right there," he continued, pointing to a fulmar petrel that was well within range to port and obviously bent on circling the bow. "Notice how I lead before pulling the trigger!" I watched. The fulmar went on. The gun roared. And scores of neat little splinters sprang up and away from the distal half of the wooden bowsprit as the fulmar sped safely on. "Gosh," whispered JB, as he put the gun between his feet on the deck, steadied himself by grasping the railing with one hand, and with the other pointed to a distant chunk of ice in back of the ship. His voice became louder: "See that piece of ice back there? Has a funny shape, hasn't it?" He continued to point. Then came his whispered "Look that way and keep on looking. I'll take care of the bowsprit later. Those shot marks won't hurt the ship!" He laughed as he looked at me, his accomplice, and the laugh was good to hear, for it sounded like that of the hale, capable, sometimes mischievous JB whom I'd come to know so well. It was the last laugh I was to hear from him while we were at sea.

As we neared the head of Ungava Bay I too became seasick, not violently so but enough to rob me of appetite and make me feel utterly worthless. While we were waiting for the incoming tide to deepen the water at the mouth of the Koksoak River, someone caught a cod, a big chunk of which we boiled in a tin bucket on a Primus stove on deck. The broth revived me.

We were at Chimo from August 28 to September 4. The post had no propeller of the right sort, but the sails could be repaired and that work started immediately. JB felt better ashore, and he actually shot some specimens, but he was not by any means in good shape. I collected birds each day, most of them small woodland species but also three shorebirds: a semipalmated plover, a solitary sandpiper, and a common snipe. My walks took me several miles up the Koksoak. Wherever I went I found blueberries and bake apples, the latter a low-growing, buff-colored fruit, shaped like a blackberry, not very sweet, but wonderfully refreshing when fully ripe. I ate dozens of them.

After the *Albert Revillon* left Chimo on September 5, we were at sea continuously for more than three weeks. They were difficult weeks. JB was in his bunk most of the time. He insisted that he was more comfortable lying down, that he wasn't at all hungry, that losing weight would do him good. He and I both knew that his shoulder needed a doctor's attention. I went to his cabin several times each day, trying to cheer him, asking if there were something special that might be cooked for him, telling him of birds, seals, or whatnot that I'd been seeing. Though obviously weaker as the days passed, he was never anything but cheerful, and this hurt a little, for I knew that he was putting on that front especially for me.

Off Resolution Island at the east end of Hudson Strait, on September 9, I shot several fulmars, specimens that I was more than glad to have, for preparing the skins would keep me busy. Scraping away all that fat took time, to be sure, but what was time for if not for scraping fat? Bitter thoughts of this sort lingered. In the hold I lost one of my favorite skinning tools, a scalpel. Though I moved literally dozens of stones, I never got to the bottom of the pile and never found the scalpel. There seemed to be nowhere to put the stones while I was moving them, nor did the pitching and rolling of the schooner help.

During the slow sail southward from Resolution Island, the Buttons, and Cape Chidley, the *Albert Revillon* kept well out from shore. I tried to recognize places that I'd seen six years before—Mount Blow-me-down, the saw-toothed Kiglapait Range, the Bishop's Mitre, near Cape Mugford, the cliff called the White Handkerchief, with its pale diamond-shaped patch—but the weather was so foul and the strip of land off to starboard so vague and dark that I gave up. I wasn't feeling hearty by any means, and the realization that JB was weakening sobered me. Meals became steadily less appetizing. Chunks of tough bully beef were served over and over, dwindling as pieces were hacked off. A huge container of orange marmalade, on the table forever and ever, became positively revolting. No one, as far as I could see, made the slightest attempt to catch a fish. Somehow it never occurred to me that I myself might have tried to catch one.

I didn't mind the hardness of the bench on which I slept. Indeed, that bench was a sort of ringside seat for all the goings-on. I slept fitfully, being half-aware of everything that happened. One night, fully clothed as usual and as usual half-asleep on my bench, I realized that the saloon had become uncomfortably cold, for I had pulled a blanket over me.

When the chief engineer came for a mug-up, he drank it perfunctorily, then, realizing that the fire was almost out, he lifted that hinged third step, snatched up some wood, tossed it into the stove, and returned to his quarters. The wood did not ignite. Someone below deck must have noticed that the fire needed further tending. At any rate, in the chief came again, this time in a huff, yanked a lid off the stove, dashed some kerosene onto the wood, and again departed. I took it for granted that he knew what he was doing and said nothing. Indeed, for all I knew, the fire was now burning properly.

The explosion sent the stove's lids clattering. No real harm was done. Nothing outside the stove caught fire but when the mate, furious because someone had been careless, came storming down from the deck, he put his right foot through the opening where that third step should have been and fell forward, barking his shin badly. He could easily have broken his leg.

I did not blame the mate for being angry. The string of expletives from him may best be described as a continuation of the explosion. The words and phrases sizzled while the poor man slammed the stove's lids back on and righted the teapot, all the while holding his other hand over his barked shin. So spellbinding was all this that I simply gaped. I still wasn't quite sure that I was awake. The situation was not in the least improved when the mate learned that it was the chief engineer who had failed to replace that third step.

Not once on the voyage southward did JB complain. He knew that he was sick, but he did not even hint that Captain Murray might put in to Nain or Battle Harbour on the chance that a doctor might be found there. I confess that I let myself think snide thoughts about the "Godforsaken tub" we were in, but JB's fortitude reminded me that I should be glad, genuinely glad, for this opportunity to test my own inner resources. I felt not the slightest desire to win the friendship of any of the crew. What did it matter whether they liked me or not?

When, during those solitary hours, I did some soul-searching, I realized that God did not wholly forsake any tub as long as it stayed afloat with compass, tiller, rudder, sail, and crew all working. JB's worsening condition alarmed me, but I came to feel that our skipper was doing his best, that the wind was pushing us right along, that the ice was far from being the threat that it might have been, and that as long as we stayed well out from shore there was little danger of running onto a reef.

I did no praying, no praying at all, though I remembered that hoping might well be a form of prayer. I did think a great deal about God. Why was He so important to me, to all of us? It mattered not a whit what He was called—whether God or Manitou or Sedna or Allah. Was it because we all needed Something infinitely bigger than ourselves to worship, Something much more powerful, Something truly all-powerful? Were such phrases as "Alpha and Omega" part of some cleric's canny plan designed to exonerate all of us, no matter how grievous our sinning, on the grounds that God, the Omniscient, the Omnipotent, had created us with a bent toward sinning and that it was therefore *He* who was to blame?

There was no Bible aboard, as far as I knew. I felt no need for one. I recalled certain words from the Scriptures now and then, words that I had long since learned to love. "Blessed is the man that walketh not in the counsel of the ungodly, nor standeth in the way of sinners, nor sitteth in the seat of the scornful." As the slow days of that last week passed, I gave up trying to decide what my responsibilities might be were my friend and companion to die. Without saying so much as a word of prayer, as such, I knew that I was praying most of the time. I couldn't help myself. There was no way to avoid it. Something told me that the forces that kept us afloat and moving southward were benign. They were God Himself, or part of God, God enough. Forgetting them, failing to acknowledge them and their goodness would not be fair, no matter how many or how powerful the untoward forces that might be operating too.

Off Anticosti Island in the Gulf of St. Lawrence, a handsome little bird of prey, an immature merlin, came aboard exhausted. I climbed the rigging for it, capturing it easily. Alas, we had not a thing for it to eat, and it died.

The stouthearted John B. Semple did not die. Thin, wrinkled, pale, and shaky, he was put ashore with me at Rimouski, and we traveled home by train. His damaged shoulder was operated on . . . successfully. When he gave me the details he laughed a little, and his laugh was good to hear. And this time it reminded me of a big table edged with molding, a cookstove with its lids clattering, and a companionway with its third step missing.

HARRISBURG AGAIN

WHEN I RETURNED to Harrisburg in the fall of 1926, I found that the newspapers had been expressing the fear that our expedition had been lost at sea. My sister Dorothy was now finishing a course in nurse's training at Johns Hopkins Hospital in Baltimore, Maryland; my sister Evie was attending school at a state teachers college in Indiana, Pennsylvania; and my parents were living once more in Bethany, West Virginia. The family home was a pretty white cottage situated at the corner of a two-acre tract that rose, steeply at the north end but gently otherwise, from a stretch of Buffalo Creek that murmured companionably all year round, except when silenced by ice or by weather so dry that the riffles between pools disappeared. This property we had owned since 1924, when, bursting with confidence and pride over my suddenly increased income, I had insisted that a real home be established.

The cottage was one of the oldest buildings in town. On the first floor it had four principal rooms, each with a fireplace; a central hallway leading from front porch to back porch; and a kitchen at a lower level in the rear. Upstairs were two bedrooms, a bath, and a wide hallway, at one end of which I kept a metal caseful of West Virginia bird specimens. Under the whole house was a thick-walled basement that was wonderfully cool in summer and warm in winter. I loved that basement. Near its one window, a big one, I often wrote notes, made drawings, or prepared specimens when I visited home during vacation periods. Father, who was good at carpentering, had lined one wall of the library from top to bottom with bookshelves; hardwood flooring had been added downstairs, except in the kitchen; and all four fireplaces had been faced with large, smooth-edged flat pebbles from the creekbed. Mother herself had worked at this. She and Evie had helped to pick up the stones and to set them in concrete. The freshly painted house, with its large, many-paned front windows (some of the glass was so old that things seen through it wobbled a bit) and four chimneys, had distinction. We decided to name it Pebble Hearths. I had long yearned for a permanent home that I could be proud of. Bestowing a name may have been a little pretentious, but I craved something like status—not so much for myself as for the family. That name plus the realization that the house, with its big rolling lawn, stately elms, huge silver maple, and old russet apple tree, was truly beautiful and truly our own gave me a feeling of belonging.

When I drove to Bethany for a short visit in the fall of 1926, I took with me a parrot that had been given me, cage and all, by a photographer who had helped me with editing film. The parrot, which had lived most of its life in Austria, could not talk in any language known to me, but it was an interesting pet. It had, however, to be watched. Allowed to fly about the rooms at Pebble Hearths, it quietly notched the wood all the way around a card table's edge with its powerful bill—an activity it might have felt no need for had we provided it with a hickory knot or a hand-ful of Brazil nuts to chew on. Where the parrot got the name Perdida (a Spanish word meaning loss or waste) I do not know. *Any* name spoken seductively sufficed to lure it closer, for it loved having its head plumage rumpled. Its yellowish orange eye rarely lost a coldly calculating expres-sion, however, one that seemed to say, "Scratch my head if you will, but do the wrong thing and off goes your finger." It was excited by loud noises. The highest note in the old Stephen Foster song "Swanee River" made it screech at the top of its voice. Years later, when it happened to get out of the house and fly off, the whole town looked for it. Nowhere could it be found. At last Evie suggested that we try singing "Swanee River" in the yard. Sure enough, from a big sycamore down Buffalo Creek a way came Perdida's answering screech. Look though I did for the green bird among the high green foliage, however, I could not see it. Nor would it come down to me. We never saw it again.

In the fall of 1926, in Harrisburg, I moved from the Engineers' Club to a house well out on State Street, east of the capitol. Here the whole second floor was mine, so I had excellent light for painting and enough room for entertaining. Busy though I was with game commission work, which necessitated a good deal of traveling, I became acquainted with interesting people in the city, especially a Mrs. Froelich, a musician who found that I liked to sing and who coached me in some of the fine *Lieder* of Brahms, Schumann, Franz, and Schubert. This woman, whom I liked greatly but never first-named, helped me memorize such songs as Brahms's famed lullaby, whose German words I remember to this day.

Mrs. Froelich, her husband, a writer named Helen R. Martin and her husband, an editor named Effie Riemensnider, and a delightful widow named Josephine Knight Baldwin belonged to a congenial group who entertained each other, and these kind people took me in. Presently, through them, I found myself lecturing at a meeting of the Pennsylvania Historical Society, my subject being the extinct passenger pigeon.

Leo Luttringer and I made a point of swimming, diving, or riding horseback every week. Our horses were fine animals of the 109th Cavalry. Infrequently, we took a walk, looking for birds. If one bird demanded my attention more than others in Harrisburg, it was the starling, a species I had seen little of in Pittsburgh or West Virginia. On the state arsenal grounds, starlings roosted by the thousand in fall and winter. So spectacular were the flocks that people came from afar to watch them. Observers who discussed the birds with me before coming for a look were advised to bring umbrellas.

Leo and I decided to capture some starlings at a large barn in which they roosted. Armed with flashlights, we climbed about snatching birds from the rafters. So close together in rows were they, and the clutching power of their toes was so great, that when we pulled one dazed bird from its perch it grabbed the bird next to it, that bird grabbed the one next to it, and so on, making possible the catching of whole strings of starlings at once.

Among my most interesting activities were visits to the state's many game refuges. I was after facts concerning the deer herd primarily, but I had wonderful opportunities to observe other wildlife. Near Shade Gap, a mountain village in Huntingdon County, I chased a small band of wild turkeys up a forested slope, never getting a clear look at them, though their tracks in the snow told me exactly where they had been. When they flew up well ahead of me, one bird, with wings set for the long glide back into the valley, passed directly overhead at treetop level. The sound its great body made ripping the air apart was almost frightening.

At another refuge, I found a dead porcupine in the snow. Kicking the carcass loose and turning it over, I exposed to the cold air and full light a half-dozen short-tailed shrews, each of which darted into a separate burrow under the leaves. I thought at first that they were mice, but they were far too pointed of nose for mice. The porcupine had lain there for weeks, frozen stiff and dry as a mummy, but it had sheltered the tiny shrews—and, for all I knew, furnished them with food—so I replaced it carefully. Beaver damage that I helped investigate was more than the mere cutting down of trees. Most tree felling in the wilds made little difference to anyone, but, when the dams backed water up over stretches of important thoroughfares, everybody was up in arms. Along highways where deer had been hit repeatedly by cars, or barely missed, DEER CROSSING signs had to go up. The extent of havoc wrought by bears, especially on beehives, had to be estimated officially. There was much argument over how big a Pennsylvania black bear might grow to be. The heaviest on record was, I believe, well over six hundred pounds. I was never in charge of projects dealing with these matters, but I was a sincerely interested observer and a reporter of sorts. No day afield passed without my learning something that was new and important to me.

One trip that I was obliged to make was anything but pleasant. Word reached Harrisburg that a refuge keeper named John Fenton had been bitten on the hand by a copperhead while clearing brush. Since I was the only bureau chief on hand at the moment, it was up to me to find antivenin and drive to the refuge as fast as possible. The poor man was in a sorry state—purple of face, so swollen of tongue that he could only mumble, and badly nauseated but unable to vomit. A doctor from the nearest town had done what he could. The antivenin probably did not help much, if at all. Never in my life had I felt so ignorant, so utterly ineffectual, as I did while trying to comfort that stricken man and his wife. There was something so shorn of pretense about the scene—the plain little house, the distressed faces, the marks of the two fangs at the base of a finger, the funny little tourniquet that had been used to keep the poison from spreading. Even the artificial flowers on the kitchen table were as honest in their way as the geranium that bloomed near a window: they were evidence that someone wanted home to be an attractive place, a place to enjoy. John did not die; indeed, he lived to be past ninety; but he never regained full use of his hand and arm.

Occasionally I witnessed an arrest. In the middle of one dismal night, a man who had been caught red-handed jacklighting deer begged me to intercede in his behalf, not with a magistrate at some future date but on the spot with the game protector, for he felt that his name would be forever smirched if he were jailed or heavily fined. At another time, well away from the nearest village, I did what I could to help a man who, apprehended for some violation, was wounded savagely in the foot when his high-powered rifle, carelessly propped against a tree, fell to the ground and went off just after he had put in a long-distance telephone call for legal help.

While far afield, I was informed by telegram that I had been elected president of the recently organized Harrisburg Community Theater. This worried me, for I knew that my work with the game commission would suffer were I to give any such presidency much time. The theater movement prospered, despite shortness of funds. We put on plays, gave benefits, occasionally brought a big-name actor from New York to take a leading part, eventually hired a part-time director. Though not of much help to the organization, I thoroughly enjoyed becoming acquainted with the many enthusiastic amateurs who did the acting, made props, managed publicity, and sold tickets.

After a talk that I gave in Gettysburg, I became acquainted with Elsie Singmaster Lewars, a gifted writer who lived at the edge of the famous battlefield. Invited to her home for a weekend, I participated in family prayers led by her father, head of the Lutheran Seminary in Gettysburg, and was given a guided tour of the battlefield. In big open fields I observed upland sandpipers (called plovers in those days) that presumably were nesting, though I failed to find either eggs or downy chicks. Above the trees on a hill called Little Round Top, several turkey vultures circled. My hostess' definitive work on the Battle of Gettysburg had been one of Theodore Roosevelt's favorite books.

Many of Mrs. Lewars's stories were about her fellow Pennsylvania Germans. My favorite was about a proud young father who, when asked for the name of a recently arrived baby, replied: "Well, we wanted to call her Roos [Ruth], but my wife she couldn't say Roos right, and we thought Marssa [Martha] would be nice, but I couldn't say Marssa right, so we decided to call her Wyeolet [Violet], and Wyeolet's what she is!"

Urged by Mrs. Lewars—whose writings appeared under her maiden name—to attend a Bach festival, I went with her and a few of her friends to Bethlehem, Pennsylvania, there to be thrilled by the trombone choir's clarion chords as they soared out from a tower on the Lehigh University campus and by carefully trained human voices as they joined in repeating one of musical history's major works. At luncheon I met Teddy Roosevelt's sprightly widow, who obviously enjoyed telling me of ornithologists known to her, among them Frank M. Chapman. That afternoon, we found in the old Moravian cemetery the big, homely, ground-level gravestone of one Benjamin Miksch, probably among the earliest of my forebears to come to America. On the slab was the date 1743, but I do not know whether that was a year of birth or of death. I do recall that a letter had been left out of that unspellable, unpronounceable word

Miksch. Added above the other letters, and smaller than they, the correction had obviated the need for ordering another stone. What a frugal lot have we, the Moravian Miksches, always been!

At my office in Harrisburg there was fresh excitement almost every day. On one occasion I received from Altoona, Pennsylvania, a box in which, according to the accompanying letter, there was a barn owl that had "died soon after being caught." Leo opened the package, tossed the owl onto its paper wrappings, and commented that the specimen might make a nice skin for the Carnegie Museum. Imagine my surprise when, half an hour later, I heard paper rustling, turned in the direction of the noise, and saw the barn owl on its feet, slowly blinking its deep-set eyes. Too convincingly had it played possum: thought by one and all to be dead, it had been wrapped, packaged, and mailed at least twenty-four hours before I received it. We let it go not far from the city.

Another owl, a tiny saw-whet that had been sent in alive, lay motionless on its back on the lectern in front of me throughout an hour-long talk that I gave at the Civic Club. I put it to sleep at the first of my talk by stroking its underplumage as it lay in my hand. In conclusion, I called attention to the supine form, touched a clawed foot with a finger, and watched the little "carcass" pop to attention, glare at me with its orange yellow eyes, and snap its bill fiercely, much to the delight of all within hearing distance.

One day a crate arrived—in it a raven that freed itself by pounding slats loose with its powerful bill during the noon hour, while everybody was out for lunch. At large in my office, it sneaked about craftily, eventually finding the feet under my desk and untying the laces of a shoe. A letter explained that this bird had been in captivity for some time, that its penchant for thievery had become so unremitting that its owners had thought best to rid themselves of it. Its worst habit had been pulling clothespins from wash freshly hung out to dry. Enjoying the whole syndrome of wet garments hitting the ground, women shouting, and doors banging, it had made its Monday rounds, always managing to avoid brooms waved and sticks hurled, always flying to some roof from which to croak its immense satisfaction. During the rest of the week it had visited garages, taking nuts, nails, screws, bolts, and small tools that it could carry off and hide. It liked to scare the wits out of sleeping cats by dropping small stones on or near them. This creature of doubtful ethics certainly could not be kept in my office. Colonel Luttringer, Leo's father, had a cage made for it at the state arsenal, where it had a grand time gloating over baubles sent to it by admirers. It was especially fond of costume jewelry. Dead starlings given to it for food it plucked neatly, arranged in rows, and looked at as if in admiration—except when it was very hungry.

A handsome golden eagle that had been caught by one foot in a steel trap was sent in from the mountains. The foot had been damaged very little. When Fox Movietone News learned of the bird, they wanted photographs. With its feet firmly held, it was surprisingly docile. It made not the slightest attempt to bite me, though it might have torn me to bits with its claws. The photographers wanted eagle and me outdoors, in full sunlight, with the capitol's dome as background. All went well until the eagle suddenly spread its great wings, hitting me in the face with one, and started off. Though I did not let go, I was pulled along for several yards in spite of my resolve to stay put. Presently I got my free arm around the big wings and regained control. "Great, just great!" yelled the cameraman. "Come back and do all that over again!"

A crippled great egret, snow-white and about three feet tall with head held high, was brought in. A bone in one wing was broken, though there was no open wound. Leo fetched a bucketful of small fish from a hatchery, and we watched the heron catch and swallow these without taking the time to kill them. Perched on the rim of the bucket, the half-starved bird wobbled perceptibly as the doomed fish thrashed about inside it, doing their best to get out.

A young weasel brought in by some boys became an extremely interesting, though not at all cuddly, pet. Never did it curl up in my lap, or stroke my leg as a cat might have, or evince the slightest pleasure at having its head or back scratched, but it obviously enjoyed being allowed to leave its cage, bound around over a tabletop, and leap from the table's edge across to me. If I stood as far as three feet away, it had to size things up and muster its resolve, but, having made the jump successfully, it acted as if wonderfully pleased, climbing swiftly upward, nibbling at my neck, ears, or chin, and eyeing me mischievously. Never did it really bite, though I knew from the feel of them that its teeth were needle-sharp. Occasionally it romped quite playfully, chasing the end of a string or pulling at a small object dragged in front of it. Our name for it was Stoat.

Very much on my mind were the colorplates for Mr. Todd's forthcoming *Birds of Western Pennsylvania*. Mr. Todd did not know how publication of this major work would be financed, but he went ahead with his manuscript, meanwhile paying me personally for the seventy-some drawings that I made. Most of these I did while on vacation in West Virginia. Only one of them—that showing the semipalmated and least sandpipers—was composite. I made a point of drawing such accessory material as leaves and flowers directly from living plants, never from memory. Pulling a weed, placing it in water, and drawing it at arm's length was easy enough, but taking paper and drawing board to a tree and delineating the leaves as they hung was laborious. After penciling in the branch, I would cut it, take it to the house, fasten it at eye level, and work out the details. Dogwood leaves in the wood thrush drawing were done in precisely this way. The weed in the grasshopper sparrow drawing

Northern Three-toed Woodpecker   Sketched in pencil and watercolor along the Abitibi River, Ontario, in the later summer of 1923 but used as an illustration for this chapter since the species was sighted at its northernmost limit on the east coast of Hudson Bay on August 9, 1926.

was pulled up, set in water, drawn in detail in the shade, then taken out into full sunlight (where a grasshopper sparrow would surely be) before colors were added.

What I continued to say about the value of birds of prey and the evils of the bounty system led the men of the field force to request that I explain the great flights of hawks that took place every fall along a narrow part of Kittatinny Ridge near Drehersville, about sixty miles northeast of Harrisburg. I had heard of the flights, to be sure. Sportsmen from Drehersville, Reading, and Pottsville had been gathering there to shoot hawks for years. At first the shooting had been just for fun, but dealers in guns and ammunition had encouraged the belief that hawks should be destroyed, more and more gunners had espoused the cause, and the whole thing had come to be considered commendable. Cold fronts were known to bring good flights, so everybody had watched the weather. The shoots had become social events. Literally thousands of hawks had been slaughtered.

My suggestion that thermals and updrafts—not to mention landmarks visible to the hawks, all species of which were believed to migrate by day—might be responsible for the funneling past Kittatinny Ridge was sound enough, though the idea was far from original with me, and I could only guess that keeping to the left of certain ridges or to the right of certain rivers was more than accidental.

One game protector in particular, Archie C. Smith of Lavelle, Pennsylvania, continued to keep me informed about the hawk shooting. On October 17, 1927, he told me of several hawks that had been shot that very day, among them eighteen sharpshins that he was saving for me. The following day I met him at Drehersville and went with him to a well-known shooting spot on what he called Blue Mountain. There, stretching straight down through the woods from high on the ridge, was a cleared strip along which the gunners lined up in such a way as to prevent any low-flying hawk from passing without being shot at by someone. Hawks happened not to be numerous that day—living hawks, that is; dead hawks there were by the hundred. We picked up literally bushels of them, mostly sharpshins and redtails. I made no effort to count them or to find every one, for they were scattered widely. Most of the carcasses were south of the strip. The shooters evidently had learned that the hawks were harder to hit when coming head-on downwind than when leveling off after passing over.

On October 20, Smith and I returned to Blue Mountain. Sharpshins were moving this time, almost continuously in fact though not in great numbers, and flying low, just above the treetops. I wanted to know what these southbound birds had in their stomachs. Had they caught prey near the spot at which they had slept, or were they obtaining food *while migrating?* What I was observing suggested that low-flying hawks might pounce on prey without much of a pause and without any turning back. The five sharpshins that we shot that morning each had eaten at least one recently caught small bird.

Two days later, Smith picked up the hawks that a handful of sportsmen had killed during a nine-hour period on that date—a total of ninety sharpshins, thirty-two redtails, sixteen goshawks, eleven Cooper's hawks, and two peregrine falcons. How many hawks had been wounded no one could say. Leo Luttringer and I weighed and examined the specimens, and I published a paper on our findings in the *Wilson Bulletin*. Someone's editorial comment that the shooting at Drehersville was doing some good at last, since the hawks' stomachs were being examined officially, had a hollow ring for me. No one needed to be told afresh that sharpshins fed largely on little birds or that goshawks and redtails caught poultry and small game as well as rodents and snakes.

Let no reader consider me in any way responsible for the bold moves that made Hawk Mountain a sanctuary within a few years. In 1934 a determined and militant conservationist, Rosalie Edge, who had heard of the hawk killing through a friend, Richard H. Pough, and who clearly saw how little good such talking and writing as mine had accomplished, leased the mountain from a lumber company for $500 and made it off limits to hunters. The move made the hawk shooters furious, but there was nothing they could do. The following year, Mrs. Edge and her organization, the Emergency Conservation Committee, exercised an option to buy the fourteen hundred–acre mountain for $1.50 an acre. Six hundred more acres were donated by a foundation twenty-nine years later. Hawk Mountain is known today the world over. Thousands of people visit it every year, thrilling as they watch the handsome birds pass. Foggy days may be disappointing, but, when the weather is clear and sharp, beauty of a very special sort pours down from the north.

In the fall of 1927, I helped the Harrisburg Art Association assemble a total of 108 paintings, drawings, and etchings of birds and mammals. These were displayed at the public library from December 9 to 19. Among the watercolors were seven by my beloved teacher, Louis Agassiz Fuertes, who had been killed in an automobile accident the preceding

July. One evening I gave a gallery talk dealing with the anatomy, color patterns, and facial expressions of birds. Within touching distance as I spoke was a living barred owl, an untethered, uncrippled, perfectly healthy wild bird that someone had brought in the preceding day and that I felt sure would remain quietly on its perch as long as the room stayed well lighted. Alas, I forgot that a sudden noise would surely startle it. At the close of my talk, there was a burst of applause and off the bird went, sweeping low over the cringing audience, whose gasps of alarm did nothing to calm the owl down. No damage was done, and the speaker was profoundly thankful that his model had been content to circle the room without jettisoning that which had accumulated in the nether part of its digestive tract during an inactive day.

In the spring of 1928, I photographed two wild turkey nests, one holding eight eggs (an incomplete clutch) on May 5 on a game refuge in Clearfield County, central Pennsylvania, the other on another refuge in an adjoining county near the town of Lock Haven. At the latter nest, which held seventeen well-incubated eggs on June 6, the day I photographed it, the brooding hen was remarkably confiding. I made no attempt to touch her but moved about within only a few feet of her and took several photographs. The nest, of dead grass and leaves, was among small angular rocks. Though not well sheltered from above, it was screened on all sides by mountain laurel, none of which I removed. The hen's neck was stretched out in front of her when I first went to the nest, but as I set up the tripod and camera she lifted her head and moved it about snakily while hissing and grunting. Occasionally, when disturbed by a distant noise, she called *quit!* When assured that no danger threatened, she stopped hissing, lowered her head, and stretched her neck out in front of her. I was told that the nest had held eighteen eggs the preceding day.

The nest was only a quarter of a mile from the refuge keeper's house and barn. A pet red fox—that might, conceivably, have stolen the turkey egg—amazed me with its tameness. Freed from its roomy cage at the end of the barn, it shot off through the woods, making me fearful that it was gone for good; but no, back it came and around the barn it ran, by this time with tongue hanging out but showing no other sign of fatigue. After it had rounded the barn a second time, the refuge keeper crouched and whistled, and into his circled arms the fox leaped. How wonderfully happy it looked as it stuck its nose up to be rubbed! I had never seen a really tame fox before.

At a place called Torrance Junction, where I was obliged to change trains while on a lecture trip, I found on the station platform stout crates holding red foxes on their way to Rolling Rock, an exclusive club near Ligonier. The Prince of Wales was to be entertained there with a fox hunt, and the foxes were from Sears, Roebuck and Company.

A man whose office was at the opposite end of the building from mine asked what I knew about squirrels, one of which had been scratching at his window as if trying to get in. Its visits were paid at about the same time morning after morning. My first guess was that it had been fighting its reflection, trying to vanquish a rival. At my suggestion, we opened the window at about the time of the daily visit, hid in back of a door, and watched. The squirrel appeared, paused on finding the window open, moved hesitantly to the inner sill, jumped to the floor, bounded across the room and up onto a chair, jumped again to the writing level of a desk, and, pushing aside papers in a certain pigeonhole, reached a nut. With this in its teeth, it retraced its route precisely and departed. How long the nut had been there no one could say, but we found no other nuts in pigeonholes, so the squirrel had either smelled that nut or remembered exactly where it had been cached.

The year 1928 was important in my young life, for during that year appeared my first hardback book, *An Introduction to the Birds of Pennsylvania*, a modest work brought out by the Mt. Pleasant Press of Harrisburg, my lengthy report on the birdlife of Pymatuning Swamp, published in the Annals of the Carnegie Museum, my first article in a major magazine—a story in the *Atlantic Monthly* about my crawl through the hollow log after the turkey vulture's nest—my first full-page colorplates for Frank M. Chapman's bimonthly magazine, *Bird-Lore*, and my formal description of a new genus and species of South American swift. The form described, *Micropanyptila furcata*, was eventually to be known as the pygmy swift. The two specimens on which my description was based were in the Venezuelan collection that Mr. Todd had asked me to work up four years before, at the Carnegie Museum. Unable to identify the birds at that time, for they had agreed not at all either with other specimens available for comparison or with published descriptions, I had shown them to Charles Hellmayr, a distinguished ornithologist from Chicago who happened to be visiting the museum. Hellmayr looked at them closely through his thick-lensed glasses and said: "New! Undoubtedly new. A new genus, in fact!" I was elated, of course, but also puzzled. What should my next move be? Rather than discuss the matter with Mr. Todd, whose prerogative it might have been to name the form himself, I

*Pygmy Swifts   Life-size watercolor made
in 1923 or 1924 from specimens of a then-
undescribed species collected in the state
of Zulia, Venezuela, by M. A. Carriker, Jr.
The drawing was first reproduced in 1928.*

made a detailed, almost feather-for-feather life-size drawing of the two birds in flight (plate 8), decided on a scientific name that in my opinion would suffice, and, following the style used by my peers, prepared a description. As the months passed after my move to Harrisburg, I wondered what should be done. My fellow bird students had a right to know about the unnamed swift from Venezuela. Mr. Todd was generous to a fault. He checked my measurements of the specimens and gave me their catalog numbers, thus making my paper entirely acceptable to the world of science. The description, complete with a halftone reproduction of my drawing, appeared in the April 1928 issue of *The Auk*.

The colorplates for *Bird-Lore* were to illustrate a series of scholarly papers by Dr. Chapman on the molts and plumages of American bird species known to occur north of Mexico and the West Indies. Fuertes had been illustrating these papers, so Chapman's request that I continue the series was a compliment of the highest order. My first plate showed two pileated woodpeckers. Several other woodpecker plates portrayed two or more species each, the one exception being that of the ivorybill, a bird I had never seen alive. I cringe when I look at that plate today, for neither bird shown there has the ivorybill's pale glaring eye, a feature I was to marvel over while sketching a pair direct from life at their nest hole in northeastern Louisiana a few years later. Four plates of the *Bird-Lore* series were not of woodpeckers—one being of kingfishers, one of trogons, one of cuckoos, and one of anis. My chief criticism of these plates is that certain details (e.g., the woodpeckers' feet) too often appear to have been cut out and pasted on the paper.

My friendship with Chapman, never at all close, began while I was plotting the distribution of Pennsylvania's bronzed and purple grackles, a project on which I never reported. The two forms, now considered subspecies of the common grackle, were thought by some taxonomists to be separate species. Chapman had amassed such a vast array of specimens from various parts of North America that he was able to show me purple extremes unlike any I had ever seen or imagined. In the midst of one of our sessions at the American Museum of Natural History, he suggested that we forget grackles for a while and go to the New-York Historical Society for a look at the John James Audubon original drawings kept there under cover, lock, and key. That hour or so with Audubon's incomparable work was an experience of a lifetime. The colors were so pure and fresh, the paper so astonishingly clean! With Chapman and me were Robert Cushman Murphy, author of the two-volume classic, *Oceanic*

Birds of South America, and John T. Zimmer, editor of *The Auk.* Chapman himself had gone out of his way to arrange this special viewing.

That spring I found it hard to settle down to game commission work, for Mr. Todd had made clear that he expected to borrow me for another of his North Country expeditions—this one to the Canadian Labrador, the north shore of the Gulf of St. Lawrence. The area would be of special interest to me, since Audubon himself had visited it about a century before.

The Board of Game Commissioners granted me leave. Our party of five—Mr. Todd, John B. Semple, J. Kenneth Doutt (curator of mammals at the Carnegie Museum), the faithful Paul Commanda, and myself—convened at the city of Quebec, boarded the Clark Steamship Line's sturdy little vessel, the *North Shore,* on May 16, and traveled eastward for four days—as far as the village of Natashquan, near the mouth of the river of the same name. There a forty-foot powerboat with an auxiliary sail, manned by a French Canadian named Cormier and his son, awaited us. Held up by drifting ice, we stayed four more days at Natashquan Point; then, moving eastward by easy stages, and camping ashore, we reached the mouth of the Little Mekatina River on June 24. After a stay there of several days, we returned to Quebec. The expedition, Mr. Todd's Number 12, ended July 8.

My memories of that brief summer trip have to do chiefly with human behavior. JB Semple was his old self, full of mischief, unfailingly optimistic, and fond of teasing everybody except the taciturn Paul Commanda and the two volatile French Canadians. The one and only Mr. Todd had with him his rubber bathtub. When he requested the privacy of the tent, Semple, Doutt, and I scattered as best we could, hoping quite uncharitably that Mr. Todd would drown in his tub. Paul, dependable as the round of day and night, and by this time used to us "scientists," took us all in stride. Cormier *et fils* lived on their boat; we saw very little of them. Only occasionally were we really bothered by mosquitoes and blackflies. At one camp the four of us in the big tent were wakened during a heavy downpour at night by the gurgle of a little stream running full tilt amongst our sleeping bags. We suffered no real hardships, had no narrow escapes. My one continuing regret was that I had no watercolor outfit with me. All that I had for drawing was a small sketchpad, pencil, and eraser.

During breakfast one morning at Natashquan Point, JB Semple reported seeing some big common mergansers at the river mouth. This

species, unlike the red-breasted merganser, was considered rare in the
Gulf of St. Lawrence. "You should have collected one of them!" said Mr.
Todd. "Any sighting of this sort needs confirmation." To which I added:
"One bird would have been enough!" (Skinning the specimen would
have been my job; a merganser would be fat; from my standpoint, one
common merganser would have been more than enough!) Whereupon JB
was pummeled at considerable length by questions aimed at proving his
identification wrong. That evening, as we sat around the campfire, JB was
at his contrite best. "About those big mergansers that I reported this
morning," he said disarmingly, "I want to modify my statement. I didn't
see any."

JB's pronouncements were sometimes so amusing that I wrote them
down for reference, so to speak. After an indifferent meal at an indifferent
restaurant, he was wont to say, "Not so bad, really, what there was of it;
and plenty of it, too, such as it was!"

A merlin's nest that I found near the mouth of the Kegashka River on
June 7 was about fifteen feet up in a small spruce at the top of a hill.
There I took photographs the hard way, first moving the five eggs to the
ground, then attaching the camera a few inches above the nest with lens
pointed straight down, carefully replacing the eggs, and, holding my
breath while hanging on to the tree, releasing the shutter for a full second
of time exposure.

On June 19, at Ile du Lac, we visited a mixed colony of double-
crested and great cormorants. The nests were on narrow ledges well
down from the top of a sheer cliff several hundred feet high. The great
cormorant was very rare in the New World, so our permit allowed us to
take only one specimen. That heavy bird Kenneth Doutt captured by
dangling a wire noose over its head from the top of the cliff. With the
fresh specimen before me, I made a pencil sketch on which, using the
letters y and gw, I indicated just where the bill and naked skin of the face
were dull yellow and where grayish white. Tiny round spots in a row all
the way around each eyelid were dull gray blue. The irises were a clear,
startlingly beautiful, faintly greenish blue. Alas, my watercolor paints
were a thousand miles away!

Near camp at the mouth of the Little Mekatina on June 26, I was
lucky enough to happen upon a Lincoln's sparrow nest holding four eggs.
This was something I had especially wanted to find, for I knew that
Audubon had based his description of "*Fringilla Lincolnii*" on a specimen collected along this very stretch of coast. The photograph that I took

turned out so well that Mr. Todd used it in his classic work. In passing, it may not be amiss to state that Audubon named his Lincoln's sparrow not after Abraham Lincoln but after one Robert Lincoln, a young man referred to in Elliott Coues's *Check List and Ornithological Dictionary* as a "sometime companion of Audubon."

Just after leaving one camp, our powerboat ran aground with all hands aboard. Cormier *et Cie* went simply wild. Over went much of their firewood, chunk by chunk. In vain we tried to calm the two men, to assure them that the tide might still be coming in, that no harm had been done to the boat, etc. But calm down they would not. The boat was theirs, not ours, said they, and they, not we, knew about shipwrecks. They feared the worst. No one volunteered to lighten the load further by jumping overboard. So helpless we stood and sat, looking at each other for a suspenseful quarter of an hour. As the boat swung free, Cormier *et Cie* glared at us. We had permitted them to do all the suffering.

An unexpectedly high moment came for me as we were traveling on the *North Shore* from Harrington Harbour back to Quebec. A fellow passenger proved to be one Sam G. Ford, a Newfoundlander who had established a trading post for the Hudson's Bay Company on Southampton Island at the north end of Hudson Bay in 1924. As I talked with this fine man, I learned that he had known, known well in fact, natives who had seen blue geese in summer and found their nests. "Where were the nests?" I asked eagerly. "Over west of the trading post at the southwestern corner of the island. It's a place called Cape Kendall. The birds have a big colony there," answered he. Before the *North Shore* had reached Quebec, Sam Ford and I had worked out an important plan. To visit Cape Kendall during the breeding season of the blue geese, I would be obliged to overwinter on Southampton Island. Getting to Southampton would mean a trip on the famed Hudson's Bay Company's supply ship, the *Nascopie*. With Sam's help I would do it.

In the fall of 1928, the dome of the capitol in Harrisburg received a thorough cleaning. As the work progressed, the citizenry could not help noticing how very grimy the structure had become. When floodlighted at night, the cleaned parts had a luminosity, almost an opalescence, that forced one to remember some of the world's other magnificent buildings—the Taj Mahal, St. Peter's in Rome, the Capitol in Washington, D.C. Night-migrating birds on their way south flew about the dome in such numbers that I feared many were being killed, but workmen found none dead or crippled on the roof, and I found not a one on the ground.

Toward midnight on October 15, Leo Luttringer and I, equipped with the proper permit, climbed the scaffolding, there to find ourselves in the midst of a veritable swarm of little birds, most of them juncos and chipping and white-throated sparrows. The bewildered creatures fluttered close to the dome without actually striking it. Those that alighted did so on the sloping walkway or its handrail. Nowhere was the walkway rickety, but it was not overwide and we were glad for the handrail, not only for the support it afforded but also because birds that alighted there were easy to catch. Among the hundreds of juncos and sparrows suddenly appeared a solitary sandpiper, which uttered a sharp cry when it saw us. And well out from the dome, never at all close to us, floated a short-eared owl. Against the ghostly pallor of the owl's light-reflecting underwings, the forms of little birds crossed and recrossed endlessly.

Early in the spring of 1929, I had an accident that might well have killed me. I had agreed to talk at an evening meeting in Lock Haven. On my arrival there by train, John Ross and another officer of the commission's field force met me. Knowing that I'd be interested, John told me of a wild gorge in which peregrine falcons had been seen from time to time. "The place is back in the mountains, a couple of miles south of McElhattan." When I learned that we could drive to within a short distance of the gorge, I begged to be taken there for at least a look at the place.

Off went the three of us. No change to field clothes. Plenty of time before the meeting and talk. A fine March day. After leaving the west branch of the Susquehanna, the dirt road climbed steadily, finally becoming a mere logging trail. Unable to drive farther, we got out. To our right loomed a bold, angular knob. As we slowly climbed, a deer splashed across the stream that the trail followed. Off on a high slope a ruffed grouse drummed.

I now perceived that much of the knob's south face was sheer cliff. As we approached, I fully expected to hear the grating fanfare of an annoyed peregrine, but no such sound greeted us. Peering through the trees, I looked for a patch of white droppings—a sure sign that peregrines had established an aerie there, but no white patch could I find. Instead I saw a great mass of sticks about fifty feet above the rubble at the cliff's base—the nest of a raven. Even as I called attention to this discovery, out flew the raven. The great bird headed southward across the gorge, croaked three times, and disappeared.

Perhaps my companions should have argued me out of attempting the climb. But I had climbed cliffs before. I must have stated in no uncertain terms that I knew what I was doing. At any rate, up I started. And all wènt well. Following a narrow ledge, I reached a point directly below the nest. The remaining part of the climb, though vertical, was not without good handholds that became footrests. I took care not to use my knees or elbows lest my business suit be soiled or torn. I was almost within touching distance of the nest's foundation when the big rock that I was pulling myself upward on suddenly came loose, debris clattered, I tried in vain to find another good handhold as the loose rock plummeted, and down I went. Fortunately the falling rock was ahead of me. Fortunately my descent was impeded by some vines. Fortunately my neck was not broken when I struck the coarse talus at the cliff's base. Some ribs and upper dorsal vertebrae were fractured and a collarbone was sprung, but I was able to get up, to brush myself off a bit, to retrieve my watch, which had slipped from a vest pocket and was lying unbroken, faceup, on a rock, to reassure my companions, who were white-faced with solici- tude, to walk to the car, and to stay cheerful despite the pain on our way to the hospital.

Indeed I was a very hero: not a peep of complaint, not a word of regret, save one or two over being unable to give the scheduled talk. No one chided me. No one said a word about what a blasted fool I'd been. John and his fellow officer were kindness itself. Everyone at the hospital was positively angelic. Friends visited me from Harrisburg. One person, one only, a Philadelphia newspaperwoman, gave me my just deserts. The limerick that she wrote was silly, but it was wonderfully well con- structed. Here it is:

> Doc Sutton once had a cravin'
> For catchin' a Lock Haven raven.
> But he stepped off the edge
> Of a fifty-foot ledge,
> And the pieces were hardly worth savin'.

How I wish I could remember that young lady's name: it should be immortalized along with that of Edgar Allan Poe!

THE FAR NORTH

X-RAY PHOTOGRAPHS at the hospital in Lock Haven made clear which bones had been fractured. The doctors seemed to feel that no very serious damage had been done. They bound my rib cage with what felt like strips of tarpaulin and discussed the details of my accident almost gleefully. They could not say how long I'd be convalescent. Very much on my mind was the year I was planning to spend in the Far North. I would have to be in shape for that. I had decided to give up my work in Pennsylvania and to enroll as a graduate student at Cornell University in Ithaca, New York.

When that faithful and beloved friend, my sister Dorothy, came to the hospital to see me, I must have worn her down badly with discussing my plans. I would be overwintering on Southampton Island (I told her), at the north end of Hudson Bay. My headquarters would be the Hudson's Bay Company's recently established trading post at a spot called Coral Harbour on the big island's south coast. I would travel to Southampton on the company's annual supply ship, the *Nascopie*, which would leave Montreal in mid July and reach Coral Harbour about a month later.

At Cornell I would work directly toward a doctor of philosophy degree, bypassing the master's, since I would be obtaining during my year in the North a vast amount of data from which could be extracted enough for a dissertation on some aspect of the birdlife. Cornell's residence requirements would be met in part by the fieldwork itself. I would, in other words, be a graduate student *in absentia* for a year. The Carnegie Museum would purchase my collection. I would go after and preserve everything—birds primarily but also mammals, fishes, mollusks, insects (especially butterflies and moths), and plants, including shrubs, mosses, lichens, and fungi. John B. Semple would provide the money for buying the collection and would drive me to Montreal to see me off on the *Nascopie*. While lying there swaddled with tape, talking my plans over with Dorothy, I was impatient, to say the least. "Get me out of here!" I felt like yelling at every doctor or nurse who passed by. Dorothy, in her somewhat professional way, calmed me down. So did Leo Luttringer, who knew of my plans, though I had not yet asked him to type my letter of resignation.

When I returned to Harrisburg, I lived for a time with Leo and his wife, Mildred, whose nickname was Midge. These two were wonderfully kind . . . and imaginative. My first real outing was a trip to a circus with them. Leo had learned that a baby dromedary had been born the day before. The little thing was not very strong and the circus people wanted it surely to survive, so it was not on display, but Leo obtained permission for the three of us to observe it at close range. It had the most extraordinary eyelashes I had ever seen. Curved gently, they stuck out like a heavy fringe, each hair well over an inch long. They would be of real service, I knew, during a dust storm in dromedary habitat, but as I stood there marveling I could not resist the very unscientific thought that they were the Lord's way of keeping the overly curious from seeing too much of those big, translucent, bewilderingly innocent eyes.

On my feet again, I enjoyed Harrisburg as I never had before. This was partly because I had decided against ever again holding a political job. Though a registered Republican, I was irked by requests for donations to the party, for never could I see clearly how my money was to be used. Halfheartedly, I said that I believed in the two-party system, though it often seemed to me that the two parties stood for the same things. The idea of being loyal had appeal, to be sure, but why be loyal to anything that I did not fully understand? What I wanted to be, first of all, was not a loyal member of any organization but, rather, an ornithologist knowledgeable enough to draw birds well, write good books, and teach younger people. If questions shot at me professionally were to deal with such a truly puzzling phenomenon as bird migration, I would try to be honest but, rather than embarrass all concerned by emphasizing my ignorance, I would discuss theories as intelligently as possible, call attention to certain well-documented facts, and recommend participation in the bird-banding program, a worldwide effort that had already brought to light amazing information concerning the seasonal movements of birds.

During the early summer of 1929, my correspondence with the Canadian government and the Hudson's Bay Company became urgent. Certain official permits had to be obtained. Several extras not regularly stocked at trading posts—sackfuls of Irish potatoes and crates of apples,

oranges, lemons, and onions—were to be ordered. "Perishables like potatoes will be welcome while they last," said HBC letters, "but, if they
freeze, don't expect to enjoy them after they thaw." Never was a truer
statement put on paper. A few of the oranges, carefully guarded against
freezing, became almost as dry and hard as croquet balls by Christmas.
Most of the onions went *their* way, not ours. Not a word did letters have
to say about the behavior of processed cheese in really cold weather. On
one dog team trip, when my Eskimo friends and I stopped for a mug-up,
a packet of some company's best cheddar turned so powdery in the cold
air that it blew away, right out of the foil in which it had been wrapped.

I am ahead of my story. For photography, which I knew would be
essential, I bought a small motion-picture camera, a 3A Eastman Kodak, a
tripod, a portrait lens, and a photometer. Never having been a photographer, I looked upon all this as a necessary evil. I would take the old
Fuertes paint box, of course, and a good supply of Strathmore watercolor
paper. I would take a Krag rifle and two double-barreled 12-gauge shot-
guns, each with a short auxiliary tube of .410 caliber that fitted into the
right-hand barrel but that would not be used in the left-hand barrel, for
that barrel was choked to give the shot a denser pattern and greater
carrying power. Ammunition for the tube, designed to scatter well, would
be especially useful for small birds and for wing shooting. John Semple,
an expert on firearms and ammunition, knew which parts of my guns
would be most likely to cause trouble, so he made spares of those parts
and drew diagrams showing me just how they worked.

I had grown to like the men with whom I had associated in Pennsylvania, especially the district supervisors, county game protectors, and
refuge keepers, many of whom were scientists at heart, eager to discover
new facts and put them to use. The Board of Game Commissioners made
a mighty, and a continuing, effort to keep themselves and their em-
ployees free of politics, but the struggle was unceasing. One member of
the board, Francis Coffin, of Scranton, I liked especially well. He and his
wife, Anna, an ardent conservationist, had entertained me often in their
home. They gave me a fine wristwatch that I would wear during my
sojourn in the North and for many years thereafter. My last visit with
them was at Lacawac, a beautiful lake in the Pocono Mountains. There I
had the novel experience of catching one after the other the four species
of game fishes regularly found in that area—a large-mouthed black bass,
a small-mouthed black bass, a pickerel, and a walleye or pike perch.
Each of these was of fair size, and I caught no other fish. The accidental

haul amused my hosts and their other guests, for everyone knew that I was not a dyed-in-the-wool angler.

Among those who put me aboard the *Nascopie* was one of my favorite professors at Bethany College, a slender, spirited woman named Pearl Mahaffey, who had taught me Spanish. The crew showed Miss Mahaffey their vessel with justifiable pride, for the *Nascopie* had won renown for her performance, year after year, in far northern waters.

The long voyage to Southampton was anything but tedious. Every day Dudley Copland, an employee of the company, gave me a lesson in the language of the Inuit, the Eskimos. I wrote down nouns, adjectives, adverbs, verb stems, and short sentences by the dozen and memorized them thoroughly. I watched the oceanic birds eagerly, being especially impressed with the variation in color pattern among jaegers. Near Cape Dorset, along the south shore of Baffin Island, I had a wonderful look at a white gyrfalcon that flew over the ship.

Arrival at Southampton was gala. Eskimos from all over the southern part of the island had come to the trading post, there to consume large buns, baked beans, and other "foreign" foods prepared in quantity for ship time. There was no pier, so big motorboats plied noisily between the floating dock and the *Nascopie*, taking bales of furs, walrus hides, and casks of oil aboard and bringing ashore trade goods, provisions, my pile of gear, and me.

Sam Ford and his nineteen-year-old son Jack welcomed me heartily, showed me the upstairs room that would be mine, and made me part of the celebration. To prove to one and all that I was a person of consequence, they insisted that I join them in scattering handfuls of hard candy on the beach for the kids. The black-haired, black-eyed, brown-skinned youngsters scrambled hither and yon, laughing and squealing, allowing no bit to go ungarnered. Said Jack, in that quaint lingo of his, "The people likes you, Doc. They intends to help you with all of the bird work you plans to do. The people here knows their birds. They has names for all the different kinds." I can hear that eager young voice even as I write. It had a warmhearted, respectful tone that meant much to me at the moment, for, despite my remembering that a polar bear was a *nanook* and a seal a *netchek*, I was a stranger in a strange land with a long way to go to prove that I was real, not make-believe. The tone in Jack's voice never changed during the year we had together. Nor has it changed as the decades have passed since 1930. Even today, that much younger man considers me more knowledgeable than I really am. Of course I know more about some things than he does, but I marvel when I contemplate what he knows that I don't. He has had a lifetime in the North. He speaks the language of the Inuit fluently and has been a man of affairs. Had he elected long ago to become an ornithologist, he'd be a better one than I by this time.

On the beach that day in August of 1929 was a sturdy crate holding a young polar bear bound for a zoo in England. Before the crate was taken aboard, it was dunked, bear and all, into the cold ocean. Even after the cub had shaken, pawed, and licked itself dry, it was a long, long way from being white.

After about three days of ship time, the Eskimos who were not employed by the company, the Roman Catholic mission, and the Anglican church folded their canvas tents, climbed into their boats, and departed. No one traveled by *komatik* (dogsled) for there was neither snow nor ocean ice to travel on.

Outstanding among the Eskimos who remained was John Ell, Sam Ford's right-hand man, an extremely capable full-blooded member of the Aivilikmiut, the walrus-hunting tribe from Repulse Bay. John could speak more than a word or two of English. With pride he was to tell me that he had learned such English words as "yes," "no," "many," "much," "near," and "far," and—now that I had come to live in his country—he would learn *American* from me.

The name John Ell was short for John L. Sullivan, the famous pugilist, whose strength and prowess the Eskimos had heard about over the radio. John's Eskimo name as I wrote it down was Amaulik Audlanat, but I was to discover that there was no way, no way at all, for anyone to be sure that I had spelled the two words correctly or, indeed, that the several syllables were actually two words rather than three or more. These fine people had no printed literature, no dictionary, no spelling, no letters, no alphabet. What Dudley Copland had taught me was a lot of sounds. What I had written down were syllables spelled so as to be pronounceable by me. Some sounds had been too much for my alphabet, for they had been produced in the back of the mouth, between cheeks and molars. I am not poking fun when I say this. I can poke fun at what I tried to pronounce, for the sounds I made were amusing at times, but, spoken by the Eskimos themselves, the syllables were as mellifluous as a brook's murmuring.

Oh, not all the Eskimo that I heard and learned was gentle! When a driver yelled *Ow-ka!* or *Howk!* at his dogs, he meant them to veer left or right and, if they didn't veer, and promptly, they felt the sting of his whip. If, at camp, the dogs became too noisy, the command *Palaghit!* (Shut up!) shouted from inside the *igloo* (snowhouse) or *tupek* (tent) was harsh enough to silence them instantly.

Another important Eskimo at the post was John Ell's wife, Mary Ell, who washed the dishes and swept the floor every day at Sam's house. When Mary came to do her work, she often brought a winsome little boy named Peter who, lifted from the hood of Mary's *kooletah* blouse, scampered quietly upstairs and down, learning all sorts of things about this foreigner's world. Peter fell in love with my lemming traps, the small hatchets I had brought along for trading, the tools I used in preparing specimens, in short, with almost everything I possessed. If I wanted to entertain him, all I needed to do was set a mousetrap for him to sneak up on with a broomstraw. "Careful," I warned him, lest the trap snap shut on his fingers. Thus did a mousetrap come to have the Eskimo name *kayafoo*, which was, of course, what I seemed to call it.

Other Eskimos lived with John and Mary Ell and little Peter, among them old Shoofly, whose face had been tattooed when she was young. In the early days, Shoofly had seen many a whaler and independent trader come to Repulse Bay, stay a while, and go. With her kinfolk, she had lived a while at Duke of York Bay, in the rough northern part of Southampton, and she had been among the first of the Aivilikmiut to be moved to Coral Harbour when the post had been established there in 1924. She had become a matriarch of the Aivilik people, an *angegok*, or soothsayer, wise enough to communicate with the spirit world.

Toward the end of August, Sam Ford and John Ell took me by motorboat to the flat southwestern part of Southampton, to the much talked-of nesting ground of the blue goose. En route we stopped at a place I called Four Rivers, where I ran down a half-grown whistling swan and saw four *tuteeghuk*, or sandhill cranes, two adults and two full-grown young birds, all flying well. When we reached the area in which the blue geese had nested, we witnessed the departure for the south of hordes of geese, both blues and snows. John Ell explained to me that the Aivilik name for the blue was *khavik* and, for the snow, *khanguk*.

Almost every day in early September, there was talk at the trading post about the great *akvik* or bowhead whale that John Ell had wounded with a harpoon gun the preceding summer somewhere between Coral Harbour and Seahorse Point, the southeasternmost corner of Southampton. It was common knowledge, apparently, that the wound had been bad, for the water had been red where the whale had sounded. But even the powerful John Ell deemed it wise for old Shoofly to consult with the spirits about the *akvik*. Had the creature really died? Had its carcass come to the surface and drifted northward to Southampton's shore rather than southward to Coats Island?

I made no attempt to learn what the spirits said to Shoofly. For all I knew, the old woman had simply thought the matter over, pieced together what she knew about currents, tides, and winds, and decided on her own that the whale had died and drifted to Southampton's shore. Almost certainly she had long since discussed the wounding of the animal with all who had seen it and the bloody water. At any rate, it was decided that the dead whale should be looked for, since the *shookak*, or whalebone, was valuable. Also it was decided that I should be a member of the search party.

Thus, in the big open motorboat, with Jack Ford, John Ell, and Kayakjuak, another fine Eskimo, as my companions, did I enter the Inuit world as it then was. The boat was crowded. I heard English only when Jack sent a word or two my way. On our second day out, we found ourselves suddenly surrounded by a pod of walruses—weirdly beautiful animals that rolled in the water, hissing and coughing through their whiskers, glaring at us with tiny eyes that seemed to be ringed with red and white. So excited were the Eskimos that they paid no attention to anything but their guns. The boat went wild, charging around in circles. Some of the poor brutes were probably killed, but no one made the slightest move toward retrieving a carcass. I was appalled by the thought of the waste until assured by Jack that the dead animals would float to shore and be found and used later. The faces of those frightened, defiant *aiviut*, glaring at us from the water within a few feet of the gunwale, linger in my memory. I am reminded of them when I contemplate drawings by William Hogarth and Hieronymus Bosch.

We saw thousands upon thousands of oldsquaw ducks that day. The birds had been molting. Their feathers covered the smooth ocean, looking at a distance like the fluffy dust that gathers under beds. Not one of the feathers was really wet. Each rested on the water lightly, its downier parts catching the afternoon sunlight in such a way as to give the sea's surface a rosy glow.

John Ell called attention to the fact that all the gulls were flying in the same direction toward shore northeast of us. This, said he, might be because there was something to eat there. John himself was the first to sight the whale carcass, a tiny black spot in the distance. Among the gulls overhead suddenly appeared a raven, a *toolooghak*, a species needed for my collection. As the bird circled our boat, I shot it. To my surprise, no one shouted approval. Jack Ford might have said, "Good shot, Doc," but he made no such comment. Every man watched silently as I lifted the specimen from the water and shook it. Said Jack, in a voice that was downright solemn: "The people watches these ravens, Doc. They tells what's going to happen by what the ravens does. You seen that one fall on its back, didn't you? Well, that maybe means something. Maybe it means we'll see a bear or something." In spite of my scientific training, I accepted what he said without argument. I sensed that my companions had been disturbed by the killing of the big black bird or by the way it had fallen. It was a creature of omen.

We had no way of knowing how vile the whale carcass was until we got downwind of it. A yawning cavern had been eaten away in its belly by bears and foxes. Alas, fully half of the precious whalebone had rotted away from the roof of the mouth and been carried off by the waves. More than once, I heard the word *toolooghak* as the Eskimos discussed their dismay. As one of the men climbed from a vast fluke up onto the whale's back, I expected to see him break through the skin, but on he went toward the head, sinking deep with every step. Jack said, "They all says that the raven back there gives them a sign." I could not help thinking that in the minds of these, my companions, the whalebone would all be in place had I not shot that raven!

A bit dejected, I decided to be by myself for a while, so off I strode, heading for a spit half a mile eastward. I happened upon a Baird's sandpiper, which I shot. When I had got about two-thirds of the way to the spit, I noticed a flat, ten-foot-long object lying half-buried in the sand at the water's edge. It looked like a thin old plank with frayed edges. When I kicked it loose, I saw at once that it was a slab of whalebone. At almost the same instant, I perceived that half-buried slabs of the same sort lined the shore ahead of me as far as I could see. The missing baleen! The precious *shookak!* As I hurried back with the news, the very wind seemed to rejoice. Said I to Jack, "Tell everybody that I'm glad I shot the raven and that it hit the water the way it did!" Within an hour the *shookak* had been stacked tepee-fashion far enough back from the water to be beyond the reach of the highest tide. Jack said, "They's all glad that you got your *toolooghak* back there, and they's glad it hit the water with its back!'' Thought I: *If only the world's multitudinous beliefs could all be as flexible as this one!*

At Seahorse Point we were to see much of *nanook*, the polar bear. The handsome creatures had drifted south on pans of Foxe Channel ice, but the ice had melted or moved on, for the sea was clear of it. From one eminence we counted eleven bears at one time, all on cliffs not far from water. The Eskimos shot four of them. One that I happened upon while picking my way down a rocky slope was only a few rods from me, pawing in the turf for mushrooms and berries. Having only a shotgun, I backed off, glad that the meeting had been short of confrontation. But, as I circled downwind, thoughts of another sort entered my mind. How fine to be known as the greenhorn fresh from the South who had killed a *nanook* with a mere shotgun! I could use the specimen, too. It would be gratifying to see my name on the label. The ideas nagged, kept nagging, becoming an obsession. Remembering what John Semple had told me about ringing a shotgun shell so as to let the shot move en masse like a bullet from the barrel, I found my jackknife, ringed a shell holding BB shot, and started after the bear.

When I found it again, it was in the water not far from a seal that it had hauled out onto the shore and partly eaten. Presently it climbed out of the water, shook itself, and returned to the seal. Watching it carefully, I continued downslope, gaining confidence as I drew closer, for the bear's eyes, though often directed my way, seemed not to be seeing me. When I had got as close as I could without letting myself down a fifteen-foot sheer wall of rock, I tried to think through what might happen in case the wounded animal charged. The wall just below me would surely be to my advantage, for the bear would have to climb it. I decided to stay where I was. If the wounded bear rushed me, I would give its open mouth a blast from the gun's right-hand barrel.

The sound of a rifle shot and the plop of a bullet in the water reminded me that I was not the only hunter of *nanook* at Seahorse Point. What if someone that I could not see was actually shooting at *my* bear? Refusing to consider further the fact that I had had no experience with ringed shotgun shells, I reviewed the situation swiftly and decided in favor of trying. I raised the gun, aimed it carefully, lowered it. I was not breathing easily. Thought I, *this temporizing is bad; if this indecision continues, I'll never get a bear.* I raised the gun again, aimed at the broad face, and fired.

The bear shook its head, rose to its hind feet with a visceral roar, swung wildly with both front paws, about-faced as if expecting attack from another direction, dropped to all fours, about-faced again. Obviously it had been little more than stunned, though it was angry and in pain, for its roaring continued. The shot must have scattered, hitting several parts of the head and neck, though there was no gaping wound.

If my teeth were not chattering, they should have been. Four words I uttered, though not loudly enough for the bear to hear: "Well, it's your turn!" That was precisely how I felt. Remorse had set in. Carried away by visions of grandeur, bent on making a name for myself, I had hurt a magnificent wild creature, robbed a wilderness scene of its loveliness. How I ached as I crouched there, wondering what might happen next! Failure to kill the bear had hurt, but recognition of the shallow motives that had led to the failure was hurting more.

The bear continued to mutter as it lifted its nose into the wind, smelled the sea, and started for the shore. As it moved off, disappearing behind rocks, my heart quit pounding. I did not leave my ledge, however, until I was sure that the bear had gone. When I last saw it, it was swimming strongly toward a rocky islet a hundred yards offshore.

I have debated with myself at length over whether to recount here the above-discussed episode. I have put it on record in hopes that other young men, eager to prove their mettle or win renown, will not make the same sad mistake.

That night we devoured bear steaks fried in a big skillet. They were delicious. It seemed to me that I'd never in my life been so hungry. Every bite that I swallowed seemed to make me hungrier. No one teased me for my attempt to get a bear with a shotgun. I had my own feelings about the matter, though.

What I have said above about my sojourn on Southampton Island is a twice-told tale, for my book, *Eskimo Year*, published in 1934, tells the whole story. In that book I did not, however, make sufficiently clear how I failed as a photographer. The movie camera worked by fits and starts until midwinter, then quit. Even with the photometer as a guide, I overexposed almost every picture that I took with the Kodak in really cold weather. Of my fifteen hundred or so stills, only about fifty were usable. Best of them all by far were those of a female snow bunting whose nest was so completely hidden under a flat rock that I had to remove the rock to see the nest at all. To my surprise, the bunting returned promptly to her eggs even when the rock was gone. She was remarkably confiding. So used to tripod, camera, and me did she become that she accepted crane flies from my fingers. Indeed, when she saw one of my crane flies coming, her bright eyes sparkled with anticipation. After I had taken several shots of her on or near her nest, I replaced the rock.

Many a time have I relived in memory those wonderful months with Sam and Jack and the Inuit. In many ways that year was the finest of my life. I have wondered which persons, which scenes, which occasions I would remember the longest.

Would it be the immaculate interior of my first snowhouse, with its lighted stub of candle, the halo of rime circling the tiny flame, and the opal-colored shadows on the curved walls? That little flame spelled all the difference between the comfort of home and the merciless cold of out-of-doors.

Would it be the northern lights, those ghosts of the long-departed playing a game in the sky; or the December sun perched on the horizon at high noon, flanked by a bright parhelion at either side; or the *sheenah*, the vapor cloud, hanging over the open floe where the cold, cold water was so much warmer than the air that it *steamed*; or the humming of wires at the post when the air fairly snapped with frigidity; or the chorus of the huskies that accompanied every ringing of the mission bell and that continued long after the ringing had stopped, permitting even the *king-miatsut*, or puppies, to participate; or Sam's cheerful greeting when the thermometer read only 20 below rather than the usual 50: "Spring's here, everybody! Next thing you know we'll be seeing violets"?

Or would it be that Saturday evening along toward Christmas when, listening to a special broadcast from Radio Station KDKA in Pittsburgh, we all heard my mother playing the piano and the Beta boys from Bethany College singing songs that I knew so well, and John Ell, perplexed by Sam's statement that the young men who had been singing were my brothers, made this charming comment in his best English: "Mus' be very many family"?

Or would it be that *komatik* trip on which, doing my best to make the twenty-foot walrus-hide whip flick the dog that needed flicking, I realized that in back of me the whip's wicked tip had missed Jack Ford's nose by only an inch, sending a cigarette from his lips off into oblivion, and Jack had responded not with an oath or a scowl but with a laugh so loud and wild that every dog in the team, bewildered by a sound unlike any it had ever heard, turned its head around for a look?

Or that frozen-solid can of "specially selected" French peas that I had with me on a caribou hunt in the East Bay country, that I put on the Primus stove to thaw, and that exploded, sending its scalding contents to the igloo's curved roof from which, plucked from the snow with taxidermic forceps, each and every blessed pea was retrieved and eaten?

Or the houseful of male snow buntings that Jack Ford and I rescued during the last of the winter's blizzards, sweet little creatures that never once alighted on the hot kitchen stove, though they gathered happily under it, that sang for all they were worth right there in the house when the sun came out, and that quieted down instantly when one of them, recognizing that what it was perching on was the stuffed skin of a gyrfalcon, gave a sharp cry of alarm?

Or that fine young Aivilik, Tommy Bruce (pronounced "Tahmee Bloose" by the Inuit), whose real name was Acheevak, who took me on an ill-starred *komatik* trip into the foothills of the Porsild Mountains northeast of the post, whose canvas *tupek* the wind and snow almost pulled apart while we were inside it, who laughed when I quoted doggerel to him though he did not understand a word of what I said, and who, using his own tongue, reported on our return: "The Bird Man and I had a good time. We did not become lonely. The Bird Man talked to me, and I talked to the Bird Man"?

Or the three big rocks that the Eskimos put at the head of each sleeping bag in our *tupek* at the floe—rocks that proved to be the frozen contents of three walrus stomachs, each containing hundreds of delicious clams that we chipped off one by one and ate raw?

Or the relief I felt when Jack Ford yelled, "It's all right, Doc. The baby's come! You scared it out of her"? I'll never, never forget that message, shouted across the snowy expanse. The poor Eskimo woman, Pahmeeolik's wife, had been in labor for a long time, but the baby would not arrive. Finally Sam had said to me, his face as serious as I'd ever seen it, "You'd better get your tools and go over. I know you're not a surgeon, but you know more about such things than I do, and the people know that you have all those tools." In a kind of a daze, I had cleaned the scalpels and scissors and forceps, boiled them fiercely, and put them in a washbasin, ready for the trip to the little house beyond the Roman Catholic church. Then came Jack's hearty message, and I felt relief more truly blessed than any I had ever felt.

Or would it be, perhaps, the radio message that came that winter night telling one and all that Dewey Soper, a Canadian, had discovered the blue goose's nesting ground at Lake Amadjuak in the southwestern part of Baffin Island? Soper had been on his way out with the news even as I had been traveling northward on the *Nascopie*. The message had hurt a bit, for I had dreamed fond dreams of going down in history as the man who had discovered the blue goose's nest, but the pain wasn't great, nor did it last very long. When summer rolled around (I told myself), I'd be finding a blue goose nest of my own, maybe many of them. What was more to the point, I was discovering every day, almost every hour, things that were more important than any bird's nest: things about myself that had sorely needed discovering for a long, long time.

Did I do what I set out to do on Southampton Island? Did I actually find the blue goose there? Answering these questions demands more than a word. I did not visit the southwestern part of the island during the breeding season, though that capable Eskimo, Tommy Bruce, went there for me. Near Cape Kendall he found a big colony of blue geese and snow geese. He shot *and prepared as specimens* eight adult blues, all of which he brought to me on July 9, 1930. They were not in very good shape for, not expecting Tommy to skin out his specimens, I had given him no preservative. To the crossed legs of each nicely stuffed skin he had tied a bit of thick paper on which, using syllabics, he had written important data. He collected three sets of eggs, too, but by the time the nine crudely blown specimens reached me the sets were hopelessly jumbled, for Tommy did not mark any of them.

Scattered pairs of blues and snows nested widely in low country well away from the big colony at Cape Kendall, and many pairs were obviously mixed. One mixed pair, the male a snow, the female a blue, nested on Prairie Point directly across South Bay from the post. About eight miles east of the post, a pair of blues had a nest with four eggs. These eggs I collected. The male of the pair was a pure blue, and the female a blue with a white belly. In the light of what we now know, both Tommy Bruce and I might have looked in vain for pairs in which both males and females were all blue, strictly speaking, for the species now called the snow goose is two-phased or two-morphed throughout much of its range. There is now no such *species* as the blue goose. There is, rather, the highly variable blue phase or blue morph of the snow goose. And taxonomists continue to wonder why the greater snow goose—the big geographical race that breeds in northwestern Greenland and in far northeastern parts of the Canadian arctic archipelago and that winters solely on the Atlantic coast of the United States—should have no blue morph.

Epilogue:
CORNELL UNIVERSITY

THE RETURN to the United States in 1930 after my year on South-ampton Island was almost as time-consuming as the voyage northward in 1929. The *Nascopie* took me as far as Chesterfield Inlet on the west coast of Hudson Bay where, while wondering how I'd get farther south, I made good use of my time collecting bird specimens and drawing mushrooms that I found within walking distance of the Hudson's Bay Company's trading post. Toward the end of August, the motor yacht *Nowyah* carried me south to Churchill, at the mouth of the great river of the same name. Here huge grain elevators were being built, a round-house was operating at the end of steel, and the famed Hudson Bay Railroad had actually made one run from Winnipeg. That train took me back to the telephones, corner drugstores, restaurants, hotels, theaters, and dentists of the world I had almost forgotten.

At Cornell, life was bewilderingly full. The chairman of my doctoral committee was Arthur Augustus Allen, an industrious, even-tempered, handsome man who had won fame through his bird photography, his articles in *Bird-Lore*, his experiments with the recording of bird songs, and his successful rearing of ruffed grouse in captivity. Single-handed, he had made Cornell an important center of ornithological research. He, his scholarly wife, Elsa, and their several children lived on Kline Road, a winding street that led steeply down from Cayuga Heights to the level of lake and town. The Allen place was in the woods. It had no formal lawn. There was no telling what interesting creature might be seen there in a cage or shed.

An immature bald eagle that had been captured on a farm near Ithaca and brought to town Dr. Allen agreed to care for. Kept for a short time in a small wire enclosure, then in a room fifty feet long and fifteen feet wide, the great bird refused for fifteen days to eat. It was offered fresh fish, rabbit, mouse, and chicken, but to no avail. Finally, hoping to stimulate the eagle's predatory instinct and hunger, Dr. Allen gave it a little black hen *alive*. That evening, to the utter amazement of all concerned, the two birds went to roost side by side in what appeared to be perfect bliss.

For thirty days eagle and hen occupied the room together, the hen "scratching out a living during the day and each night going to roost beside the eagle." Those who heard of the strange relationship were dumbfounded. When, after fifteen days of incarceration, the eagle gave up its hunger strike, it was soon eating any kind of food that Dr. Allen gave it, but it did not touch its companion, the little black hen. Friends who witnessed the miracle offered the suggestion that the eagle had lost its predatory instinct as a result of captivity. To test this, a living sister of the little black hen was introduced into the eagle's room. That day Dr. Allen had scarcely closed the door "before the eagle pounced on the newcomer and devoured her." Presently, after a month of what had looked like amiable companionship, the eagle "turned on the hen that had roosted with it and gobbled her up" too!

Dr. Allen's explanation of this all-but-incredible behavior, which he wrote about in his 1951 *Stalking Birds with Color Camera*, may well be quoted here:

> During the 15 days of fasting the eagle was gradually adjusting itself to an entirely new environment. The mental picture of the habitat in which it had been accustomed to live and hunt its food had suddenly been obscured and was being replaced by another entirely different. Until the adjustment had been made, even physiological functions largely ceased. By the time the adjustment had been made, the mental picture included the little black hen, not as an item of food but as a companion.
>
> The same holds for the little black hen. She had been summarily removed from her companions and placed in a new environment with another companion the like of which she had never seen before. Because of its size she immediately conceded its dominance, and it mattered little if it had a more curved bill and larger feet than the roosters of her acquaintance.
>
> When it grew dark, her social instinct required that she roost with the flock, and she flew to the perch and moved along until she was as close as she had been the night before to a less lordly fowl.
>
> The relationship between them might have endured indefinitely had not something suddenly stimulated the killing reaction in the eagle.
>
> Falconers know that a bird in distress will lure hawks from a long distance, and a tethered pigeon that can be made to flop awkwardly is regularly used as a lure in catching wild hawks. For example, when search-

ing for duck hawks migrating along Atlantic beaches, a falconer often will bury himself in the sand, tie a pigeon to his wrist, and conceal his head under a bushel basket. Upon seeing the pigeon, the hawk swoops down upon it, only to be seized in his turn by the falconer.

It may well be that the little black hen suddenly expressed alarm or helplessness and thereby stimulated the killing instinct that put the touching story to an end.

A memorable feature of that first fall as a graduate student was the seminar in ornithology, a weekly forgathering that Dr. Allen called his "séminaire," a French pronunciation that he never explained. The seminar was well attended. The speaker, though usually a member of the faculty or a graduate student, was sometimes a distinguished person from afar. Part of the evening's program was a long-drawn-out checking of birds seen during the preceding week. Amusing it was to hear a hearty voice reporting "4,760" crows observed "flying toward their roost over near Etna," followed by a sheepish "6" from another part of the room and an even more sheepish "2" from another, until the week's grand total of crows was finally settled upon and recorded.

If anyone reported an improbable species, there were rustlings of disapproval, these followed by questions, a detailed description of the moot bird or birds, more questions, more description, until everyone was convinced that the species reported had or had not actually been seen. Ithaca winters are not severe as a rule, but they are snowy and gray, hence not conducive to the overwintering of birds that usually move southward at that season. I recall a January seminar at which someone reported a chipping sparrow, a species that had rarely, if ever, been seen at Ithaca in winter. The report was greeted with sounds of skepticism. "But I saw that bird's reddish brown cap very distinctly," said the observer in self-defense. He could hardly have chosen words more certain to prove his identification wrong. Almost everyone in the room knew that when a chipping sparrow molts into its winter plumage it *loses* its reddish brown cap. So thumbs went down, so to speak, and the argument ceased.

A duck whose molts I had made a point of studying while on Southampton Island was the oldsquaw. I may or may not have given a seminar talk on that species, but I did prepare a paper developing the idea that the bold black-and-white plumage worn in winter by the drake was actually the courting dress, the attire worn while pairs were forming before migration northward to the breeding ground. Dr. Allen went

over my manuscript carefully, giving me the benefit of his wide experience with waterfowl. My paper, "Notes on the Molts and Sequence of
Plumages in the Oldsquaw," was published in *The Auk* in 1932.

Albert Hazen Wright, affectionately known as Uncle Bert, was a
second member of my doctoral committee. He and his wife, Anna, a
sister of Dr. Allen, were at work on a handbook dealing with the frogs and
toads of North America. Part of every day these two dedicated her-
petologists fed, photographed, and wrote about their cold-blooded
captives, many of which were sent to them alive in the mails. Professor
Wright had an abiding interest in baseball. His lectures sometimes wandered far from reptiles and amphibians to players whose batting average
he had been watching or to teams whose performance he considered
worthy of note. I sometimes wondered why he let himself get so far from
his avowed subject, but I always enjoyed what he said. His discourse was

*Sharp-shinned Hawk   Head and foot of a bird in first winter plumage, captured near
Ithaca, New York, on November 9, 1930.*

characterized by frequent use of the wholly unneeded word "now," a habit for which he became so well known that his wife decided he should be cured of it. She took down some of his sentences verbatim and showed these to him. One had to do with the habits of rattle-now-snakes. The *Handbook of Frogs and Toads of the United States and Canada* was published in 1933 by the Comstock Publishing Company, whose offices were just across Fall Creek gorge from the Cornell campus.

The third member of my committee was Walter King Stone of the Fine Arts Department, a gifted painter whose nickname was Stoney. Professor Stone had known Fuertes well and through Fuertes had heard of me. He and his wife were warmhearted and lovable. Their Thursday-evening at homes were delightful. Their charming old house stood on the bank of Fall Creek upstream from the deep impoundment known as Beebe Lake. Country folk usually called the creek a crick, so the Stones decided to name their house Lumbago—from the crick in its back.

Working with Stoney and Professor Olaf Brauner, I made some oil paintings in the Fine Arts Department's studio on the campus. For one of a goshawk I used as my model an adult specimen that had been beautifully mounted by Fuertes. That painting I still own. Another was of a barnyard rooster reaching upward toward an ear of corn hanging at the end of a string from the ceiling. My model was stuffed, the painting was representational enough to record the taxidermist's mistakes, and the dangling corn was altogether improbable, so the general effect of the work was surrealistic. Fellow students who happened by approved of the fact that what I was doing was not at all scientific. I could hear them whispering to each other about what they thought the picture's title should be. *Manna from the Skies* was obviously aimed at ridiculing all things religious.

Before receiving my degree, I would have to demonstrate proficiency in two modern languages aside from English. Since many important ornithological works had been (and were being) published in German and French, those two languages were settled upon as mine. I had not had any French as an undergraduate, but the language had always appealed to me; furthermore, during the long, far northern winter of 1929–30, when nine-day blizzards had shut me in, I had (with a little French dictionary in hand) translated Pierre Loti's fine novel, *Pêcheur d'islande*, from beginning to end. Among volumes available to us candidates for the degree was E. L. Trouessart's *Les Oiseaux utiles*, a factual rather than a literary work. From this I read while being examined, finding it not difficult, partly because I knew something about the habits of European birds.

As for German, I realized that I needed instruction, so I enrolled in a class for beginners, enjoyed the semester under the guidance of a quick-witted young teacher, and wound it all up with a lecture *from me* on the world's birdlife. My audience was the class, a small one. Aided by maps and colored charts, some so big that a fellow student had to help me hold them up, I went on at great length, using such resounding agglutinative German words as *Kirschkernbeisser* (cherry pit biter)—a nicely descriptive name for the huge-billed bird known in England as the hawfinch—when I knew them and resorting to English when I had to.

My fellow graduate students in ornithology were well worth knowing. One of them was Austin Rand, who would presently be recognized as an authority on the birdlife of Madagascar. Another was George B. Saunders, who was interested in the taxonomy and distribution of the New World's two species of meadowlark. Others were Wilfred A. Welter, whose studies focused on the long-billed marsh wren, James Crouch, whose bird was the cedar waxwing, and Victor Coles, who had us all wondering about the turkey vulture's sense of smell. As for Adger Smythe, Victor Gould, Richard Weaver, Elizabeth Kingsbury, Lawrence Grinnell, Dorothy Compton, F. C. Edminster, and L. S. Vijjakich, my memories are mixed: I cannot recall what their special interests were or what their status was in 1930 and 1931.

As for Peter Paul Kellogg, who may also have been a graduate student, I continue to be perplexed. He was so busy giving radio talks, managing ornithological affairs during Farm and Home Week, and assisting with Dr. Allen's many projects that I considered him not a student but a member of the faculty. Albert R. Brand was on deck, too, a successful stockbroker who had decided to devote his time and energies to investigating the field of sound recording. He may have been a graduate student, but I suspect that he was in a special category of his own.

The grad that I came to know best was Olin Sewall Pettingill, Jr., a New Englander fresh out of Bowdoin College. This young man's dignity, reticence, and sincerity appealed to me deeply. He was a crack bird photographer. With me he went over the many pictures I had taken on Southampton Island, most of them worthless. He enjoyed what I had to say about the North Country—its Eskimos, its caribou and seals and bears, its aurora borealis, its huskies. He liked the way I had been into things as Pennsylvania's state ornithologist and as a traveler to various parts of Canada. We hit it off, becoming close friends. We shared the third-floor apartment at the Fuertes home at the corner of Thurston and Wyckoff avenues only a few blocks from the campus. Each morning we breakfasted with Margaret Sumner Fuertes, Louis Fuertes's widow. Those breakfasts were occasions, every one of them.

Sewall's dissertation was to deal with the biology of the American woodcock. He was afield at all seasons, for he was as much interested in his bird's overwintering as in its migrations and nesting behavior. During that first fall and winter, he was obliged to spend much time becoming acquainted with the literature dealing with his bird and its Old World cousin, the Eurasian woodcock.

My fieldwork was done, so I settled down to studying my notes, ascertaining what my most important findings were, and writing a dissertation. My data on mammals were of interest to William J. Hamilton, Jr., the mammalogist at Cornell, who consented to coauthor my paper on them. My ornithological data fell into place readily since, having kept day-by-day notes on separate species sheets, I could proceed without an elaborate indexing of diary.

That first winter in Ithaca passed swiftly enough. In the late spring of 1931 I returned to Churchill, Manitoba, with my old friend John B. Semple, who, fired by what I told him of the Harris's sparrows I had seen there the preceding August, decided that we should go to the area to find that species' nest. Though the Harris's sparrow had been made known to science almost a century before, it had remained one of North America's mystery birds, for its eggs had never been discovered. With Semple, Bert Lloyd, and me on that memorable—and successful—expedition to Churchill went Sewall Pettingill. The idea that Sewall would one day be director of Cornell's Laboratory of Ornithology never entered his thoughts—or mine.

My lengthy report on the birdlife of Southampton Island slowly took shape. At the Carnegie Museum, William J. Holland and Andrey Avinoff were so pleased with my collection of far northern butterflies and moths that they had virtually every specimen photographed in color. The handsome composite photographs were reproduced as full-page colorplates in volume 12 of the museum's Memoirs. In this same volume appeared also my lengthy paper on the birds, the above-mentioned report on the mammals, a paper on the fishes by Arthur W. Henn, and papers on the plant life by O. E. Jennings and others. The volume appeared in 1932, the year in which my degree was awarded. So cooperative were the Carnegie Museum's editors that I was able to submit to the graduate college at Cornell three copies of the published paper rather than three copies of typescript.

After taking my degree, I decided to stay on at Cornell as curator of the Louis Agassiz Fuertes Memorial Collection of Birds. My office was on an upper floor of McGraw Hall, one of the three oldest buildings on the campus. During my stay in that building, I continued to hear much about a proposed move to another part of the campus. Before the move was made, I realized how fond I had become of the old building. The following nostalgic essay, written on a gray day late in the fall of 1935, explains to some extent why I felt as I did.

Parasitic Jaeger   Sketched from a specimen shot near the mouth of the Churchill River, on the west coast of Hudson Bay, on July 4, 1931.

OLD McGRAW

I.

In a few days our Laboratory of Ornithology will be leaving McGraw
Hall for new and finer quarters in Fernow Hall, half a mile away on the
border of what is called the Ag Campus. In Fernow ornithology will have
ever so much more room. There will be space for the bird collections,
for the graduate students' stalls, and for taxidermic and photographic
laboratories. Fernow Hall is modern and fireproof. McGraw isn't.

But I, for one, shall miss old McGraw. Here at my tall window I look
down across a broad slope of campus to the roofs and treetops of the
town, to the inlet and lake, to the distant hills that are so neatly patched
with fields and dotted with orchard trees. Yesterday the first snow of
winter fell. Today the spruces and hemlocks are so white they do not
stand out very clearly against the buried lawn. Strong wind from the lake
moves the maple branches and rattles the Virginia creeper vines as it finds
its way through the cracks about my window. Every automobile that
passes carries a wet mass of snow on its top, hood, and fenders. The street
that leads past the Baker Dormitories is covered with deep slush. If the
weather turns much colder and the roads become slippery, the boys at
the Theta Delt house will be turning out en masse to cheer the motorists
whose cars, failing to make the grade, will slither this way and that with
an awful roar and slide back downhill or into the curbing.

I came to Cornell five years ago. This window in old McGraw, with
its passing automobiles, its sky and clouds, and its sunsets above the
dark hills, has been mine for five years. I have become very fond of this
window.

There has been much talk these past five years about the shortcomings and inadequacies of McGraw. Our funny old museum on the second
floor has been the butt of many a joke. In order to make more room for
laboratories and incoming collections, the cases of stuffed birds, stuffed
mammals, and skeletons have gradually been shoved closer and closer
together, so that nowadays persons who are unfamiliar with our building
find their way across or about the second floor only with great difficulty.
Here in my office, which is one floor above the museum but which is
really part of the big room's balcony, I frequently hear some bewildered
person asking: "Can you tell me where I can find Professor So-and-So?"
And Professor So-and-So, having heard the query, for partitions in

McGraw all seem to miss the ceiling by inches, says quite distinctly: "Here I am. Just go on through the museum, out to the hall, go up two flights of stairs, turn right through a doorway, and go down a short flight of stairs. Be careful, for it's dark there. In fact, you'd better turn on the lights. The switch is near the doorway beside a sort of box. Then go straight ahead toward the only window you can see, and you'll find my door."

McGraw is so full of specimens, elevator shafts, storerooms, sinks full of living bullfrogs, refrigerators full of dead cats, gunnysacks full of hawks, owls, and crows whose stomachs are to be examined, and tubs full of field mice whose reproductive cycle and period of gestation are being studied that I long ago gave up trying to tell the uninitiated how to find my room. "Do you know where McGraw is?" I ask. And, having received an answer in a whole-souled affirmative, I say: "Come to the building at five minutes of four and I'll meet you at the entrance." Which reminds me that McGraw faces not Lake Cayuga but rather the university's chief quadrangle. In the middle of the building's back are steps leading up to what appears to be a nicely designed entrance, but as far as I know that entrance is never used, and no walkway leads from it in any direction.

II.

McGraw is a building of strange sounds. Even at midnight there is a low chatter of typewriters in the grad lab and an incessant croaking of bullfrogs from big sinks in the basement hall. In the laboratory where experiments in the recording of bird songs are being carried on, there are the wildest of yells, roars, crashes, and shrieks as dials are turned and films projected. (Lowered in pitch and augmented in volume, the recording of a yellow warbler's cheery little song sounds for all the world like coal roaring down a chute into somebody's cellar.) The tapping of the Geology Department's hammers at work upon fossils ceased a year or so ago, when the Department of Buildings and Grounds made a special investigation, found walls gaping and floors sagging, and decided that there were several tons too many mineralogical and paleontological specimens on the fourth floor. But the clatter of bottle washing in the zoological laboratories continues undiminished, and there is always the tramp of feet, the opening and banging shut of doors, the thumping of pipes, the whistle of steam escaping from radiators, the dripping and roaring of water faucets, the whining of the band saw in the carpenter's

shop, the peculiar moaning of the emery wheel, the booming of professors' voices about supraorbital this and sphenoid that, and the wailing
of some torch singer over the radio that one of the students recently
installed in the Laboratory of Ornithology.

Two years ago, I kept in my office for a short time two Boston bull
terrier pups. They had a pen near the window at one end of the room.
They were frolicsome animals, at times noisy. Just below me was a
laboratory full of aquariums where hundreds of brightly colored tropical
fishes were being bred for experimental work on cancer. One day a little
girl, who was looking through a half-open door at the fish, heard my
terrier pups quarreling. "What's *that* noise?" the little girl asked the janitor, who happened to be passing. "That's them little dogfish in there
barking! You mean to tell me you can hear 'em? They're awful small, you
know!" And there were inquiries about the barking dogfish at McGraw
for weeks thereafter.

A pygmy shrew brought to me last spring and kept in a cage near my
desk was an interesting captive, though not a pet. The tiny creature required meat in surprising quantities. What I gave it as a rule was freshly
killed mice—house mice, white-footed mice, jumping mice, field mice,
whatever was obtainable. A full-grown house mouse, though considerably larger than the shrew, went the way of all flesh with unbelievable
rapidity. A field mouse lasted longer, for the field mouse is much larger
than a house mouse. When the shrew gave birth to three young ones, I
was hard-pressed to provide food. The grads all helped. One day after I
had provided mother and babies with an adult field mouse, I asked some
friends in to see them. When I lifted the cage's top, we could see
nothing but the field mouse. Not a shrew was in sight. Afraid that the
voracious little beasts had killed and eaten each other, I lifted the mouse
by its tail and out poured the four shrews. They had eaten their way into
the mouse and gone to sleep there.

A few months ago, with the help of governmental funds, the
mounted birds and mammals in the museum got a more or less thorough
cleaning. Three women from downtown did the work. Never shall I
forget some of the remarks made by those women as they polished the
glass eyes of monkeys and walruses and lions and warthogs. They never
dreamed, I suppose, that anyone could hear them. Their talk was of a
frank, biological nature, dealing with such subjects as pregnancy, wean-
ing of infants, behavior of mated animals toward each other, and one
phase or another of the reproductive process. Some of us who heard this

talk wondered if we ought to let the women know that we could hear them. The discussions waxed so torrid and were so breathtakingly interesting that we decided it only discreet and well-mannered to keep our silence, even to stop listening at times. We were completely faithful to the former of these decisions, not to the latter.

McGraw is, as I have said, a building of strange sounds. But its odors are stranger. Enter the heavy outside door on the first floor and immediately you will smell the sharks. These gray-skinned carcasses come to our building by the carload, destined to be skinned and picked to pieces by students who will one day be removing our tonsils and appendixes. The odor of a freshly captured shark I do not know, for I have never captured one, but our McGraw sharks have an odor that must be their very own. About it there is little if any tang of briny deep. Formaldehyde is among the least noticeable of its component parts. The cats that are dissected during the second semester and that are stacked in the basement in vast heaps awaiting their hour also have about them an odor of formaldehyde. But, compared with any of McGraw's dead sharks, any of McGraw's dead cats is a gentleman.

Those whose paths lead to and from McGraw blame the hardworking premeds for all the vile odors that cling to their clothing. But, as a matter of solemn fact, we ornithologists are not guiltless. Only a week ago the Pennsylvania Board of Game Commissioners showered us with dead goshawks whose stomachs were to be examined. Many of the hawks had been dead a long time. Some of them were, indeed, so badly decomposed that we could not breathe near them without choking. But we went ahead with our examination of stomachs and preparation of specimens, firm in our belief that mankind has been unfair to the birds of prey. So completely just to all alike is McGraw's system of ventilation that the air currents carried the odor of Pennsylvania goshawks hither and yon. And we who were responsible could hear our ancient foe, the Department of Geology, saying "Whew!" and "Phoo-ey! What in thunder's that!" We were a little pleased when we heard the grumbling. After all, why shouldn't the world know about the more serious and more disagreeable sides of bird study? Ornithology is not, and never was, all sweetness and light.

The museum has the odor of nearly all museums—the close, dry odor of mustiness that I enjoy. Some specimens have odors that are peculiarly their own. A golden cuckoo from Africa has a scent of honey about it that will not leave its iridescent plumage. Fulmars and petrels have their own not wholly unpleasant aroma of oil and stale fish. And as for skunks and such foxes and great horned owls as have caught skunks, mention is sufficient.

Our heating system has its odors. The alcoholic specimens in the herpetological collection and the live bullfrogs and fishes downstairs have their odors. Some of the grads eat their meals in the grad lab, and the odor of their coffee, peanut butter, and scorching stew wanders daily about the building.

Among the most memorable of McGraw's odors is that of the roughing-out room. Here, in the drafty tower, the crudely skinned carcasses of birds and mammals are given to ravenous hordes of dermestid beetles, whose larvae devour the flesh but leave the bones. In this way, rather than through a boiling process, are our best osteological specimens prepared. The beetles are our workmen. The only pay they ask is vile carcasses, the viler the better. In the roughing-out room, the fumes of ammonia are so strong as to be all but overpowering. Had Edgar Allan Poe spent two minutes in this chamber of horrors, he might have written a mystery thriller the likes of which are not on the world's bookshelves today.

The worst, the very worst, McGraw odor within my memory had nothing to do with any course in zoology. One of the grad students, having volunteered to make a drum following directions in a Boy Scout manual, obtained the fresh skin of a cow, put this in a caldron he had lugged to the third floor, poured a potent solution of some sort over it, and let it soak until the hair came off. Faithfully, day after day, the student visited this "double-double-toil-and-trouble" pot, sousing the hide noisily, making sounds that announced to one and all how he, the dedicated craftsman, was suffering. In time the hair came off, the skin was stretched, the drum made. The wonder was that any of *us* still had our hair!

III.

Such a place of sounds and odors and stuffed and bottled specimens is McGraw. But ever so much more interesting than odors and sounds and specimens are the human beings who live and work here: professors who arrive ten minutes before eight o'clock in the morning to draw diagrams on the blackboard or to round up their classes for a field trip to the inlet; grads with guns, burlap sacks, and binoculars; ichthyologists in hip boots, carrying heavy nets; red-cheeked undergraduates who clomp upstairs, laden with coats, galoshes, textbooks, and notepaper.

To me the most interesting of all these are the grads, for they spend a great deal of their time here, laboring upon their dissertations, conversing with their fellows about their problems, attending seminars and lectures, eating their frugal meals, changing their clothes for field trips, and, now and then, waxing boisterous over a game of cards late at night.

Four years ago we had a tousle-headed grad student whose passion was reptiles. He had charge of the preserved herpetological specimens, if I remember aright, but his real passion was the living creatures—turtles, terrapins, tortoises, lizards, and, in particular, snakes. He had bags, boxes, and drawers full of snakes. He was mailing or shipping snakes, or getting snakes from somewhere, or talking about snakes most of the time. He had to feed his charges of course. He fed live toads and frogs to them. At feeding time a multitude gathered.

One day a lot of his snakes got loose in the building. Rumor had it that some mischievous undergraduate had set them free. No one knew just how many there were. There was a flurry of searching, and several of the reptiles were found. Our tousle-headed friend moved crates and cases, cleared shelves that had not been cleared for decades, and went upstairs and down with an expression of anxiety on his face, but many of his pets he could not find.

During the following six or eight months, snakes appeared from time to time throughout the building. A stenographer would hear an unfamiliar rustle near a wastebasket and turn to see a pretty little red-bellied snake flicking its tongue at her. We would hear a blood-freezing scream and run to find a co-ed sitting weakly in a chair, telling her friends of a huge black snake that had dropped from a shelf onto the open dictionary she had been consulting. Snakes continued for weeks to appear unexpectedly, coiled innocently near a window where sunlight might warm them or gliding noiselessly among jars of specimens. Fortunately, not one of them was poisonous. Whether all of them eventually were found or accounted for, no one can say. My guess is that there may yet be a snake at large, or two, roaming about old McGraw.

Three years ago a long and lanky grad from Florida spent most of his time in McGraw. He was a good sort, friendly, manly, a crack rifleshot. He had to save money howsoever he could. He had no room or apartment anywhere, as far as anyone knew. He slept on gray army blankets on one of the long tables in the Zoo 8 lab. Many a time I came up to my office that winter to find him asleep on his table, his long toes sticking out from the blankets, his mild snore pervading the room. He was not a student in the Zoo 8 course, but those of us who sat in on the eight o'clock lectures rarely failed to hear him shaving behind a cabinet back at the sink. *Scraa, scraa!* came the sound of his razor gouging away at a tough beard. And there was the somewhat tantalizing odor of his breakfast cooking on the gas jet.

Long and Lanky had a big pot in which he boiled a sort of perpetual mulligatawny. He would buy himself five cents' worth of beans and five cents' worth of carrots and find some bread crusts somewhere and throw all of these into the pot with the bodies of red squirrels and chipmunks trapped in Fall Creek gorge, at the rifle range, or along the borders of the campus. I used to wonder if he ever really got enough to eat. One evening I came up to the lab to find him preparing a meal for four back among the bookcases. On the table were plates and bread and butter and shining radishes and crisp celery. In the all-welcoming pot a fine stew was bubbling. Long and Lanky and a pal were to entertain two lady friends that evening at dinner.

Had you spent in McGraw as many hours as I have spent, morning hours, noontime hours, midnight hours, you, too, would have heard of our ghost. You, too, would by this time have been surprised at finding this ghost—not a mere creaking of stairways, tapping on windows, or clanking of chains but a living man whose face is fine and sensitive, whose hair is silken and white, whose tread is noiseless. They tell us that the Ghost of McGraw came of a fine family. That he was once an athlete of renown, a gifted photographer, the author of a book. But now he is a wanderer, without home and family, without friends, sometimes without proper food and clothing. He has a way of appearing at the most preposterous times. More than once I have been working in my office late at night when, hearing the sound of the doorknob's slow turning, I would glance about to see the Ghost, cap in hand, standing not far from me, smiling, asking in a gentle voice how my work was coming or how the birds were faring or whether I had seen certain members of the faculty recently.

I wish the Ghost of McGraw came to see us more frequently. He is such a well-bred, thoroughly friendly being. I wish he weren't so shy. I wish he wouldn't always feel that he is taking too much time. I wish he'd sit down and let me study the light and shadows on his hair and the lines of his face. A face such as his would be worth striving for. But he comes when I do not expect him, and, before we have a chance to settle ourselves for a chat, he has moved quietly on with a "Good-bye! I probably shall be seeing you soon again!" He never looks at me as he speaks. Never! Always he is looking in some other direction or at the cap twirling in his hand. To call the expression of his face wistful is to miss the mark sadly, as so much of our discourse misses the mark. But the look there gives me the feeling I sometimes have when I look into the eyes of a snow leopard as it paces back and forth behind the bars of a cage.

Yes, I know I shall miss old McGraw. I will get some good work done in the new building. There will be much talk of advancement and enlargement and efficiency. But it will be years, oh, probably a great many years, before Fernow has a ghost, and from my new office I shall not be able to see the sunset far above Cayuga's waters.